Second Verse, Same as the First

Second Verse, Same as the First

★ ★ ★

The 2012 Presidential Election in the South

★ ★ ★

*Edited by Scott E. Buchanan
and Branwell DuBose Kapeluck*

The Citadel Symposium on Southern Politics

The Diane D. Blair Center of Southern Politics and Society

The University of Arkansas Press
Fayetteville
2014

Copyright © 2014 by The University of Arkansas Press

All rights reserved
Manufactured in the United States of America

ISBN-10: 1-55728-648-5
ISBN-13: 978-1-55728-648-2

18 17 16 15 14   5 4 3 2 1

∞ The paper used in this publication meets the minimum requirements of the American National Standard for Permanence of Paper for Printed Library Materials Z39.48–1984.

Library of Congress Control Number: 2013950787

Contents

List of Illustrations vii

Foreword. ix

Preface. xiii

Introduction:
    Southern Politics and the 2012 Presidential Election. . . . xv
    Branwell DuBose Kapeluck and Scott E. Buchanan

Part I The Setting and the Nominating Process

1. Demographic and Issue Cleavages in the
   Southern Electorate. 3
   Patrick R. Miller

2. The 2012 Presidential Nomination Process. 21
   John A. Clark

Part II Elections in the Deep South

3. Alabama: Republican Dominance and Democrats
   Fighting to Survive 37
   Shannon L. Bridgmon

4. Georgia: Even Redder. 51
   Charles S. Bullock III

5. Louisiana: For Republicans and Obama,
   Second Verse, Same as the First 69
   Robert E. Hogan and Joshua D. Hostetter

6. Mississippi: Democrats Struggle in an Increasingly
   Dominant Republican State 83
   Stephen D. Shaffer and David A. Breaux

7. South Carolina: "It's Déjà Vu All Over Again" 101
   Cole Blease Graham and Scott E. Buchanan

Part III Elections in the Rim South

8. Arkansas: Another Anti-Obama Aftershock......... 123
   Janine A. Parry and Jay Barth

9. Florida: *Sí, Se Puede!* 143
   Jonathan Knuckey and Tyler Branz

10. North Carolina: No Longer Federal Red
    and State Blue? 171
    Charles Prysby

11. Tennessee: Republican Ascendency Affirmed 185
    J. David Woodard

12. Texas: Big Red in the 2012 Elections 199
    Brian Arbour

13. Virginia: Obama's Unexpected Firewall 213
    John J. McGlennon

Conclusion: Toward Two-Party Competition
in the South?................................233
   H. Gibbs Knotts

Notes...245
Contributors 277
Index...281

Illustrations

Tables

1.1. State-Level Political Characteristics 5
1.2. Obama Vote Percentage by Group 7–8
1.3. Changes in Race and Democratic Vote in Largest Counties, 2000 versus 2011–12 11
1.4. Issue Preferences among Southern Voters, 2012 15
1.5. Political Behavior of Latinos, 2012 18
2.1. Republican Nomination Contests, 2012 25
2.2. Republican Primary Outcomes in the South 28
3.1. Alabama Partisan Control of Political Institutions, 1982–2010 39
3.2. Alabama Federal Elections Results, 2012 43
3.3. Alabama Presidential Election Exit Poll Results, 2000–2012 46
4.1. Georgia Republican Presidential Primary Exit Poll Results, 2012 56
4.2. Georgia Voter Presidential Election Preferences, 2012 59
4.3. Georgia General Assembly Partisan Makeup, 1963–2013 65
5.1. Louisiana Republican Presidential Primary Results, 2012 72
5.2. Louisiana Republican Presidential Primary Exit and Entrance Poll Results, 2012 74
5.3. Louisiana Voter Turnout in Presidential Elections, 2008, 2012 77
5.4. Louisiana Votes for President, 2008, 2012 78
6.1. Mississippi Federal Election Results, 2012 94–95
6.2. Mississippi Voter Ideology and Perceptions of Candidate Ideology, 2012 95
6.3. Mississippi Demographic and Attitudinal Sources, 2012 97
7.1. South Carolina Republican Presidential Primary Exit Poll Results, 2012 107
7.2. South Carolina Republican Presidential Primary Vote by County, 2012 109–10
7.3. South Carolina Presidential Election Vote by County, 2012 112–13
7.4. South Carolina Federal Election Results, 2012 115–16
8.1. Arkansas Presidential Primary Voter Turnout, 1976–2008 126
8.2. Arkansas Presidential Election Polls, 2012 130
8.3. Arkansas Federal Election Results, 2012 131
8.4. Arkansas Presidential Election Republican Vote by County, 2004, 2008, 2012 132–34
8.5. Arkansas Presidential Election Exit Poll Results, 2012 135–36

8.6. Arkansas Registered Voter Turnout and Presidential Vote in Ten Most-Populous Counties, 2012 140
9.1. Florida Federal Election Results, 2012 155–56
9.2. Florida Presidential Vote Demographic Analysis, 2008, 2012 158
9.3. Florida Presidential Election Vote by Region, 2012 159
9.4. Florida Presidential Election Exit Poll Results, 2012 161–62
9.5. Florida Megacounty Partisan Change in Presidential Elections, 1992–2012 170
10.1. North Carolina Election Results, 1992–2012 172
10.2. North Carolina versus U.S. Republican Presidential Vote, 1988–2008 175
10.3. North Carolina Vote by Political Orientation, 2012. 177
10.4. North Carolina Vote by Demographic and Social Variables, 2012 .. 178
10.5. North Carolina U.S. House Election Results, 2008, 2012 180
11.1. Tennessee versus U.S. Attitudes on Political Issues 190
11.2. Tennessee Republican Primary Poll Results and Actual Vote, 2012 . . 192
11.3. Tennessee Presidential Election Partisanship, 2000–2012 193
12.1. Texas Election Results, 2012 201
12.2. Texas Republican Vote Trend, 1948–2008 206
12.3. Presidential Votes in Select Large-State Suburban Counties, 2012 . . . 207
13.1. Virginia Presidential Poll Monthly Averages, January to November 2012 215
13.2. Virginia Presidential Election Results, 2004–2012 223
13.3. Virginia Presidential Results for Select Localities, 2004–2012 . . 224–25
13.4. Virginia Federal Election Results, 2012 227
13.5. Virginia Presidential Election Exit Poll Results, 2004–2012 229

Figures

9.1. Florida Presidential Vote by Race, 2012 169
11.1. Tennessee Population Distribution 188
11.2. Tennessee Division between Democrat and Republican 195
C.1. Racial Context and Support for Obama, 2012 236
C.2. Decreasing Gap in Percent Urban, 1950–2010 238
C.3. Urbanization and Support for Obama, 2012 239
C.4. Population Growth and Support for Obama, 2012 241
C.5. Prospects for Two-Party Competition in the South 243

Foreword

Southern Politics and the 2012 Presidential Election

The contemporary American South continues to be one of the most rapidly changing regions of the country. Dramatic changes in population, economics, and partisanship have altered the political landscape of not only the region but the entire nation. Prior to the civil rights movement, the Solid South stood as a monument to de jure segregation, the politics of race, and the power of the Democratic Party over local, state, and national elections. Following the civil rights movement, the South's transformation from a once solidly Democratic stronghold to a consistently Republican region was one of the most dramatic political changes in American political history. The wide-ranging effects of this development on electoral behavior and public policy are difficult to assess, but it is unquestionable that the New South remains as important to American politics as the old. With 153 Electoral College votes, a Solid South represents over half the necessary 270 electoral votes necessary to win the presidency. Over twenty years ago, in *The Vital South: How Presidents Are Elected,* Earl Black and Merle Black paraphrased W. E. B. DuBois by arguing that "as the united South goes: so goes the nation" (344). Given the historical forces that have moved the South to act as a unified voting bloc, it is no coincidence that many of our recent presidents have hailed from one of the former Confederate states. The surprising success in 2008 of the first African American presidential candidate and the Democratic Party across several southern states suggests that Republican dominance of the region may be in decline. Not only did several southern states support a northern liberal Democratic candidate, but they supported the nation's first African American presidential nominee. In a region better known for Jim Crow segregation than racial tolerance, such outcomes beg for scholarly investigation.

Despite the signs of possible two-party competition in the South, the 2012 presidential election reminded us of the solid control that the Republican Party maintains across the region. Republican presidential candidate Mitt Romney won nine of the eleven former Confederate states. Further, at the state and the local levels, the Republican Party continued to increase its standing. Despite the millions of dollars spent on campaigns across the country by the Democratic Party and changes in states like Florida and Virginia, the Solid South remains securely in Republican control. In many ways, the voting patterns in 2008 were repeated or even exaggerated in 2012. In the 2012 presidential election, white voters supported the Republican candidate in greater percentages than they did in 2008. We find similar patterns among urban voters versus suburban and rural voters, as well as older voters versus younger voters. The changing demographics of the South continue to be the only indication that two-party competition will ever again return to the South.

The Presidential Elections in the South Series

Since the 1984 presidential election between then-president Ronald Reagan and former vice president Walter Mondale, our colleagues at The Citadel have drawn attention to the importance of the South in presidential elections. Every four years, these scholars have facilitated important insights into presidential elections, and this book series has not only advanced our systematic understanding of southern politics but also served as a catalyst for countless articles and books focusing on the politics of the region. Through this 2012 edition of the series, aptly titled *Second Verse, Same as the First,* we can more clearly understand how President Obama and the Democratic Party won the presidency while winning only two southern states. Furthermore, we can learn a great deal about the successful Republican Party strategy of leveraging frustration with (and even animosity toward) President Obama and with politics in Washington that created substantial gains in Republican Party strength in state houses and in senates across the South. Some of the gains were, of course, because the Democratic Party largely ignored many southern states and focused the presidential campaign in battlegrounds outside the South.

Fittingly enough, Diane D. Blair was an important contributor to this series in the past. Consequently, the Blair Center of Southern Politics and Society's collaboration with The Citadel and sponsorship of this important book series is not only appropriate but also an exciting opportunity.

The Diane D. Blair Center of Southern Politics and Society

The Blair Center was established by a congressionally appropriated endowment granted in the fall of 2001. The center is a part of only a handful of research centers across the nation established by congressional appropriation and one of the only centers established to honor an individual who was not a former member of Congress. The Blair Center is dedicated to supporting interdisciplinary scholarship, study, and outreach relevant to southern politics.

Diane Divers Blair was born on October 25, 1938, and was raised in Washington, DC. She received her bachelor's degree from Cornell University in 1959 and worked in Washington, DC, for the President's Committee on Government Contracts, in a Senate committee on unemployment, and as legislative secretary and speechwriter for Sen. Stuart Symington of Missouri. She moved to Arkansas in 1963 and received her master's degree in political science from the University of Arkansas in 1967. She debated Phyllis Schlafly before the Arkansas legislature on Valentine's Day 1975 on behalf of the Equal Rights Amendment, and in 1992 she was selected to cast one of Arkansas's ballots in the Electoral College.

Diane Blair taught at the University of Arkansas for thirty years and established a record of accomplishment unparalleled in its combination of serious scholarship and practical involvement in both local and national politics. In May 2000, Blair was awarded an honorary doctor of laws by the University of Arkansas, and she was twice nominated to the board of the Corporation for Public Broadcasting by President William Jefferson Clinton and twice confirmed to that position by the Senate. She served two terms as chair of the Corporation for Public Broadcasting, and the corporation has now named its governing board after her. She was appointed by Governor Dale Bumpers in 1971 to serve as chair of the Governor's Commission on the Status of Women, by Governor David Pryor in 1976 to chair the Commission on Public Employee Rights, and by Governor Bill Clinton in 1979 to serve as a member of the Arkansas Educational Television Network commission, on which she served until 1993 and which she chaired from 1986 to 1987. In 1992 she took leave from the University of Arkansas to serve as senior researcher for the Clinton presidential campaign and again took leave in 1996 when she served as senior advisor to the Clinton-Gore reelection campaign.

In addition to establishing a breakneck record of service to her state and nation, Blair was an accomplished scholar, teacher, and mentor. She published two books, the first an analysis of Sen. Hattie Caraway, the first woman elected to the U.S. Senate, entitled *Silent Hattie Speaks: The Personal Journal of Senator Hattie Caraway* (1979). Her second book, *Arkansas Politics and Government: Do the People Rule?* (1988), continues to serve as a primary text in Arkansas high schools, colleges, and universities. She also authored fourteen chapters in edited volumes and authored or coauthored over ninety articles in various publications. Her research interests focused primarily on women and politics, state and local government, and the politics of Arkansas and the South.

Blair was three times named Outstanding Faculty Member by University of Arkansas students, and in 1982 she was one of the first recipients of the Fulbright College Master Teacher Award. In 1995 she was honored by the Midwest Political Science Association for her body of work in political science, and the Southern Political Science Association now has a competitive annual award in her name given to a scholar, chosen by committee, who successfully combines rigorous analyses of contemporary politics with a commitment to political activism. Future activities of the Blair Center will continue to honor her through excellence in researching and teaching southern politics and society, as well as through a commitment to service in the state and the region.

> Todd Shields, PhD
> Director
> Diane D. Blair Center of
> Southern Politics and Society

Preface

This is the eighth volume in a series of analyses of presidential elections in the South between 1984 and 2000 that resumed, in book form, with the historic 2008 presidential election. A state-by-state study of the 2004 presidential election was not done as an edited book but did appear in a special double issue of the *American Review of Politics*. While the presidential election is the focus of each volume, other important aspects of contemporary southern electoral politics are addressed, as well. Previous volumes examine congressional and state elections, as well as the overall status of party development and competition in each southern state. This volume continues the general organization of previous editions, with an introductory chapter, a chapter on presidential primaries, and a chapter on issues in the 2012 presidential election, as well as chapters on each of the eleven southern states of the Old Confederacy and a conclusion summarizing lessons to be drawn from the 2012 election cycle.

This study of the 2012 presidential election in the South benefitted greatly from the institutional and financial support of the Diane D. Blair Center for the Study of Southern Politics and Society. We are grateful for the interest expressed by the Blair Center's director, Todd Shields, and for his continued support of this project.

We appreciate the support of those who made this book possible or who contributed to the atmosphere in which it was created. The Citadel Foundation provided indispensable financial support. The Citadel Symposium on Southern Politics, a biennial conference that for over three decades has brought together a community of scholars engaged in the study of southern politics, helped to develop the network of contributors involved in this study.

Finally, we thank Lawrence J. Malley, the director of The University of Arkansas Press, for his support, patience, and guidance during the publication process.

Introduction

Southern Politics and the 2012 Presidential Election

Branwell DuBose Kapeluck
Scott E. Buchanan

As readers of this volume well know, the South occupies an important place in the study of American presidential politics. First, the eleven states of the former Confederacy tend to vote as a bloc. This tendency toward one-partyism elevates the relative importance of the region nationally. The South is also culturally distinct from other regions in the country in ways that affect political attitudes and behavior. Southerners are more likely to be born-again Christians and are more politically and socially conservative than their fellow nonsouthern citizens.[1] Finally, southern states (and the Sunbelt more broadly) have experienced significant population growth in the postwar period due to industrial growth, a warmer climate, and an increasing number of retirees moving south. This growth has translated into more representation in the U.S. House and the Electoral College. The South had 127 Electoral College votes in 1944, which was almost a quarter of the total and just short of half of that needed to win the election.[2] In 2012 the southern states' share of the Electoral College was 160 votes. This is 30 percent of the total Electoral College votes and 59 percent of the total needed to win.

Until 1964, the South was a source of strong electoral support for Democratic presidential candidates, though there was evidence as early as the 1948 presidential election that the region's place in the Democratic coalition was contingent upon the party turning a blind eye to black civil rights. This Dixiecrat revolt may be seen as the beginning of the region's divorce proceedings, with the final split occurring in the civil rights era of the 1960s.[3] The eventual move to the Republican Party was gradual, however. The Wallace candidacy in 1968 siphoned off the electoral votes of five southern states. While Texas remained in the Democratic column in 1968, Richard Nixon won South Carolina in what turned out to be a harbinger of the future. Nixon carried the South in 1972, and he won 78 percent of the vote in Mississippi, his largest margin of victory in any state. Carter, with the lone exception of Virginia, won the South in 1976, though he won only his home state of Georgia four years later. Reagan's election in 1980 cemented the GOP's ascendancy in the region.

The Democrats were able to make significant inroads in the South during the 1990s by nominating a southerner, Bill Clinton, for president. The Clinton-Gore ticket carried four southern states in both 1992 and 1996, though this success was not continued in 2000. Despite Vice President Al Gore at the top of the ticket, George W. Bush carried the entire South, including Gore's home state of Tennessee. Four years later, John Kerry failed to carry any state in the region. Something interesting happened in 2008, though. The Democrats nominated Barack Obama, the nation's first black major-party presidential candidate. Hawaii-born Obama, hailing from the Land of Lincoln, was about as nonsouthern as possible. Obama won the presidency, however, with the help of three southern states, Florida, North Carolina, and Virginia. Four years later, Obama, despite a struggling economy, held on to Florida and Virginia and lost North Carolina by only 2 percentage points, Romney's closest win in the nation.

It is clear that in the past few decades the South has become an increasingly pivotal region for presidential candidates of both parties. Awareness of the region's influential position in American politics prompted the creation of the biennial Citadel Symposium on Southern Politics in 1978, which continues to meet in Charleston, South Carolina, every even-numbered year. While the scholars involved in the symposium have collaborated on a number of books on southern politics, presidential politics in the South has emerged as a theme that has generated a series of books (and one edited journal) covering every presidential election since 1984. The initial book was published by Praeger, which continued publishing the books through the 2000 election. Analysis of the 2004 presidential election in the South was published in a special edition of the *American Review of Politics,* which has also regularly published some of the best papers from each Citadel Symposium. The editing for all of these works was done by the late Tod Baker, Laurence

Moreland, and Robert Steed, all Citadel professors and founders of the Citadel Symposium. In 2008 Citadel professor DuBose Kapeluck joined the presidential election project. With the retirement of professors Moreland and Steed, Professor Scott Buchanan joined The Citadel faculty in 2009 as director of the Citadel Symposium on Southern Politics and, with Professor Kapeluck, is coeditor of this year's book.

The format of all the books in this series follows the state-by-state structure used in V. O. Key's *Southern Politics in State and Nation*.[4] The states included are those eleven states of the former Confederacy. Along with a discussion of the presidential election in the state, contributors include commentary on important congressional and statewide elections, as well as some discussion of trends in state legislative elections. We also include chapters on the issues driving the 2012 election and on the nomination process in the southern states and a conclusion.

By all accounts, 2008 marked an extraordinary and historic presidential election. It was historic because Barack Obama became the country's first black president. What was extraordinary was that Obama was the first nonsouthern Democrat to win a southern state since 1968. Moreover, he won three: Florida, North Carolina, and Virginia. Given this historic accomplishment, an important question in 2012 was whether Obama could maintain his vote margins in these states. Was the bloom off the rose? The Obama administration's positions on gay rights, its tax increases, and the passage of the controversial Patient Protection and Affordable Care Act (Obamacare) were significant headwinds for his reelection bid in the conservative South. Furthermore, voter tendency to blame sitting presidents for weakness in the economy posed daunting problems for Obama in all regions of the country. Would the Obama campaign be able to mobilize its voter base in 2012 as well as it had four years prior?

With pundits wondering aloud about the challenges the president's campaign faced, the Republican Party faced its own challenges in the region, as well. At one point there were twelve announced candidates in the Republican presidential primary. The winnowing process was divisive, pitting Republican against Republican. Emerging victorious by late April 2012 (though Ron Paul continued his bid for the nomination) was Mitt Romney. How would Romney, former governor of Massachusetts (and architect of Romneycare, the Massachusetts state health care plan structurally similar to Obamacare) and active leader in the Church of Latter Day Saints, fare in the South, a region rich with evangelical and politically conservative voters?[5] Would Romney's relatively moderate stances be sufficient to bring back into the Republican fold the moderate voters in those southern states that defected in 2008?

A theme that emerges in the following chapters is that the South in 2012 was continuing to change politically. This is nothing new. As noted in these introductory comments, the South has evolved politically a great deal in the past several decades. Until recently, the conventional wisdom was that the region was politically monolithic. The events of the 2008 and 2012 elections suggest otherwise.

It appears that in-migration has softened southern partisan rigidity. It is not so much that *native white southerners* have changed politically but that southern votes have undergone dilution. Peripheral southern states with large urban populations are becoming less Republican at the presidential level. North Carolina, Florida, and Virginia have all joined the ranks of battleground states (though Florida has had this distinction for some time). Indeed, a case can be made that Georgia will be in this category by 2016—or 2020 at the latest. One notable exception is Texas, a peripheral, fast-growing state that is home to three of the top ten largest cities in the country. Texas has become, if anything, even more red, as have most of the remaining states in the region.

Though this book's primary interest is with the details of the presidential election in the eleven southern states, the authors also cover important electoral outcomes in down-ticket races. While the region became at the presidential level, perhaps, an even paler shade of red in 2012, the GOP did do well in many congressional, gubernatorial, and state legislative races. In North Carolina, for instance, the state came under unified Republican control for the first time since the 1890s. It is interesting that the seed planted during the region's top-down realignment, which has only recently exhibited some cracks at the presidential level, has found fertile ground at the local and state levels. This cross-pressure between state- and national-level politics may mark the next chapter in the South's unique political history.

I

The Setting and the Nominating Process

1

Demographic and Issue Cleavages in the Southern Electorate

Patrick R. Miller

The 2012 election season opened with many uncertainties about the course of the presidential contest. Barack Obama cruised to a relatively easy victory four years before, but he faced major challenges in his first term. Though the national economy was slowly recovering by virtually every measure, unemployment remained stubbornly high, and many Americans lacked optimism about the recovery. Would Americans credit him for a turnaround or blame his policies for being ineffective? Health care reform had become a controversial point for conservative elements such as the Tea Party. Would there be backlash for it against Democrats, as there had been in the 2010 midterm? Would Republicans rally behind their nominee, Mitt Romney, given his Mormon religion and history of taking more liberal issue positions as he campaigned in Massachusetts?

Ultimately, what looked at many points like a close race concluded with little unexpected drama, a 4-point Obama popular vote majority and a 332–206 electoral vote rout. Indeed, in both the Electoral College and exit polls, little had changed since 2008, despite Obama's first-term challenges. His coalition, including Florida and Virginia in the South, held together, though the coin-toss state of North Carolina, which had landed in Obama's column four years previously, narrowly flipped into the Romney camp. The great headline of the election, at least for the media, became America's changing demographics, especially its growing Latino population, which swung strongly to Obama and reached a double-digit share of the electorate for the first time. This chapter examines the issue and demographic divisions in the southern electorate, focusing on comparisons with national trends and demographic transitions in the region.

The Political Terrain of the South

Population changes in the South continue to grow its electoral strength. Reapportionment in 2010 added seven electoral votes to the region, bringing it to 160 votes—59 percent of the 270 needed to win the presidency. Southern electoral votes accounted for 13 percent of Obama's total, but a stunning 57 percent of Romney's. Though the region's three 2008 swing states reprised their role in 2012, three additional states—Georgia, Mississippi, and South Carolina—were decided by roughly 10 points each. Indeed, as Table 1.1 shows, Mississippi and Louisiana were among the few states that shifted toward Obama as compared with 2008.[1] Barring any seismic shifts in the overall political terrain, long-term population trends in the region, especially growth of racial minorities, may well bring more southern states into competitive status in upcoming cycles.

Table 1.1 covers the general political terrain heading into the election. Democratic candidates hoping to compete in the region faced an electorate with a Republican and conservative tilt. Republican growth region-wide is evident in the reported partisanship of Gallup respondents in the first half of 2012.[2] Only Arkansas, Florida, and North Carolina maintained Democratic pluralities, though every southern state was more Republican than the national average. Republican margins in other states ranged from 3 points in Virginia to 13.6 points in Alabama. Obama did outperform Democratic strength by substantial margins in some states, such as South Carolina, where his vote share bested Democratic identification by 7.2 points. Only in Arkansas did he underperform Democratic identification, falling 4.6 points short.

Southern ideological conservatism remained strong, though some issue preferences in the 2012 exit polls—taxation, immigration, and abortion, specifically—suggest that voters were more attached to the conservative label than to conservative policies.[3] This is not surprising, as a significant number of Americans describe themselves as conservative in surveys but actually embrace more liberal issue positions, a phenomenon political scientist James Stimson calls "conflicted conservatism."[4] Florida and Virginia generally reflected the nation's ideologi-

Table 1.1. State-Level Political Characteristics

	Obama % (v. 2008)	Partisanship		Ideology			Pres. approval		Uninsured	Unemployed
		Dem.	Rep.	Con.	Mod.	Lib.	App.	Dis.		
AL	38.4 (-0.3)	36.0%	49.6%	50.6%	32.0%	14.6%	36%	58%	18.0%	8.1%
AR	36.9 (-2.0)	41.5	40.8	45.3	33.5	18.6	38	55	21.5	7.2
FL	49.9 (-1.0)	43.0	42.3	38.8	35.9	21.6	46	47	22.9	8.5
GA	45.5 (-1.5)	40.3	44.3	43.8	35.1	18.0	45	48	21.5	8.7
LA	40.6 (+0.7)	40.3	45.1	45.6	34.8	15.2	40	51	20.4	6.6
MS	43.6 (+0.6)	40.1	47.1	48.2	32.9	15.4	44	52	23.5	8.9
NC	48.3 (-1.4)	43.4	43.2	41.2	35.3	20.3	45	48	20.2	9.3
SC	44.1 (-0.8)	36.9	48.8	43.7	36.2	17.1	40	55	20.0	8.6
TN	39.1 (-2.6)	38.1	46.5	44.2	34.6	17.9	37	57	17.1	8.2
TX	41.4 (-2.2)	38.3	44.1	42.6	34.4	19.4	42	50	27.6	6.6
VA	51.1 (-1.5)	41.2	44.2	38.8	37.3	20.4	46	48	14.3	5.7
National	50.9 (-2.0)	44.0	40.0	38.0	36.0	23.0	46	46	17.1	7.9

Sources: Dave Leip's Atlas of U.S. Presidential Elections, vote share, http://uselectionatlas.org; Gallup Daily tracking polls, party identification, gallup.com/poll/156437/heavily-democratic-states-concentrated-east.aspx; Gallup Daily tracking polls, ideology, http://www.gallup.com/poll/160196/alabama-north-dakota-wyoming-conservative-states.aspx#1; Gallup Daily tracking polls, presidential approval, gallup.com/poll/156389/thirteen-states-give-obama-majority-approval.aspx; Gallup-Healthways Well-Being Index, percent uninsured, gallup.com/poll/153053/Texas-Widens-Gap-States-Percentage-Uninsured.asp; and the Bureau of Labor Statistics, unemployment, bls.gov/web/laus/laumstrk.htm.

cal mood, whereas the other states showed a clearer rightward bent. Though Americans are more reluctant to label themselves as liberal as their real issue preferences would suggest, southerners across the region reject that identity at an even higher rate. Nevertheless, this disinclination toward liberalism clearly did not prevent Obama from being at least reasonably competitive in much of the region, as his vote share far outperformed the liberal bloc in every state.

Indicators more relevant to Obama and his policies showed a mixed bag for the president. His disapproval rates in the first half of the year were above the national average in all southern states.[5] Nowhere in the South did he score net positive approval, though his net negatives were only 3 points or less in Florida, Georgia, North Carolina, and Virginia. Obama was forced to defend Obamacare in the campaign, and the South might have intuitively presented a tempting target for the president, as every state in the region except Virginia was at or above the national percentage of uninsured citizens in 2011.[6] Indeed, six of the ten states with the highest rates of uninsured were in the South, with Texas leading the nation. Obama's regional performance, however, suggests little correlation between real health care conditions and his vote share. Four states in the region had below the national average unemployment rates in October 2012, but Obama triumphed in only one, while nearly capturing North Carolina, the state with the highest unemployment.[7] Ultimately, little real relationship existed between actual conditions, in this case on the economy, and the Obama vote.

Demographic Patterns in the General Election

The National Election Pool pared back its exit polling in 2012, cutting surveys in nineteen uncompetitive states.[8] Respondents from those states are still represented in the national exit poll, but the long-standing series of state-level surveys is now gone. The most severe consequence of this cut for scholars of southern politics is that it is not possible to talk in broad terms about the "southern electorate" or "southern voters" in the 2012 race. Rather, analysis is limited to a nonrandomly selected series of states that may not be representative of regional dynamics.

In the South, polls for only the three swing states, plus Alabama and Mississippi in the Deep South, were done. Table 1.2 shows the Obama vote by group for those five states, with the change in that vote from 2008 in parentheses.[9] The data generally show stability, with most shifts in voting minor. Indeed, most changes are so small that any differences may simply reflect sampling error between surveys across years rather than true change. Further, it is difficult to generalize most patterns of change across states. For many groups, Obama gains in some states as compared with 2008 but loses support in other states within the same group. It is impossible to determine whether this pattern captures sampling error between states or genuine state-specific dynamics.

Race

Unsurprisingly, race persisted as the major divide in southern voting.[10] Obama's white support eroded in all states but Alabama as compared with 2008. Deep South whites were markedly more Republican in their presidential voting than were Rim South whites. The subregional difference is likely exaggerated, however, since the five states chosen for exit polling were among Obama's best and worst performances among

Table 1.2. Obama Vote Percentage by Group

	AL	FL	MS	NC	VA	National
Race						
Black	95 (-3)	95 (-1)	96 (-2)	96 (+1)	93 (+1)	93 (-2)
White	15 (+5)	37 (-5)	10 (-1)	31 (-4)	37 (-2)	39 (-4)
Latino	—	60 (+3)	—	68 (—)	64 (-1)	71 (+4)
Asian	—	—	—	—	66 (—)	73 (+9)
Gender						
Female	44 (+2)	53 (+1)	46 (-1)	51 (-4)	54 (+1)	55 (-1)
Male	33 (-3)	46 (-5)	40 (+2)	45 (+2)	47 (-4)	45 (-4)
Race and gender						
Black female	95 (-1)	96 (-1)	96 (-2)	99 (-1)	95 (+1)	96 (0)
Black male	96 (-4)	94 (-1)	95 (-2)	92 (+5)	91 (+2)	87 (-8)
White female	16 (+4)	41 (-1)	11 (-2)	33 (-5)	40 (0)	42 (-4)
White male	14 (+5)	33 (-9)	9 (0)	30 (-2)	34 (-3)	35 (-6)
Latino female	—	61 (+6)	—	68 (—)	—	76 (+8)
Latino male	—	58 (-2)	—	—	—	65 (+1)
Age						
18–29	48 (-2)	66 (+5)	55 (-1)	67 (-7)	61 (+1)	60 (-6)
30–44	44 (-3)	52 (+3)	44 (-2)	51 (+3)	54 (+3)	52 (0)
45–64	35 (-1)	48 (-4)	45 (-5)	47 (+4)	46 (-5)	47 (-3)
65 and over	31 (-9)	41 (-4)	22 (—)	35 (-8)	46 (0)	44 (-1)
Income						
< $50,000	45 (-3)	59 (-3)	54 (-5)	55 (-2)	60 (-2)	60 (0)
≥ $50,000	30 (-2)	43 (+1)	27 (-2)	45 (+2)	47 (-2)	45 (-4)
Evangelical						
Yes	10 (+2)	21 (0)	5 (-1)	20 (-5)	17 (-3)	21 (-3)
No	60 (-4)	62 (+1)	73 (+2)	65 (-3)	64 (0)	60 (-2)
Place						
Urban	38 (-9)	56 (+4)	—	59 (-7)	64 (+2)	62 (-1)
Suburban	33 (-3)	51 (-2)	45 (+17)	45 (+1)	49 (-2)	48 (-2)
Rural	48 (+15)	35 (-6)	39 (-3)	39 (-4)	45 (-2)	39 (-6)

continued >

Table 1.2. (continued)

	AL	FL	MS	NC	VA	National
Party identification						
Democratic	90 (+5)	90 (+3)	92 (+3)	91 (+1)	94 (+2)	92 (+3)
Republican	1 (-2)	8 (-4)	4 (-2)	4 (0)	5 (-3)	6 (-3)
Independent	23 (-10)	50 (-2)	30 (-5)	42 (+3)	43 (-6)	45 (-7)
Ideology						
Liberal	82 (+5)	86 (-5)	83 (+6)	85 (-2)	92 (+2)	86 (-3)
Moderate	47 (-2)	53 (-4)	56 (+1)	57 (-6)	56 (-2)	56 (-4)
Conservative	11 (-5)	20 (-1)	18 (-4)	17 (+2)	11 (-7)	17 (-3)

Sources: 2012 and 2008 National Election Pool exit polls.
Note: Entries are Obama vote percentage by group. Changes from the 2008 Obama vote for that group are in parentheses.

southern whites four years previously. Though southern whites were generally more Republican than the 39 percent of white support Obama received nationally, his share in Virginia and Florida was comparable to the national vote. Whites were roughly 70 percent of the electorate nationally and in all polled southern states except Mississippi (59 percent). If minority voting patterns are static, these data suggest that 35 to 40 percent of the white vote is the Democratic target to construct a successful multiracial coalition both nationally and in the current southern swing states.

Black voters stayed almost unanimous in their Obama support regionally. Their higher-than-normal turnout from 2008 was largely flat everywhere except Mississippi, where their vote share increased 3 percent.[11] Obama received roughly two-thirds of Latino and Asian votes in states where those data were available. Hispanics increased 3 points to 17 percent of the Florida electorate but remained a stable 2 to 5 percent of the electorate in the other states. Asians barely registered in Deep South exit polls but were 1 to 3 percent of the voters in Rim South states. Despite these comparatively small numbers for Latinos and Asians in most southern states, their combined vote, even if only 5 percent of a state electorate, is critical to Democratic aspirations of winning electoral votes in the region's swing states. Generally, southern electorates became marginally less white in all states sans Alabama, a small but important change that could portend greater regional competitiveness in the future as the South diversifies.

Gender

Every southern state exhibited a gender gap of at least 6 points, but crossing race and gender shows that this gap was largely a function of race. Minority women drove the gender gap regionally, as substantial male-female differences among whites appeared only in Florida and Virginia. Curiously, the 8- and 6-point gaps among whites in those states were, respectively, larger than the 2-point differences each state showed in 2008. In 2004, however, Florida whites exhibited a gender gap of just 3 points, but white men and women in Virginia differed in their support for Democrat John Kerry by 8 points. Given this irregular fluctuation over time, it is difficult to discern whether long-term changes in the white gender gap in those two states are a function of mere sampling error or genuine electoral dynamics.

A 9-point difference emerged in national Obama support between black men and black women. That difference was a mere 1 percent in 2008, but most southern states showed little to no such gap among African Americans. North Carolina, where a 7-point gap appeared between black men and women, is the closest to a significant gender difference in this racial group in the states polled. That state also showed a 13-point gap among black voters in 2008, far exceeding the next closest black gender gaps of 5 percent in both Louisiana and Virginia that year.

Age

Young voters were critical to the 2008 Obama coalition, but many commentators speculated that their enthusiasm would wane in 2012.[12] Nationally, turnout of voters under thirty actually increased 1 percent, and their turnout was essentially flat across the South, remaining at about 20 percent of the electorate at both levels. The Obama vote in this group fell 6 percent nationally and 7 percent in critical North Carolina but increased 5 percent in Florida. Indeed, he won voters under thirty everywhere but Alabama and captured the thirty-to-forty-four segment in the three swing states.

Evangelical Whites

Despite doubts that white evangelicals would turn out for Romney, given his Mormonism, they declined as a share of the electorate only in North Carolina (-9 percent) and Virginia (-5 percent).[13] Their share of the vote remained at 26 percent nationally and ranged from 23 percent in both Virginia and Florida to 50 percent in the Deep South states. Evangelical whites voted strongly for Romney, but Obama won by substantial margins among nonevangelicals in all five states.

Size of Place

Republican growth in the South has been fueled by suburban and, more recently, rural voters, but Obama successfully outpaced recent Democratic performances in 2008 across all types of communities.[14] The change in the Obama vote by size of place, rather than fluctuating consistently across the region, varies by state. In suburban communities, for example, Obama gained in two states, Mississippi and North Carolina, but dropped in three sampled states, whereas Alabama was the only sampled state where Obama improved among rural voters. Florida and Virginia urban areas showed increased support for Obama compared with 2008. Again, the extent to which these shifts are driven by real voting changes versus the greater sampling error that accompanies subgroup estimates in surveys is unknown.

Across time, however, the geography of presidential competition across the South is changing. Republicans have generally won the region in recent decades by accumulating huge margins in growing suburban counties and, later, whiter rural locales. In many of the largest southern counties, however, Democrats have rebounded in the past decade, partially due to the growing diversity of those counties. Using 2000 as the baseline, Table 1.3 shows how the three largest jurisdictions in each state changed racially between the 2000 census and the 2011 American Communities Survey and how the county vote for Al Gore compares with the 2012 Obama performance. In Jefferson County, Alabama, for example, Obama won with 52.6 percent in 2012, an increase of 5.2 percent over Gore. Jefferson is now 47.8 percent minority. The white population share declined 6 percent by 2011, with blacks and Hispanics increasing their shares about equally.

Gore won only one-third of these counties, but Obama topped Romney in two-thirds. The difference is even starker when extending the comparison back another twelve years to Michael Dukakis in 1988. He lost all but two of these counties: DeKalb (50.2 percent) and Fulton (56.2 percent). Even in suburbs like Gwinnett County, Georgia, and Virginia Beach, Virginia, Democratic performance has generally improved in these vote-rich jurisdictions. Thus, it is not just counties with

Demographic and Issue Cleavages in the Southern Electorate ★ 11

Table 1.3. Changes in Race and Democratic Vote in Largest Counties, 2000 versus 2011–12

State	County	2012 Dem. %	Δ Dem. Vote %	2011 Minority %	Δ Population %			
					White	Black	Hispanic	Asian
AL	Jefferson	52.6	5.2	47.8	-6.0	2.6	2.4	0.4
	Mobile	45.0	3.1	39.3	-3.7	1.2	1.3	0.3
	Madison	40.0	-2.6	31.7	-5.0	1.1	2.8	0.2
AR	Pulaski	54.8	1.0	43.2	-7.8	3.2	3.6	0.9
	Benton	28.6	-3.7	20.7	-10.8	1.5	6.9	2.0
	Washington	40.1	-1.6	21.4	-10.9	1.1	7.6	0.8
FL	Miami-Dade	61.6	9.0	85.5	-4.7	-1.0	7.2	0.3
	Broward	67.1	-0.3	56.7	-14.9	6.9	9.1	1.2
	Palm Beach	58.2	-4.1	39.9	-11.0	4.0	7.2	1.0
GA	Fulton	64.3	6.6	58.4	-4.4	-0.1	2.2	2.8
	Gwinnett	44.7	12.5	56.3	-23.7	11.7	9.6	3.6
	DeKalb	77.9	7.6	69.4	-2.1	0.2	1.9	1.2
LA	E. Baton Rouge	51.8	6.5	52.3	-8.4	5.4	2	0.9
	Jefferson	39.9	0.6	43.7	-9.7	4.1	5.6	0.9
	Orleans	80.3	4.4	68.2	4.5	-7.2	2.1	0.6
MS	Hinds	72.3	19.0	71.5	-9.1	8.0	0.8	0.2
	Harrison	36.2	-0.2	31.5	-5.4	2.0	2.9	0.3
	DeSoto	32.8	5.4	29.1	-15.1	11.4	2.7	0.7
NC	Mecklenburg	60.7	12.4	48.7	-10.7	3.6	5.9	1.7
	Wake	54.9	8.9	36.9	-7.9	1.6	4.6	2.2
	Guilford	57.7	9.1	44.5	-8.9	3.8	3.5	1.7
SC	Greenville	35.2	4.0	28.8	-5.6	0.1	4.5	0.7
	Richland	65.3	11.1	53.5	-3.9	1.1	2.2	0.6
	Charleston	50.4	6.0	36.6	1.6	-4.8	3.0	0.4
TN	Shelby	62.6	6.1	60.5	-7.6	3.7	3.2	0.8
	Davidson	58.4	0.7	41.0	-7.6	2.0	5.3	0.9
	Knox	34.4	-6.1	14.6	-3.8	0.4	2.3	0.7
TX	Harris	49.4	6.5	67.1	-9.4	0.8	8.5	1.3
	Dallas	57.1	12.2	66.7	-11.5	2.2	9.0	1.3
	Tarrant	41.4	4.6	47.4	-10.6	2.5	7.6	1.2
VA	Fairfax	59.6	12.1	43.7	-10.3	1.3	4.8	5.0
	Virginia Beach	48.0	6.4	33.4	-5.3	1.1	2.8	1.4
	Prince William	57.3	12.8	49.7	-16.4	2.5	10.8	4.1

Sources: Dave Leip's Atlas of U.S. Presidential Elections, http://uselectionatlas.org; 2000 U.S. Census; 2011 American Communities Survey.

a large, minority-heavy central city such as Birmingham or Columbia, South Carolina, where the party has gained.

Arguably, the key dynamic driving the transformation of large southern counties is racial diversification. Jurisdictions like Hinds and Dallas Counties epitomize this phenomenon. In both locales, the white population share plummeted by about 10 percent from 2000 to 2011, owing to some combination of migration of minorities to these counties, higher birth rates among minorities, and white flight to newer suburbs and exurbs.[15] The same population dynamics are undoubtedly at play in other large counties across the region. Mainly, African Americans in Hinds and Latinos in Dallas have grown their shares at white expense. Accordingly, Democratic performance in these counties has spiked as the population and, logically, the active electorate have become increasingly nonwhite. Obama performed 19 and 12 points better than Gore in Hinds and Dallas, respectively, and 29 and 17 points better than Dukakis in 1988.

To what extent recent white flight from larger counties has contributed to their political transformation, newer suburban growth does not necessarily portend Republican strength. Many booming suburban or exurban communities are swinging more Democratic. In the rapidly growing Atlanta exurbs, for example, some counties, such as Cherokee and Forsyth, have indeed remained Republican strongholds, but others—Douglas, Rockdale, Newton, and Henry—have trended toward the Democrats. Like their larger counterparts, the political balance of these newer growth counties will lie mainly in their racial balance.

Though the rural South has trended more Republican recently as rural whites who were the last vestige of the old Solid South have disappeared, those slower-growing—or even shrinking—and smaller populations have not offset the Democratic boom in more populous areas. Southwest Virginia, for example, was one of the few areas of the state where Democratic presidential nominees could reliably count on support in recent decades, especially in the coalfield counties along the West Virginia border. In 2012, though, Obama lost every county in the region. The Republican surge there, however, has been drowned out by Democratic growth in urban and suburban counties in Northern Virginia and Hampton Roads.

Issues and Voting Patterns

Issue questions were inconsistent across the state exit polls, with many more questions asked in swing state surveys than in safer states. Thus, the focus here is on major campaign issues, especially the economy and health care, for which questions are available in at least all three competitive states. Minor campaign issues such as immigration, abortion, and gay marriage were each asked in one to two states in the South, but not enough to inform a broad analysis. Generally, the pattern of issue priorities, attitudes, and candidate support by issue in the South mimics the pattern observed nationally, with some small differences.

Economy

Table 1.4 compares how respondents in southern states responded to issue items relative to those in the national exit poll. Obama support by cell is in parentheses. On the "most important issue" facing the country, southern respondents resemble the national picture on both issue priority and Obama vote by issue choice. The economy trumped foreign policy, the deficit, and health care as the most popular of the four selections available to respondents across the board. A potential problem with questions such as this is the constricted choice set. Respondents seeing other issues like education or immigration as most important can select only from among the available options, so the issue choices should be analyzed with a substantial caveat. Obama performed best among voters selecting health care and foreign policy as the top issue, though his losses among economy voters were substantial only in the Deep South.

Unemployment and inflation vied for the economic problem respondents nationally saw as the most pressing. These were also the top problems for southern respondents, though North Carolina voters were 13 points more likely to select rising prices and Virginia voters were 17 points more likely to choose unemployment. Romney won economy voters nationally by 4 points, but this national victory was built mainly on a 34-point win among those selecting taxes as the top economic challenge and a tie among those picking inflation. That pattern was generally replicated in the southern swing states. Obama won housing market and unemployment voters, lost on inflation only in North Carolina, but trailed Romney substantially among those selecting taxes.

Both southern and national electorates were pessimistic about the current state of the economy. Voters overwhelmingly rated economic conditions as either "not so good" or "poor," but only about a third at both levels felt the economy was worsening. Obama captured only moderate support from those who saw the economic track as stagnant but won roughly 90 percent of the vote among the 40 percent of the electorates who believed the economy was improving. National economic perceptions are hugely colored by partisan perceptions, but it is impossible to remove partisans who are biased in their perceptions from the analysis in order to isolate more-persuadable voters.[16] Generally, at both the national and the state level, Obama won just enough support from those who felt the economy was at least not getting worse to carry him to victory. Undoubtedly, he was aided by the fact that voters, even in the South, still placed more of the blame for the nation's economic woes on George W. Bush than on him.

Health Care

The Affordable Care and Patient Protection Act of 2010, often dubbed Obamacare, was a major controversy in Obama's first term. In the campaign, though, it was arguably difficult for Romney to attack Obama credibly on it given that he championed a very similar bill as governor. The law survived a summer 2012 Supreme Court challenge, and Obama vigorously defended it on the trail. Though national polling had shown Americans as supportive of many key provisions of the bill, opinion had been somewhat negative on the law in abstract.[17] This general negativity is evident both nationally and in southern swing states in the exit polls. Voters nationally favored repeal by 5 points, and the only southern state noticeably off that mark was North Carolina, where repeal had a 13-point margin. Yet Obama won 75 percent of the vote among North Carolinians whose top concern was health care, similar to his performance elsewhere. Obamacare, though it divided the public, did not appear to fuel enthusiasm for Romney and, if anything, may have boosted Obama among voters for whom this issue mattered.

Other Issues

Questions about illegal immigration, abortion, and gay marriage were placed on the exit polls in certain southern states, though none of those issues emerged as major themes in the presidential race. Only with same-sex marriage did any state-level electorate significantly vary from how voters nationally felt about these issues. Even on supposed wedge issues, then, southern voters appear to have converged with where the broader American public was on many of these hotly contested debates.

The Alabama poll included a question about policy toward illegal immigrants working in the country, which was appropriate given the controversy there over the strict anti-illegal immigration law HB 56.[18] Despite its strong conservatism, 61 percent of Alabama voters favored

Table 1.4. Issue Preferences among Southern Voters, 2012

	AL	FL	MS	NC	VA	National
Most important issue						
Foreign policy	4 (—)	5 (53)	3 (—)	5 (43)	4 (—)	5 (56)
Deficit	18 (16)	13 (30)	18 (32)	14 (29)	14 (28)	15 (32)
Economy	61 (38)	62 (46)	56 (32)	59 (44)	62 (46)	59 (47)
Health care	15 (64)	17 (78)	20 (66)	19 (75)	17 (78)	18 (75)
Biggest economic problem						
Housing market	—	11 (57)	—	6 (—)	8 (—)	8 (63)
Unemployment	—	36 (53)	—	31 (52)	45 (54)	38 (54)
Taxes	—	11 (40)	—	15 (39)	16 (38)	14 (32)
Rising prices	—	38 (50)	—	44 (44)	28 (51)	37 (49)
U.S. economic conditions						
Excellent/good	—	24 (91)	—	24 (91)	30 (92)	23 (90)
Not so good/poor	—	75 (33)	—	75 (33)	69 (32)	77 (38)
Economic conditions are						
Getting better	—	38 (88)	—	38 (93)	43 (92)	39 (88)
Getting worse	—	32 (9)	—	33 (7)	33 (4)	30 (9)
Staying about the same	—	27 (37)	—	28 (33)	22 (36)	29 (40)
Blame for economic problems						
Obama	—	42 (8)	—	40 (5)	43 (8)	38 (5)
Bush	—	51 (83)	—	49 (84)	51 (86)	53 (85)
Repeal health care reform						
No	—	40 (87)	—	40 (90)	47 (89)	44 (87)
Yes	—	47 (21)	—	53 (16)	48 (13)	49 (15)

Source: 2012 National Election Pool exit poll.
Note: Entries are respondent issue preferences, with the Obama vote percentage for each group in parentheses.

offering legal status to illegal immigrants, with 35 percent favoring deportation. This is relatively close to the 65 to 28 percent national divide. Though Obama won only 11 percent of the pro-deportation vote in the state, those favoring legal status narrowly supported him by 51 to 48 percent. This breaks down to Romney voters favoring deportation by a slender 54 to 46 percent margin, indicating substantial support for immigration liberalism among Alabamians who favored the Republicans.

Abortion was placed on polls in North Carolina and Virginia. Nationally, 59 percent of voters preferred abortion to be legal, and only 36 percent, illegal. The Virginia electorate was marginally more liberal than voters nationally, breaking 63 to 33 percent in favor of legal abortion. North Carolinians were somewhat more conservative, favoring legal abortion only by a 53 to 40 percent margin. Small state deviances from national numbers aside, a majority of the electorates in both states solidly favored pro-choice positions. Abortion also clearly divided voters along partisan lines, unlike legal status in Alabama. Obama carried pro-choice voters by 41 points in Virginia (70 percent) and lost pro-life voters by 58 points (21 percent). His North Carolina numbers were similar—a 39-point win among pro-choice voters (69 percent) and a 58-point loss with pro-life voters (21 percent).

North Carolina was the only southern state with a same-sex marriage item. Voters nationally supported legal gay marriage in their states by 3 points, dividing 49 to 46 percent in favor. The North Carolina electorate came down clearly against same-sex marriage, opposing it by 57 to 35 percent. In the May 2012 primary, 61 percent of voters supported Amendment 1 to the state constitution, defining marriage as between one man and one woman. The amendment grabbed national headlines for its unusually restrictive nature, putting pressure on President Obama to publicly announce his personal support for same-sex marriage just days after the primary.[19] Like abortion, marriage rights divided the electorate, with Obama winning 79 percent of North Carolinians favoring same-sex marriage and only 29 percent among opponents (versus a comparable 73 percent and 25 percent nationally).

Latinos in the South

The Hispanic population has boomed in the South since 1990, especially outside the traditional Latino population centers in southern regions of Texas and Florida.[20] They are a growing political force whose increasing Democratic bent is altering the national political terrain. Despite growth rates ranging between 42 percent (Texas) and 148 percent (South Carolina) across southern states between 2000 and 2010, their absolute share of the population is below 10 percent in all but Texas and Florida, and their share of the electorate, smaller still. The geographic concentration of Latinos within states is helping change the balance of political competition at the local level, including in many previously Republican suburbs, and even their low single-digit portion of the electorate can be critical to a swing state victory for either party.

Quality data on Latino opinion has been difficult to gather given sampling and language challenges particular to this population.[21] But Latino Decisions (LD), a firm specializing in surveying Hispanics, conducted extensive polling before the election both nationally and in targeted states with large Hispanic populations, including Florida, North Carolina, Texas, and Virginia. Unlike the exit polls, the LD data had sample sizes large enough to produce more reliable estimates of subgroup behavior.[22] Table 1.5 summarizes some of the key findings from these data, comparing southern Latinos with the national sample.

State-level Hispanic populations in the South as aggregates resemble the national Hispanic community on most political accounts. Though Obama won the Florida Latino vote, his performance there lagged 17 points behind the national numbers. Parsing the Florida numbers by national origin, this difference stemmed largely from Cuban Americans. Only 35 percent of Cuban Americans surveyed planned to support Obama, as compared with 95 percent of Dominican Americans and roughly 70 percent of voters with Mexican, Puerto Rican, and Central or South American roots. Hispanic samples in the other three states were largely of Mexican and Central American descent, with their behavior resembling their Florida counterparts. Though Obama won naturalized Latinos by 9 points more than natural-born citizens, this pattern varied by state and is likely the product of state-level differences in the nature of Hispanic populations.

The LD survey included a different set of "most important issues" than did the network exit polls. A majority of Latinos, nationally, selected the economy/jobs as their top issue, a pattern that replicates in all but two state polls. Thus, both Latinos generally and the broader electorate perceived the economy as the top issue despite question differences. Only in North Carolina and Arizona did more Hispanics rate immigration as their top concern, beating the economy by 4 percent and 1 percent, respectively. The rationale for this difference is not apparent in the polls but could stem from state-level political dynamics, such as the highly controversial SB 1070 in Arizona.[23] The Obama vote is not available by top issue choice, as in the national exit polls.

Importantly, though many Republican leaders advocated reaching out to Latino voters after the election by softening the party's stance on comprehensive immigration reform, pluralities of Hispanics across the

Table 1.5. Political Behavior of Latinos, 2012

	FL	NC	TX	VA	National
Obama vote	58%	72%	71%	66%	75%
Obama % by nativity					
U.S. born	69	71	65	52	71
Naturalized	54	72	80	75	80
Most important issues					
Economy/jobs	57	46	55	55	53
Education	12	15	21	15	20
Health care	13	8	17	10	14
Immigration	35	50	33	42	35
Other	7	6	7	8	8
Deficit policy					
Only spending cuts	14	11	16	11	12
Raise taxes on wealthy	30	30	22	28	35
Combination	42	47	50	46	42
Obamacare					
Leave in place	51	55	59	59	61
Repeal	35	26	30	28	25
GOP vote if CIR* support					
More likely	39	30	38	28	31
Less likely	8	14	10	9	11
No impact	42	46	48	52	48

Source: Latino Decisions, *2012 Latino Election Eve Poll,* www.latinovote2012.com/app/#all-national-presidential_vote.
*Comprehensive Immigration Reform

board responded that such a move would have no effect on their willingness to support the GOP.[24] This suggests that the Republican problem with Latinos goes deeper than issues, perhaps relating to a stereotype that the party is unfriendly to minorities in general. The Republican Party is often perceived by Americans as a whiter, less racially tolerant group. The existence of a few prominent Republicans from minority backgrounds often does more to help the party's image among moderate whites uncomfortable with the racial image of the GOP than it does among minorities.[25] Nevertheless, boosting the party appeal even among a minority of Hispanics would help Republicans stem the growing affinity of Latinos for the Democratic Party.

The Election in Perspective

Though not quite the cliffhanger many anticipated it to be, the 2012 election was historic, especially for what it portends about the future of race in American politics. The first African American president won reelection with a majority of the votes cast, proving that 2008 was no fluke fueled by intense anti-Bush sentiment. Whether that success in breaking the color barrier will trickle down to racial minorities, especially blacks, running down-ballot is yet to be determined. The 113th Congress will have one black senator, Tim Scott (R-SC), and a bloc of African American representatives elected mostly from districts with large black populations. America has only one black governor, just the second elected post-Reconstruction. Most Hispanics and Asians in office are elected from constituencies with at least a minority plurality, but the South is notable for having both of the nation's sitting Indian American governors (Bobby Jindall [R-LA] and Nikki Haley [R-SC]) and two of three Latinos in the 113th Senate.

Though Obama largely reassembled his winning coalition, he lost the national white vote by 20 points. Indeed, Romney's margin among whites was the same as that of Ronald Reagan in 1980, the last Republican to unseat an incumbent Democratic president. At least nationally, the old racial calculus for Republicans of overwhelmingly winning the white electorate is a faltering strategy. Democrats are finding the formula for Electoral College success from the southern Democratic playbook—maximize minority turnout, win the minority vote overwhelmingly, and stem losses among whites to eke out a victory. Thus, national electoral politics increasingly resembles southern politics of the 1970s through 1990s, with the exception that the old biracial Democratic coalition is fast becoming a *multiracial* one. The unknowns for Democrats, though, are significant: Will minority turnout fall without Obama on the ballot? Will their Latino support continue to grow? Will whites swing further to the Republicans? The answers to these questions will dictate whether Democrats can build a successful multiracial coalition in 2016 and beyond.

With exit polls from most southern states unavailable, it is difficult to make reliable comparisons between the South generally and the national political scene. Some limited generalization is possible, however, with the data from the three Rim South swing states and two Deep South states. On most accounts, especially on issue priorities and preferences, the broader southern electorate is quite comparable to the national electorate. The same is true of Latinos in Rim South states compared with Latinos nationally. Thus, at least in survey top-lines, these data provide further evidence of converging opinions between southerners and nonsoutherners, though we should not overgeneralize the results, given that so many states are missing. More recent survey data have suggested that southern opinion remains distinctly more conservative on racial and moral issues, a pattern only partially observed here.[26] Again, the limited data do not necessarily warrant declaring opinions converging on these wedge issues, but do suggest a continued need for serious surveying of regional opinion trends.

In this election the key regional differences appear demographic, especially racial. In most southern states, though they have minority populations larger than the national average, polarized racial bloc voting continues to prevent Democrats from capturing enough white voters to forge a winning coalition. Unless Democrats can sway greater white support, which may be possible given continuing migration of more liberal-leaning nonsoutherners into many of the South's booming metropolitan areas, their regional hopes hinge on longer-term nonwhite population growth. Otherwise, Democratic presidential nominees may be hitting their high-water mark in many states with vote shares in the low to mid–40 percent range. The South is guaranteed, however, at least some attention in national campaigns of the foreseeable future, as three of its largest states have certifiable swing status. As the past two presidential elections proved, the South is anything but solid for either party.

2

The 2012 Presidential Nomination Process

John A. Clark

In retrospect the nomination of Republican Mitt Romney to challenge incumbent President Barack Obama seems like a preordained conclusion. To be sure, the former Massachusetts governor was perceived to be the front-runner in a crowded field of contenders. Romney entered the 2012 campaign with experience, name recognition, and a campaign network built during his unsuccessful run for the nomination in 2008. Part of his support was based on the likelihood that he more than any other candidate could topple Obama. Nevertheless, many Republicans had reservations about Romney. They seemed to be waiting for someone better to come along and enter the race. In the end, no such alternative candidate emerged. Romney captured his party's nomination and narrowly lost his general election bid.

The real race for the Republican nomination was not as clear-cut as this account suggests. It is true that no single alternative to Romney emerged from the pack of contenders who entered the race. It is also true that there were numerous times throughout the campaign that it seemed that Romney was on the ropes or at least vulnerable to defeat. A less experienced candidate with a less extensive organization and fewer resources might not have been able to weather the challenges that the front-runner faced. Far from inevitable, the battle for the Republican nomination was heavily contested at first. Then, in the blink of an eye, it was over.

As a region, the South in 2012 did not decide the Republican nomination. It did, however, provide opportunities for candidates who hoped to appeal to voters who were wary of Mitt Romney. Had their support solidified around a single candidate, the outcome of the nomination—and thus the general election—may have been quite different.

Setting the Stage for 2012

The system through which the major political parties select their presidential nominees is in seemingly constant flux. Significant changes in 2012 involved changes in laws governing campaign finance and rules created by the Republican Party itself. In addition, an extensive series of debates exposed the candidates to potential supporters and opened them up to a level of scrutiny not previously seen. Each of these changes affected the nominating process and its ultimate winner.

Changes in Campaign Fund-raising

The Federal Election Campaign Act amendments adopted in 1974 were an attempt to clean up campaigns for Congress and the presidency. In the aftermath of the Watergate scandal, the new laws were designed to foster transparency and encourage participation by small donors rather than wealthy "fat cat" donors. With regard to presidential nominations, a hybrid system of private and public funding was created. Individual contributions were capped at $1,000, with a federal match of up to $250 to encourage support from smaller donors. In exchange for these matching funds, qualifying candidates voluntarily agreed to limit both their total spending and their spending in individual states. The total, indexed to inflation, was $42 million in 2008. A different set of spending rules affected the general election campaign.

Between 1976 and 1992, only one candidate chose to forego matching funds to avoid the spending limits. That candidate, John Connally in 1980, failed to gain traction with voters and may have discouraged other candidates from following his path. In 1996, Steve Forbes used his ability to fund his own campaign as a signal that he was not beholden to special interests. He failed to win many votes, but the old campaign finance regime was beginning to fray. George W. Bush declined to accept matching funds in 2000 yet still raised an unprecedented $60 million before the first contest and more than $100 million by the time of the Republican convention. When contribution limits were raised to $2,000 in 2002 (and indexed to inflation), it became easier for candidates to forego public funds. By 2008, most major contenders in both parties chose to raise and spend as much as they could within the constraints of the individual contribution limits.[1]

In 2012, a new wrinkle in the system of campaign finance allowed individual contributors to give as much as they wanted to support the nomination bids of their preferred candidates. Most candidates formed so-called Super PACs to raise funds in unlimited amounts. Corporations were permitted to contribute to Super PACS, too, as a result of the U.S. Supreme Court's decision in *Citizens United v. Federal Election Commission* (2010), which required that corporations be treated as individuals in the context of campaign spending. As long as the Super PACs did not coordinate their spending with the candidate's official campaign organization, the ordinary limits on contributions did not apply. Super PACs supporting candidates for the Republican nomination raised more than $43 million by the end of 2011. Restore Our Future, a Super PAC supporting Mitt Romney, raised more than $30 million before the first votes were cast. According to the Campaign Finance Institute, nearly all of Restore Our Future's contributions came from individual and corporate donors who gave $25,000 or more.[2] This total, combined with the $56 million raised by the official Romney campaign, gave the former Massachusetts governor more than three times the spending capacity of his closest competitor heading into the first contests of 2012.

Changes in Party Rules

Presidential nominations are officially bestowed at the parties' national conventions. Thus, the primaries and caucuses held in each state are important because they determine who the delegates to the national convention will be and whom they will support on the first ballot of the roll call of states. The rules governing delegate selection are drawn from a combination of state laws and rules set by state and national party organizations.

In recent election cycles, decisions by state legislatures and parties to move their nominating contests to earlier dates have created what some have called the "frontloading problem."[3] Frontloading creates a compressed calendar with little time for candidates to refocus their campaign efforts on the next states in the sequence. Given the need to compete in multiple states simultaneously, frontloading puts a greater emphasis on early fund-raising and media coverage. The first contests, the Iowa caucuses and the New Hampshire primary, are considered more important than those that come later. Candidates who falter in these contests may see their nomination hopes dashed before most voters get the chance to cast a ballot.[4]

The national parties have tried both rewards and punishments to convince states to reverse the frontloading trend. In 2012, the Republicans continued a policy from 2008 that penalized states holding nominating contests prior to a specified date, in this case the first Tuesday in March. Four states were granted exceptions to hold their contests in February: Iowa, New Hampshire, South Carolina, and Nevada. States that violated the policy risked losing half of their delegates to the national convention unless granted a waiver from the national party.[5] Some states likely delayed their nominating contests to avoid the penalty. Others may have reacted to the prolonged Democratic nomination fight in 2008, which demonstrated that states holding later contests could benefit if they were not competing for attention with the contests of other states. Whatever the reason, the frontloading problem was reduced in 2012 compared with other recent nomination cycles.

A second Republican rules change prohibited states from awarding delegates on a winner-take-all basis prior to April 1.[6] This change meant that candidates who finished second or lower in a state might be able to pick up some of that state's delegates to the national convention. In practice, only a few states were affected by this change in rules. Given that Romney sewed up the nomination fairly quickly, it is unlikely that the process was affected to any considerable degree.

Debates and More Debates

A final characteristic of the 2012 nomination race was an unusually large number of debates. Between May 5, 2011, and March 3, 2012, as many as nine candidates appeared together in twenty-seven debates. Eleven of the debates were held in southern states: six in South Carolina, four in Florida, and one in Texas. Some observers suggested that the heavy schedule helped the eventual nominee, Mitt Romney, sharpen his skills for the general election debates with President Obama. Critics argued that the debates emphasized minor differences among the Republicans instead of their shared disagreement with the incumbent president. Considerable attention was focused on gaffes and misstatements, as when Texas Governor Rick Perry could not remember

Table 2.1. Republican Nomination Contests, 2012

Date	Contest
January 3	Iowa caucuses
January 10	New Hampshire primary
January 21	*South Carolina primary*
January 28	Maine caucuses (through March 3)
January 31	*Florida primary*
February 4	Nevada caucuses
February 7	Colorado caucuses, Minnesota caucuses
February 28	Arizona primary, Michigan primary
March 3	Washington caucuses
March 6	Alaska district conventions, *Georgia primary*, Idaho caucuses, Massachusetts primary, North Dakota caucuses, Ohio primary, Oklahoma primary, *Tennessee primary*, Vermont primary, *Virginia primary*, Wyoming caucuses (through March 10)
March 10	Guam convention, Kansas caucuses, Northern Marianas convention, Virgin Islands caucuses
March 13	*Alabama primary*, American Samoa caucuses, Hawaii Republican caucuses, *Mississippi primary*
March 17	Missouri caucuses
March 18	Puerto Rico caucuses
March 20	Illinois primary
March 24	*Louisiana primary*
April 3	Maryland primary; Washington, DC, primary; Wisconsin primary
April 24	Connecticut primary, Delaware primary, New York primary, Pennsylvania primary, Rhode Island primary
May 8	*North Carolina primary*, West Virginia primary
May 15	Nebraska primary, Oregon primary
May 22	*Arkansas primary*, Kentucky primary
May 29	*Texas primary*
June 5	California primary, Montana primary, New Jersey primary, New Mexico primary, South Dakota primary
June 26	Utah primary

Source: Frontloading HQ, "The Presidential Primary Calendar (Republican and Democratic)," http://frontloading.blogspot.com/p/2012-presidential-primary-calendar.html.
Note: Contests in southern states are italicized.

which federal agencies he wanted to shut down.[7] One Romney strategist compared the debates to the television show *American Idol* rather than a serious discussion of policy ideas.[8]

The 2012 Republican Nomination Campaign

As the incumbent president, Barack Obama was unchallenged for the Democratic presidential nomination. The Republican field, in contrast, was crowded. Former Massachusetts governor Mitt Romney was the presumptive front-runner after waging an unsuccessful campaign for the party's nomination in 2008. Romney had not run especially well in the South four years earlier, although he did place second to eventual nominee John McCain in Florida. Perry and former House Speaker Newt Gingrich of Georgia seemed to have the best chance of winning the votes of southern Republicans. Ron Paul represented a Texas district in the U.S. House of Representatives, but his libertarian philosophy had not garnered much support in 2008. Likewise, Atlanta businessman Herman Cain had never held office in Georgia or anywhere else. Most of the other candidates charted paths to victory that required success in other parts of the country, including former governors Jon Huntsman of Utah and Tim Pawlenty of Minnesota, former Pennsylvania senator Rick Santorum, and Rep. Michele Bachmann of Minnesota. Several prominent Republicans mentioned as possible candidates who declined to enter the race had few connections to voters in the region. Among those who teased a run were former vice presidential candidate Sarah Palin, governors Chris Christie of New Jersey and Mitch Daniels of Indiana, and even real estate mogul Donald Trump.

The Invisible Primary and Early Contests

Political scientists define the *invisible primary* as the period of campaigning that takes place before any votes are actually cast. This is the period during which prospective candidates jockey for position in the polls, put together their campaign organizations, and set out to raise as much money as possible for the impending party nomination campaign.[9] Despite Romney's prodigious fund-raising lead, it appeared that many rank-and-file Republicans were looking for an alternative. First Perry, then Cain, then Gingrich briefly passed Romney in national polls before the first votes were cast. In each case, their support faded as quickly as it emerged. Similar fluctuations occurred in most of the key early states.

Two prominent candidates did not survive the invisible primary. Pawlenty withdrew from the race in August 2011 after it became clear that he could not raise adequate funds to mount a competitive campaign. Cain shot to front-runner status in early October, but his stock dropped just as quickly under the scrutiny that accompanies the top spot in the polls. He suspended his campaign in December amid allegations of sexual harassment and a long-term extramarital affair that overshadowed criticisms of his economic proposals and lack of experience.

As 2011 drew to a close, Romney appeared to maintain his position as the leading candidate, but his grasp on the position was tenuous at best. The new year brought the first nomination contests. By tradition, Iowa's caucuses and the New Hampshire primary are first in the nation. Candidates are expected to engage voters in these states with a type of personal, retail campaigning not seen in other states.[10] To ensure that no state could hold its nominating contest earlier, Iowa had moved its caucuses up to January 3. New Hampshire held its primary just a week later. These two early contests have played a crucial role historically in winnowing the field of candidates to just two or three contenders, a role they fulfilled again in 2012. Romney narrowly won Iowa, with Santorum finishing second (Romney's victory was later reversed when delegate totals were certified, but not before he enjoyed the media attention that accompanied the initial returns). Ron Paul placed third, followed by Gingrich, Perry, and Bachmann. The poor showing in Iowa forced Bachmann from the race the following day. An Iowa native, her path to the nomination was predicated on a strong finish in the Hawkeye State. Romney followed his Iowa success with a win in New Hampshire, making him the first nonincumbent Republican to win both Iowa and New Hampshire (or so it appeared at the time). Paul finished second this time, followed by Huntsman, Santorum, and Gingrich. Perry, who had barely campaigned in the Granite State, received less than 1 percent of the vote. Huntsman and Perry withdrew the following week.

The Campaign Turns South

The two remaining contests in January were both in the South. In an effort to attract attention to their state, Florida legislators moved their primary to January 31. Not willing to sacrifice their first-in-the-region status, South Carolina Republicans moved their primary to January 21. Both states openly violated national party rules at the cost of half of their delegates to the national convention. Party leaders did not seem to mind, however. According to one South Carolina delegate, "I think there was a consensus that the penalty was well worth losing half the delegates. Honestly, I talked to many folks who said they kind of hope we don't get these delegates back because that would embolden other states to say, 'Hey, if there's no penalty, let's all jump ahead.'"[11]

South Carolina

Between 1980 and 2008, the winner of the South Carolina Republican primary went on to win the party's nomination. More important, South Carolina has held the first southern primary each cycle since 1996. Republican voters there embrace a brand of conservatism different from that in the earlier states of Iowa and New Hampshire. John McCain, a relative moderate, prevailed over a large field of candidates that split the conservative vote in 2008. With Romney in McCain's role in 2012, a victory in South Carolina would all but cinch the nomination.

Blocking Romney's path was Newt Gingrich. The former House Speaker's campaign had picked up steam after Cain and Perry floundered. In previous election cycles, weak showings in Iowa and New Hampshire might have forced him out of the race. Gingrich's South

Table 2.2. Republican Primary Outcomes in the South

	Romney	Gingrich	Santorum	Paul
South Carolina	28%	*40%*	17%	13%
Florida	*46*	32	13	7
Georgia	26	*47*	20	7
Tennessee	28	24	*37*	9
Virginia	*60*	—	—	40
Alabama	29	29	*35*	5
Missouri	31	31	*33*	4
Louisiana	27	16	*49*	1
North Carolina	*66*	8	10	11
Arkansas	*68*	5	13*	13
Texas	*69*	5*	8*	12

Source: "2012 Primaries and Caucuses Results," *CNN Politics*, July 26, 2012, http://www.cnn.com/ELECTION/2012/primaries.html.
Note: Winning percentages are italicized.
*Candidate had suspended his campaign.

Carolina effort was buoyed by a $5 million contribution from casino magnate Sheldon Adelson to the Super PAC supporting his candidacy. The infusion of cash allowed the Super PAC, Winning Our Future, to blanket the airwaves with ads bashing Romney's record as an investment banker. Gingrich received an additional boost when Perry dropped out of the race two days before the primary. The Texas governor endorsed Gingrich, as did state house Speaker Bobby Harrell. Gingrich also received support from Sarah Palin. The 2008 vice presidential nominee stopped short of a formal endorsement, but she told Sean Hannity of Fox News, "If I had to vote in South Carolina, in order to keep this thing going, I'd vote for Newt."[12] The endorsements helped solidify Gingrich's standing as the conservative alternative to Romney.

Not everything went Gingrich's way. In the week before the primary, a group of conservative religious leaders meeting in Texas endorsed Santorum. Two days before the primary, ABC's *20/20* aired an interview with Gingrich's second ex-wife, Marianne, in which she alleged that he asked her for an "open marriage" while engaged in an affair with another woman. The interview provided the basis for the first question of the January 19 debate in Charleston. Gingrich turned the issue into an attack on the media: "I think the destructive, vicious, negative nature of much of the news media makes it harder to govern this country, harder to attract decent people to run for public office, and I am appalled that you would begin a presidential debate on a topic like that."[13] The other candidates—Romney, Santorum, and Paul—refused to take up the attack. For South Carolinians seeking a nominee that would wage an aggressive general election campaign against Obama, Gingrich showed that he would not be pushed around.

Romney, meanwhile, had difficulty maintaining his momentum following New Hampshire. The front-runner provided a weak defense of his record at Bain Capital, and his Republican rivals attacked him for not releasing his tax returns. The aura of inevitability surrounding his campaign took a hit when it was revealed that Santorum, not Romney, had won the Iowa caucuses. Despite endorsements from Governor Nikki Haley and most of the state's newspapers, Romney seemed unable to connect with South Carolina voters.

A record number of voters—more than 600,000—participated in the Republican primary. When the votes were counted, Gingrich won a dominant victory with 40 percent of the vote. He carried all but three of forty-six counties. Romney placed second with 28 percent, followed by Santorum (17 percent) and Paul (13 percent). Most analysts thought that the debates had a greater impact on the outcome than did the 25,000 television ads that ran in the two weeks prior to the election.[14]

Florida

Gingrich hoped his South Carolina victory would propel him to a strong finish in Florida ten days later. Unlike Iowa, New Hampshire, and South Carolina, states where a great deal of campaigning takes place in person, Florida is a megastate with ten television markets. The Sunshine State posed different challenges, particularly for a candidate like Gingrich with limited resources. An additional $5 million, this time from Sheldon Adelson's wife, Miriam, allowed Gingrich to purchase much-needed advertising.[15] Gingrich received another boost when former candidate Herman Cain endorsed him three days before election day.

The late push for Gingrich was too little too late. Romney's campaign took advantage of Florida's early voting laws, running ads and encouraging voters to cast their ballots in advance of election day.[16] Perhaps more important, Gingrich's intensity waned as Romney's returned. Romney emphasized his long marriage and executive experience on the campaign trail in obvious contrast with Gingrich. He was sharp during the two Florida debates, whereas Gingrich appeared unfocused and less aggressive than he was in South Carolina.[17] Gingrich's call for a colony on the moon was seen as impractical at best and shameless pandering for votes at worst. Meanwhile, Romney outspent Gingrich on television by almost four to one in Florida, and almost all of his ads were negative. Nearly two-thirds of all the ads run in Florida were attacks on Gingrich. Romney won the support of 59 percent of voters for whom campaign ads were important in choosing a candidate compared with 42 percent for whom ads were not.[18]

Romney's spending advantages and sharp attacks paid dividends. He won Florida with 46 percent of the vote to Gingrich's 32 percent. Santorum placed third with 13 percent, and Ron Paul garnered 7 percent. Santorum's effort was hampered when he interrupted his campaigning in Florida to be with his sick daughter in Pennsylvania. Even so, he had neither the finances nor the organization to effectively contest the state.

Comparing Voters' Decisions in South Carolina and Florida

The outcomes of the South Carolina and Florida primaries were starkly different. Part of the explanation is grounded in the dynamics of a rapidly unfolding campaign. Perhaps more important, the electorates of the two states differed in politically important ways. Florida's demographics were more favorable to Romney, and he was able to exploit those advantages to win the state.

African Americans made up a tiny fraction of the vote in both Florida and South Carolina, but Florida's Latino community was substantial and politically important. The four remaining candidates sought to woo Latino voters in the Sunshine State. Immigration policy took on a new salience. The only positive ad that the Romney campaign ran in Florida was shown on Spanish-language television stations. In contrast, a Gingrich radio ad attempting to portray Romney as anti-immigrant backfired when U.S. senator Marco Rubio, Florida's highest-ranking Latino public official, decried it as "inaccurate" and "inflammatory."[19] Rubio remained neutral during the run-up to the primary, eventually endorsing Romney once the nomination was nearly clinched. Latinos comprised 14 percent of the Florida Republican electorate, and they favored Romney by a margin of almost two to one.

The Republican primary electorate in Florida was less traditionally southern and less evangelical than in South Carolina. Only about one-third of Florida residents were born in the state, compared with almost two-thirds of South Carolinians. Where did those new residents come from? In Florida more than 60 percent of new residents came from outside the South. Less than 40 percent of new South Carolinians migrated from another region of the country.[20] The presence of so many nonnative southerners in Florida likely gave Romney a boost, as he appeared to be less of an outsider to people who were themselves relative newcomers to the South. Not surprisingly, Gingrich ran best in the northern and panhandle regions of the state, which are, in many ways, more like the traditional South.

In religious terms, 64 percent of voters in the South Carolina primary were whites who self-identified as evangelical or born-again Christians, compared with 40 percent in Florida. Gingrich won support from 45 percent of this group in South Carolina and 38 percent in Florida, compared with 21 percent and 36 percent for Romney, respectively. Romney's margins over Gingrich for the rest of the electorate were 5 percent in South Carolina and 27 percent in Florida. Romney's Mormon religion had been an issue for many conservative Christians in the 2008 race, and it likely was in 2012, as well. Among South Carolina voters for whom the religious beliefs of candidates mattered somewhat or a great deal (60 percent of voters), nearly half supported Gingrich, whereas only 20 percent voted for Romney. Romney did better than Gingrich among the rest of voters by a 39 to 32 percent margin.[21]

Super Tuesday and Beyond

In 2012, the so-called Super Tuesday contests were held on March 6, a month later than in 2008. The original Super Tuesday in 1988 was a regional affair with ten southern states holding nominating contests on the same day.[22] Three southern states participated in 2012: Georgia, Tennessee, and Virginia. They were joined by eight nonsouthern states stretching from Vermont to Alaska. A sweep of the southern contests by Gingrich or Santorum might have weakened Romney's ability to claim a national following. Instead, they split the South. Gingrich won in his home state of Georgia; Santorum took Tennessee; and Romney carried Virginia. Romney also won Ohio, Massachusetts, Vermont, Idaho, and Alaska, while Santorum was victorious in Oklahoma and North Dakota.

Romney's Virginia win was tarnished by the fact that only he and Ron Paul were on the ballot. Virginia election law requires candidates to submit 10,000 valid signatures to get on the primary election ballot. Virginia residents must collect the signatures, and there must be at least four hundred from each of the state's congressional districts. A lawsuit challenging the constitutionality of the requirements was unsuccessful because it was filed after the deadline for submitting nomination petitions. Thus, the 40 percent of the vote received by Paul likely included a number of "anyone but Mitt" voters.

The strong showing by Romney on Super Tuesday did not guarantee him the nomination. It did, however, give him a lead in delegates that was nearly insurmountable. Losing primaries in Alabama, Mississippi, and Louisiana did little to slow his climb toward a majority of delegates. Romney did not clinch the nomination until the Texas primary in late May. By then, both Santorum and Gingrich had suspended their campaigns, conceding defeat.

Conclusion

Although the South as a whole did not determine the Republican presidential nomination in 2012, some states played important roles in the campaign. Gingrich's victory in South Carolina blunted the possibility that Santorum would emerge as the conservative alternative to Romney.

Romney's success in Florida undermined Gingrich's claim on that role. The mixed results on Super Tuesday, both inside and outside the region, further hampered the ability of the anti-Romney forces to coalesce around a single candidate.

In hindsight, the nomination of Mitt Romney may seem like a foregone conclusion. He entered 2012 with a substantial lead in fundraising, organization, and endorsements. Candidates with these advantages rarely lose in the post–reform era of presidential nominations.[23] Romney had not yet closed the deal, however, with the voters who participate in Republican primaries and caucuses. None of his challengers was able to emerge as a viable alternative, and the race ended relatively quickly.

The dust had barely settled on the 2012 campaign when potential candidates began to jockey for position for 2016. Assessments of Romney's general election defeat often contained a bit of self-serving analysis designed to enhance the fortunes of one candidate or to undermine support for another. In addition to the Republican race, the Democratic presidential nomination will be up for grabs in 2016. Both parties' fields will likely include a number of candidates from the South or who might be expected to appeal especially well to voters in the region.

II

*Elections in
the Deep South*

3

Alabama

Republican Dominance and Democrats Fighting to Survive

Shannon L. Bridgmon

The 2012 presidential election in Alabama was relatively unremarkable on the national stage, with the state proving to be a Republican stronghold, as expected. While the state received brief attention during the primary campaign from GOP candidates, neither campaign devoted many resources to the general election. Election results displayed continuity in presidential politics, with voters supporting the Republican nominee in similar numbers as previous elections. Although presidential politics has been dominated by Republicans for over fifty years, partisan politics for Alabama state and local offices has been much more competitive over the past two decades. Despite the state's little relevance at the national level, the 2012 elections sought to answer the question, emerging from the aftermath of the 2010 statewide elections; Can a Democrat win a statewide election in Alabama? The answer was no. The future appears bright for Republican candidates at every level of electoral politics in the state, suggesting Alabama has once again returned to a one-party system reminiscent of the Solid South experience.

2010: Deep Red Realignment

For two decades state-level offices in Alabama had remained divided in terms of party control. The 2010 midterm elections yielded significant gains for Republicans across the nation, resulting in switched partisan control of eleven state legislatures. Nowhere was this partisan shift clearer than in Alabama, where the statehouse fell into full Republican control for the first time since Reconstruction. Alabama now joins six other southern state legislatures controlled by the GOP: Florida, Georgia, South Carolina, Tennessee, Texas, and most recently, North Carolina. The 2010 elections decidedly placed Alabama as a Republican-controlled state.

Alabama's partisan development is consistent with the long-term trend of voters moving away from solid Democratic voting—first in presidential races, then in gubernatorial and congressional elections, and finally in state houses—a top-down realignment.[1] The Democratic bonds in Alabama's presidential voting were frayed first in 1948. After 1956, Alabama voted Democratic only once for president, for neighboring Georgian Jimmy Carter in 1976. Congressional success for Republicans grew over the past two decades, leaving only one congressional Democrat from Alabama by 2012. In 2008, Fifth District Democrat Parker Griffith managed to hold on to a Democratic seat vacated by Bud Cramer.[2] In 2009, Griffith switched his party affiliation to the Republicans.[3] It was not enough, however, to avoid a loss to Tea Party challenger Mo Brooks in the 2010 primaries.[4] Brooks faced off against Blue Dog Democrat Steve Raby and won with 58 percent of the vote.[5] Brooks's victory in the midterm elections that fall yielded the first Republican elected to Congress from the Fifth District since Reconstruction. The lone Democrat, Rep. Terri Sewell, represents the Seventh District, a majority-minority district centered in the Black Belt. As the 2012 elections neared, Alabama mirrored other Deep South states dominated by white Republican districts with one majority-minority Democratic district.[6]

While the state has been considered red, or solidly Republican, for some time in presidential voting, both houses of Alabama's state legislature remained under Democratic control until 2010. Following that election, the number of Republican seats in both legislative houses achieved almost a perfect inversion of 2006 Democratic levels. Table 3.1 illustrates the realignment of Alabama's political institutions over the past three decades. While Republican control in the state legislature is not as severe as Democratic dominance in the 1980s and 1990s, the gradual shift and eventual Republican identification is evident. Republicans accelerated their gains beginning in 1994, gaining control in both legislative chambers in 2010. When the dust settled following the 2010 elections, Alabama Democrats were, in large part, out of power in state government. Only two Democrats were left in statewide offices, the Alabama chief justice and the head of the public service commission—neither of whom were on the ballot in 2010.[7]

The 2012 Republican Primaries

Alabama received the most presidential campaign attention in 2012 during the Republican primary elections. Holding March elections relatively early in the primary season placed the state in a more influential position in determining the party's nominee. This visibility was heightened during the Republican primary, as President Obama faced no primary opposition in the Democratic elections. Republican campaign efforts were focused in Alabama and Mississippi leading up to their primaries, as earlier contests had not produced any clear front-runner.[8]

A crowded field of contestants vying for conservative support fostered impressive mobilization efforts among Alabama Republican primary voters. The campaign tightened into a three-man race between Mitt Romney, Newt Gingrich, and Rick Santorum.[9] Each candidate focused

Table 3.1. Alabama Partisan Control of Political Institutions, 1982–2010

	House		Senate		Supreme Court		Governor
	Dem.	Rep.	Dem.	Rep.	Dem.	Rep.	
1982	97	8	32	3	9	0	D
1986	88	17	30	5	9	0	R
1990	88	17	28	7	9	0	R
1994	74	31	22	13	8	1	R
1998	69	36	24	11	4	5	D
2002	64	41	25	10	1	8	R
2006	61	44	23	12	1	8	R
2010	39	66	12	22	1	8	R

Source: Compiled by author from data supplied by the Alabama Secretary of State and the Supreme Court and State Law Library.

money and resources into the state during the two weeks leading up to the election. Both Gingrich and Santorum attended a candidate forum sponsored by the Alabama GOP the evening before the election. Mitt Romney did not participate in the event, leaving Gingrich and Santorum to outmaneuver each other in order to appeal to the most conservative supporters in the party.[10]

The primary results in Alabama reflected a larger struggle within the GOP nationally as the establishment and business interests clashed with the populist elements within the party.[11] While Romney's support held steady among business-minded and older Republicans, Gingrich and Santorum both competed for social conservatives and Tea Party elements within the party. Support among these bases was fairly evenly split between the two, reflecting the similarity in their campaign messages and experience. As former congressmen, both were Washington insiders levying heavy criticism against increased centralized power and public spending. Both candidates were also pro-life Catholics who invoked populist rhetoric against social elites. Gingrich's campaign messages in Alabama were more policy oriented and geared toward reducing the scope of government. Santorum drew heavily on faith-based language and sought to connect with voters on a personal level. Gingrich and Santorum's messages found a receptive audience in Alabama, and the battle for delegates was waged between these two men in rural areas. Santorum's momentum during the last two weeks of the primary campaign appeared to grow at Gingrich's expense.[12] While Romney's support remained steady, Santorum pulled support directly from Gingrich and opened up a wider lead in the counties he carried.

Santorum's campaign rode the shift in momentum to victory with 31.5 percent of votes cast. Gingrich and Romney essentially tied for second and third place with 29.3 and 29.0 percent, respectively. Voting patterns fell along familiar geographical lines, mirroring those patterns V. O. Key first identified seven decades ago. Throughout the state's history, geographical voting has broken between the northern and the southern halves of the state. Northern Alabama is mostly hill country and populist in political character, whereas the southern half is characterized by the wealthy agricultural interests of the Black Belt. These geographic and economic bases worked to define separate political cultures within the state, and voting patterns within party primaries still reflect these differences.[13] Santorum carried the central and northern areas of the state, whereas Gingrich prevailed in the Wiregrass region. These regional voting patterns mirrored the primary elections in

2008. Generally, the counties that supported Mike Huckabee in 2008 supported Rick Santorum in 2012, and the southern counties McCain carried supported Gingrich. Although Romney found no real support in Alabama in 2008, this cycle he carried urban counties where higher education and income levels were more prevalent.

General Election for President

The 2012 presidential campaigns in Alabama were expectedly weak, reflecting the state's safe status for Republic presidential candidates over the past four decades. Alabama did prove useful, however, to each party in terms of voter mobilization and resources. President Obama made no visits to Alabama during the campaign. First Lady Michelle Obama visited the state in the summer, making several public appearances and attending a fund-raiser for the president. Mitt Romney made one visit to Alabama after securing the nomination, attending a private fund-raiser at The Club in Birmingham and setting a state record for one event by bringing in $2 million.[14] Since the electoral results for the state were a foregone conclusion, each campaign sought to export their political resources in the state. Alabama Democrats were recruited to make calls to voters in swing states for President Obama, and some joined campaign events in Florida and Ohio. State Republicans sent over two hundred activists to the swing states of Florida, Virginia, and North Carolina toward the end of the campaign. Rep. Mo Brooks led the largest delegation of "Battleground Patriots" to Ohio to campaign for Governor Romney.[15]

What attention was directed toward Alabama during the general election was not generated by the campaigns or candidates themselves. Former representative Artur Davis, an African American Democrat who represented Alabama's majority-minority Seventh District, made quite the campaign splash in 2012. Davis, who served as the national cochair for Barack Obama's 2008 campaign, switched to the Republican Party following a dismal gubernatorial campaign in 2010. Davis voted against the Affordable Care Act and actively worked to place himself as a centrist who was not tied to the national Democratic establishment, hoping to appeal to white Blue Dog Democrats. During the process he alienated his constituents and failed to earn the support of the black political establishment, intentionally not asking for their support.[16] He lost the primary election, distanced himself from the Alabama Democratic Party, and subsequently moved to Virginia.[17] His former role as campaign chair for Obama and recent switch to the GOP in May 2012 made him a prime recruit, however, for the Romney campaign.[18] Davis addressed the RNC during a prime-time speech laced with sarcasm and regret for supporting President Obama.[19] Davis went on to stump for Romney at events, served on his Black Leadership Council, and appeared in campaign ads supporting the former governor.[20]

Congressional and Statewide Campaigns

The congressional politics of the 2012 campaign resembled most congressional races, yielding overwhelming support for incumbents. No Senate seat was up for election this cycle, and all seven congressional incumbents handily won reelection (see Table 3.2). New legislative district lines reinforced district safety for incumbents.[21] Rep. Jo Bonner (Second District Republican) ran unopposed.

Reminiscent of the Democratic Solid South, the most competitive congressional races occurred in the primaries. In the Fifth District first-term incumbent Mo Brooks faced former representative Parker Griffith in the primary and captured nearly 60 percent of the vote. Despite the district's historical moderation and overwhelming reliance on federal employers, primary voters supported the Tea Party incumbent. Brooks easily won the general election, cementing the district as safe Republican territory. Sixth District representative Spencer Bachus drew a serious primary challenge by state senator Scott Beason, cosponsor of Alabama's new immigration law. Bachus won 59 percent of the vote, indicating Alabama's Republicans were still willing to support longtime establishment Republicans against Tea Party–style challengers.

Beyond federal races, eleven statewide offices were up for election, consisting of judicial races and public service commission president. Nine of these races were uncontested by Democrats. Only two races, those for commission president and supreme court chief justice, drew Democratic candidates. Over the past two decades, Alabama's supreme court races have emerged as the most expensive and bitter of all state races, with heightened attention on elections for chief justice. Former chief justice Roy Moore emerged from the 2012 primaries as the party's nominee, essentially splitting business and establishment GOP support among his rivals.[22] Best known as the "Ten Commandments Judge," his prior removal from the court left him vulnerable moving forward to the general election.[23] Democratic candidate and Jefferson County circuit

Table 3.2. Alabama Federal Elections Results, 2012

Candidate (party)	%	Vote total	Incumbent vote % change from 2010
President			
Barack Obama/Joe Biden (D)	38	787,027	-1
Mitt Romney/Paul Ryan (R)	61	1,245,221	
Virgil Goode Jr./James Clymer (I)	0	2,957	
Gary Johnson/Jim Gary (I)	1	12,242	
Jill Stein/Cheryl Honkala (I)	0	3,366	
U.S. House			
First District			
Jo Bonner (R)**	100	196,073	+17
Second District			
Therese Ford (D)	36	102,836	
Martha Roby (R)*	64	180,339	+13
Third District			
John Andrew Harris (D)	36	97,838	
Mike Rogers (R)*	64	174,875	-5
Fourth District			
Daniel H. Boman (D)	26	69,427	
Robert Aderholt (R)*	74	197,736	+24
Fifth District			
Charlie L. Holley (D)	35	101,504	
Mo Brooks (R)*	65	188,833	+7
Sixth District			
Penny "Colonel" Bailey (D)	29	86,698	
Spencer Bachus (R)*	71	215,966	-25
Seventh District			
Terri A. Sewell (D)*	76	230,077	-10
Don Chamberlain (R)	24	73,292	

Source: Alabama Secretary of State.
*incumbent
**Incumbent Rep. Jo Bonner ran unopposed.

Judge Robert Vance Jr. was widely respected and free of controversy or scandal. Vance drew several notable Republican endorsements and large campaign contributions. Despite his fund-raising advantage, professional experience, and reputation, it was not enough to defeat Moore.

While the public service commission races are typically overlooked, the 2012 race served as a gauge for the future of the Alabama party system. The race was a rematch, pitting incumbent Democratic commission president Lucy Baxley against former state GOP chair Twinkle Andress Cavanaugh. Baxley, whose name is synonymous with Alabama Democratic politics, was the last-remaining Democratic incumbent in statewide office. Despite Baxley's popularity as a longtime political figure in the state, Cavanaugh won 54 percent of the vote.

Along with statewide races, twelve proposed amendments to Alabama's extensive constitution were submitted for voter approval. Eleven of these appeared on the general election ballot. One amendment, known as the "Medicaid Amendment," was referred to voters in a special election in September. The measure approved a transfer of $148 million from an oil and gas trust fund to the general fund. The dire fiscal situation in Alabama created a situation, like in many states, where basic government services such as prisons, roads, and matching dollars for federal Medicaid transfers were likely to see severe cuts. Both Democratic and Republican leaders worried the amendment would fail if left to fare along with the other amendments on the ballot in November. Isolating and removing the measure to a special election would improve its chance of passing, as low-information voters or those with little concern about the issue were expected to stay home for the special referendum. Also, a rejection of the measure would allow lawmakers to convene in a special session to deal with the budget shortfall before the new fiscal year began.[24] With elites of both parties supporting the measure and seeking to mobilize support, the question of the general fund served as the basic campaign issue in the state during the early general election season. The measure passed by a two-to-one margin.[25] Other notable constitutional amendments approved by voters in November included a measure for secret ballot voting for labor organizations, a symbolic vote against the individual mandate in the Affordable Care Act, and the continuation of the Forever Wild Land Trust.

The most controversial amendment proposed on the general election ballot was Amendment 4, which repealed antiquated and obsolete language from the constitution regarding poll taxes and segregated schools. The central issue of disagreement stemmed from language pertaining to

Amendment 111 of the constitution, which specifically stated citizens had no right to a public education. Proponents of the measure maintained that approval removed references only to segregation by race and would not threaten public education. No vocal opposition to the proposal based on the racist language emerged. Rather, opponents voiced support for the declared intent but feared the move would further damage public education. Opponents of the measure, including the Alabama Education Association and many black leaders, argued the remaining language would retain and reinforce the denial of a right to a public education.[26] A similar measure was proposed in 2004 that also would have eliminated the language denying the right to an education. The measure failed, however, because of fear the change would make it easier to raise taxes. The 2004 proposal failed by fewer than 2,000 votes, less than 0.1 percent. The 2012 was rejected by a wide margin, 60 to 40 percent.

Analysis

The 2012 general election yielded no real surprises. The partisan map mirrors the 2008 election. Mitt Romney carried all but two of the same counties as John McCain, and President Obama carried the same counties he did in 2008, with the addition of those two counties.[27] President Obama carried Conecuh (50.6 percent) and Bourbon (51.3 percent) Counties by slim margins. In 2008, these counties supported John McCain with 50.1 percent and 53.6 percent of the vote share, respectively. Turnout was slightly lower than in 2008, as expected.[28] Turnout among registered Alabama voters was 72.4 percent. A midsummer poll projected support for President Obama hovering around 36 percent, very close to the actual 38 percent he received. These numbers were also consistent with his vote share in 2008 (39 percent) and John Kerry's support (37 percent) in 2004 (see Table 3.3).

The results of the 2012 elections in Alabama reflect well-established trends in southern political development. Alabama continued to support Republicans in presidential elections, with support for each party's nominee mirroring those from previous elections (see Table 3.3). Exit polls reveal a continuity of presidential voting behavior among various demographic groups. President Obama fared best among African Americans (95 percent), those with incomes under $50,000 (45 percent), and those who identified themselves as Democrats (90 percent). He slightly increased his support among females, whites, conservative Protestants, and Democrats. Support for Governor Romney was in line

Table 3.3. Alabama Presidential Election Exit Poll Results, 2000–2012

	2012		2008 (N = 1,070)		2004 (N = 736)		2000 (N = 1044)	
	Obama	Romney	Obama	McCain	Kerry	Bush	Gore	Bush
All voters	38%	61%	39%	60%	37%	62%	42%	56%
Race								
White	15	84	10	88	19	80	25	73
African American	95	4	98	2	91	8	91	8
Gender								
Male	33	66	36	62	30	69	36	62
Female	44	56	42	58	43	57	47	52
Income								
< $50,000	45	54	45	54	48	50	—	—
$50–100,000	30	70	36	63	22	78	—	—
> $100,000	30	70	—	—	—	—	43	55
Conservative Protestant								
Yes	10	90	8	92	12	88	18	82
No	60	38	64	34	42	56	52	46
Party identification								
Democrat	90	10	85	14	92	7	85	14
Independent	23	75	33	64	29	66	30	66
Republican	1	98	3	97	1	99	2	98

Source: "President: Alabama," *CNN Politics,* December 10, 2012, http://www.cnn.com/election/2012/results/state/AL/president.

with that of other recent Republican candidates. He carried whites (85 percent), males (66 percent), those with incomes above $50,000 (70 percent), elderly voters (79 percent), conservative Protestants (90 percent), independents (75 percent), and self-identified Republicans (98 percent).[29] Romney outperformed McCain's 2008 standing among men and independents, building on Republican strength among those groups in the state.

The exit polling data are largely reinforced when looking at county-level voting behavior.[30] President Obama received his largest vote shares in the Black Belt counties, all of which are in the lowest income group. His weakest electoral performance occurred in counties with a less than 15 percent African American population. Higher rates of white population led to higher levels of Republican presidential voting. Again, the geographic component of the analysis is compelling. Mitt Romney's widest vote margins are found in more affluent suburban counties and in the northern Alabama Hill counties.[31] Hill counties offered the weakest support for Barack Obama, with outcomes almost identical to those of 2008 and only 1 percent lower than Kerry's 2004 margin. Likewise, other regions of the state largely maintained current electoral trends since 2000, with results mirroring the Bush/Kerry election of 2004. The notable exception is the Tennessee Valley, with Democratic support steadily declining over the past decade. This is consistent with the overall partisan voting behavior in the region in other races. The decline in presidential Democratic vote share during this period shows the area was primed for Republican success, which prompted Rep. Parker Griffith's party switch and Mo Brooks's subsequent victories.[32] The state's regional political disparity becomes more apparent when examining county changes in vote margins from 2008. Counties in the northern half of the state became more Republican in presidential voting, whereas counties in the southern area increased their vote share for President Obama.[33]

With regard to racial voting, the 2012 election may shed some light on reemerging questions of race and politics in Alabama. In 2008, Barack Obama carried only 10 percent of white Alabamians—the lowest in the nation. Did this reflect an inherent racism against a black presidential candidate, or could the results be attributed to ideology, partisanship, or other factors?[34] An examination of Democratic primary votes in Alabama's 2010 gubernatorial election could lead to the conclusion that black candidates cannot win any statewide election in Alabama. A careful review reveals a more complex picture, however. Artur Davis ignored powerful black political groups during his primary campaign, failing to master basic retail politics.[35] Although President Obama's weakest performance came in the whitest areas in the state in 2012, he actually increased his support among Alabama's white voters from 2008, carrying 15 percent of the group. Despite white Alabamians' overwhelming support of Romney, President Obama's vote share is comparable with Kerry's performance in the state in 2004.

Counties with substantial African American populations voted at higher levels for Barack Obama than did white areas; however, his vote share within that group was markedly down from 2008. How does this square with exit polling data suggesting overwhelming African

American support? Nine out of the eleven counties that are majority African American experienced drops in African American population from 2000 to 2010.[36] During the same period metropolitan and, especially, suburban counties saw a rise in African American populations.

Coupled with the overall partisan developments in the state since 2008, low support for President Obama simply reflects a lack of support for Democratic candidates in general. African American support for the president was at 95 percent, slightly down from 98 percent in 2008. Identity politics among African Americans is still the defining political influence on voting, but the slight downturn in support for President Obama reveals it is not universal or static. Thus, although established voting patterns between the races continue, early results and exit polls suggest the electorate is not voting based on race itself.

One of the most interesting points the data yield in recent elections is that aside from racial voting patterns, other indicators reveal a slump within the middle range of county-group characteristics. Lowest Democratic support occurred not among counties with the highest income groups but within those counties that had median incomes between $34,000 and $40,000. This is also evident in regard to levels of rural and urban populations, with counties between 20 and 50 percent urban supporting Republican candidates at higher levels.

Election results also confirm that party label matters. Partisanship is a strong influence on down-ticket races, as well, with most contested state and federal races favoring Republicans by similar margins. Despite the GOP's advantage, individual races may be more hotly contested by Democrats, such as the chief justice race and that for public service commission president. Although the GOP candidates prevailed in both races, the margins were much narrower. Another political truism was confirmed—the incumbency advantage remained strong for Alabama's congressional delegation, with all members facing weak opposition in the general elections. Also, recent legislative redistricting helped in keeping the districts safe for incumbents.

Boomerang Politics: The Return of a One-Party State?

Alabama Democrats seek to hold on to local offices and stave off the top-down partisan realignment process. State Democratic support rests primarily in the Black Belt, where the state's African American population is largest and dominates electoral outcomes. Northern Alabama—historically, supportive of Democratic policies as a legacy of New Deal investments—reflected white Democratic support at the local level, though it shifted support to the Republicans up the ticket. Electoral victory margins in local races for white Democrats are shrinking, however. The shift has left Alabama's Democratic base with a racial and political minority status, mimicking the political divides that came to define a one-party South.[37]

With 2010 serving as a critical election at the state level, the 2012 election solidified the trend. The governing apparatus of state government is in solid Republican control, while Democratic officeholders in the state legislature are found largely in the Black Belt, many times running unopposed.[38] The redistricting process of 2011, controlled by a new Republican legislature, strongly favored Republicans and will facilitate long-term success for the party.[39]

Conclusion

While presidential politics in Alabama continues its trend of Republican support, the top-down realignment process continues in the Heart of Dixie. Following the 2012 elections, no Democrats held any statewide office and only one Democrat served in the congressional delegation. Republican dominance in state governance will yield policies seeking to cement the new partisan order. Presidential politics in Alabama were played out largely during the primary contests, with a general election so uncompetitive for Democrats that an export of state Republicans campaigned in the battleground state of Ohio for Governor Romney.[40] President Obama's performance in the state was weaker than in 2008 and much more consistent with John Kerry's in 2004. Overall support for Democrats, whether for state offices, Congress, or the presidency, is at its lowest since Reconstruction. The political landscape in Alabama has returned to a familiar one, with the state returning to solid one-party domination and taking another meaningful step away from the state's relatively brief experience in two-party governance.

4

Georgia

Even Redder

Charles S. Bullock III

For years Georgia Democrats had greater success than their peers in the region when it came to withstanding challenges from the GOP. As recently as the early 1990s, Republicans had little to show for their efforts that began in 1964 when Barry Goldwater carried the state and helped elect a member of Congress. Prior to the 1992 election, Georgia still had only one Republican member of Congress, and no Republican had won a statewide constitutional office for more than a century. The seedbed of potential candidates for higher office, the state legislature, also remained largely off-limits to Republicans, who accounted for only about one-fifth of the membership. In less than a generation, however, the positions of the two parties have reversed dramatically. Following the 2010 elections, Republicans held all fifteen statewide partisan offices. They also had eight of the thirteen seats in the congressional delegation. In the state legislature, where Republicans had controlled both chambers since 2005, their share of the seats exceeded 60 percent.

A less thoroughgoing transformation in voter loyalties has accompanied the massive shift in partisan success in electoral politics. Exit poll results from 1992 showed Democrats as the party of choice for 42 percent of Georgia's electorate, whereas Republicans claimed 34 percent.[1]

Democrats continued to enjoy a plurality among voters through the 2000 election. By 2004, the fortunes of the parties had reversed, with Republicans claiming the loyalty of 42 percent of the electorate and Democrats retaining only 34 percent. The huge surge in African American participation in 2008 nudged Democrats back to a plurality, with the division among partisans being 38 percent Democratic and 35 percent Republican. The media has not sponsored a general election exit poll in Georgia since 2008, but a survey done by the Mason Dixon polling firm in the week before the 2010 election found that 41 percent of likely voters identified as Republicans, compared with 33 percent who identified as Democrats.[2]

The shift from a solidly Democratic state to an overwhelmingly Republican one resulted from the changing loyalties of the white electorate. African Americans, who constitute a growing share of Georgia's electorate, remain overwhelmingly Democratic. For many years the rule of thumb held that Democrats could succeed in statewide contests if they attracted at least 40 percent of the white vote, along with the near unanimous backing of African American voters. When Roy Barnes won the governorship in 1998—the last year in which a nonincumbent Democrat won a statewide post—he got 39.7 percent of the white vote.[3] Four years later when Barnes failed in his reelection bid, estimates derived using ecological inference placed his share of the white vote at approximately one-third.[4] In 2006, Republican Sonny Perdue won a second term and held his Democratic opponent to only 27 percent of the white vote. White support for Democrats continued to drop, with Barack Obama winning only 23 percent support among whites in 2008. That year's Democratic Senate nominee, Jim Martin, did slightly better, with 26 percent of the white vote.[5]

Although Obama lost in Georgia, he ran relatively competitively in 2008, securing 47 percent of the vote. For a while, the Obama team had Georgia as a secondary target. They hoped that the Libertarian presidential nominee, Bob Barr, a former four-term member of Congress from Georgia, might siphon off 6 percent of the vote so that 47 percent could yield an Obama plurality. As the campaign progressed, however, it became obvious that Barr could not come close to 6 percent of the vote, and the Obama efforts in Georgia withered.

In 2010, none of the Democrats competing for statewide offices did as well as Obama had in 2008. The strongest performance came from the Democratic nominee for attorney general, but even he could not win 44 percent of the electorate. Democrats continued to run strongly among black voters, but their share of the white vote dropped still further into the vicinity of 20 percent, although that varied across offices.

Going into the 2012 election cycle, Democrats found themselves in their weakest position ever. They held no statewide offices and only five congressional seats. Democratic officeholders were almost exclusively urban and predominately African American. With the defeat of Jim Marshall in a middle Georgia congressional district in 2010, only one white Democrat remained in the congressional delegation, and following redistricting, his hold on that seat was precarious.[6] Thirteen of the twenty Democratic state senators were black, as were forty-three of sixty-three Democratic members of the lower chamber. Although the traditional heartland for Democratic strength had been rural Georgia, by 2012 only one Democratic senator represented a rural district.

The Republican Presidential Primary

Early in the 2012 Republican presidential sweepstakes, Georgia had not one but two candidates. Former U.S. House Speaker Newt Gingrich returned from political exile to seek the presidency, where he joined Atlanta radio talk show host Herman Cain. Gingrich had served in Congress for a quarter of a century, representing metro-area Atlanta Republicans. He withdrew from politics and resigned his position in Congress once it became clear, following the 1998 GOP debacle, that he could not win reelection as Speaker. Shortly after leaving Congress, Gingrich, who had overseen efforts to impeach President Bill Clinton for his dalliances with intern Monica Lewinsky, left his second wife. Even before terminating the marriage, Gingrich had begun an extended affair with a House staffer who became his third marital partner. Having left politics, Gingrich severed his ties with his adopted state, settled in the Washington, DC, area, and concentrated on making money. Conservative groups continued to pay him handsome speaking fees. He also coauthored a series of historical novels. He kept his name before the public by appearing on Sunday morning news shows. Despite remaining a public figure, the announcement that he would seek the presidency came as surprise. Gingrich's candidacy found favor with a number of Georgia Republican activists who rushed to jump on what they hoped would be a victory train. Among those who signed on to support the former Speaker was Governor Nathan Deal.

Cain lacked Gingrich's political résumé, with his only venture into electoral politics having come in 2004 when the former entrepreneur competed for the Senate seat being vacated by Zell Miller. Cain was given little chance for success, but he exceeded expectations, finishing second to Johnny Isakson. A surprising part of Cain's second-place finish was that it eclipsed the showing of six-term U.S. representative Mac Collins. Based on that relatively strong performance by a novice candidate, Cain's name often came up when talk turned to possible statewide Republican candidates.

During the tumultuous 2012 Republican presidential sweepstakes, an extended contest that saw various aspirants rise to the top before quickly fading, Cain briefly led the pack. His catchy 999 plan, which he touted repeatedly during the numerous presidential debates, found favor with conservative voters who distrusted professional politicians and longed for simple answers to complex problems. Enthusiasm for Cain proved short lived, and by the time Georgia voted, his extramarital affair had terminated his candidacy.

Since Gingrich had last run for office in 1998 a new generation had come of age, and hundreds of thousands had moved to Georgia. Moreover, he had never competed statewide. Consequently, although political activists knew of him, millions of Georgians felt no connection, as revealed in an Insider Advantage survey conducted two weeks before the Georgia primary that found Gingrich in a statistical dead heat with Mitt Romney and Rick Santorum. This startling news prompted the former Speaker to rearrange his schedule so as to spend more time in Georgia in order to reconnect with its voters. Gingrich's flurry of activity paid off, and an Insider Advantage poll done two weeks later showed him to be the preference of 47 percent of those surveyed, while Romney had the support of 21 percent of likely Republican voters and Santorum had dropped to only 18 percent.

A comparison of these two polls shows that Gingrich's efforts had improved his status with both men and women and in all age groups. The improvement with men was particularly dramatic. In the February 20 poll, Romney and Gingrich tied, whereas in the March 4 poll Gingrich had more than doubled his support among men to 56 percent and Romney had slumped to 20 percent. Among the age groups, Gingrich's greatest improvement came with the youngest voters, those who had not been politically active when the former Speaker left the House. In late February, Gingrich had no support among voters eighteen to twenty-nine years old, more than 40 percent of whom preferred Ron Paul and about a third of whom opted for Romney. In early March almost three-fourths of these young voters preferred Gingrich, and Paul's support had evaporated.

The results of the primary closely approximated the March 4 Insider Advantage poll, as Gingrich secured his only state victory other than South Carolina. Gingrich attracted 47 percent of the vote, and Romney won 26 percent, with Santorum coming in just under 20 percent.

The exit poll results presented in Table 4.1 show Gingrich was the leading preference among most subgroups. Among the exceptions, Romney managed pluralities among the most educated (those with some postbaccalaureate education) and the most affluent (those with incomes exceeding $200,000). The brightest spots for Romney came in some of the metropolitan counties, as he won pluralities in DeKalb, Fulton, and Chatham (Savannah) Counties. He eked out a narrow plurality over Gingrich among individuals who were not evangelical, or born-again, Christians. Gingrich got half of all votes cast by evangelicals, with Santorum finishing second among these voters, taking a quarter of the vote. Of the white voters in the Republican primary, 62 percent indicated that they were evangelicals. Romney beat Gingrich by 10 percent among Catholics, while losing by 26 percent among Protestants. Romney was the preference among voters who considered Gingrich and Santorum to be too conservative. Tea Party support correlated with candidate preferences, with Gingrich doing best among the 40 percent of the voters who strongly supported the Tea Party movement. Tea Partiers gave Gingrich 53 percent of their votes.

Although the Republican primary was the only game in town, it attracted fewer voters than had participated in the Republican presidential primary four years earlier. In 2012, just over 900,000 voters participated, some 60,000 voters fewer than in 2008. An explanation for this drop-off is that with Gingrich enjoying a home field advantage, albeit one he had to work to reestablish, other candidates spent little time campaigning in Georgia and, instead, concentrated on other states holding primaries on the same day as Georgia. In 2008, the three leading candidates were extremely competitive, with Mike Huckabee winning a 34 percent plurality, followed by John McCain with 32 percent and Romney with a respectable 30 percent, 4 percent better than in 2012.

Table 4.1. Georgia Republican Presidential Primary Exit Poll Results, 2012

	Total	Gingrich	Paul	Romney	Santorum
Gender					
Male	52	*47*	9	26	17
Female	48	*43*	7	27	22
Age					
18–29	8	*27*	27	22	22
30–44	19	*34*	15	23	26
45–64	48	*48*	6	27	18
65 and over	24	*53*	2	28	17
Education					
No college	17	*54*	4	20	21
Some college	30	*49*	10	20	20
College graduate	33	*43*	9	28	19
Postgraduate	19	32	7	*40*	19
Income					
< $30,000	9	*44*	10	21	24
$30–49,999	15	*44*	13	22	20
$50–99,999	36	*45*	9	22	23
$100–200,000	30	*46*	6	29	16
> $200,000	10	37	3	*43*	17
Tea Party					
Strong support	40	*53*	5	21	20
Some support	29	*42*	9	28	22
Neutral	22	*41*	11	30	18
Oppose	6	19	21	*35*	14
Evangelical					
Yes	62	*50*	6	19	24
No	38	36	12	*38*	12
Religion					
Protestant	77	*48*	7	22	22
Catholic	13	31	6	*41*	21

Source: Exit polls conducted by Edison Research of Somerville, New Jersey, for the National Election Pool, which consists of ABC News, the Associated Press, CBS News, CNN, Fox News and NBC News.

Note: Winning percentages are italicized.

General Election

Very early on, some analysts considered Georgia potentially in play. Hesitancy to put the Peach State among the solidly Republican states in 2012 stemmed from the relatively strong Obama performance in 2008 and the size of Georgia's African American electorate. In 2008, the Obama campaign spent almost $4 million in Georgia to operate thirty-three campaign offices with fifty-two paid staffers and almost five thousand volunteers and received 47 percent of the vote.[7] In 2008, blacks cast 30 percent of the votes in the state. Strong mobilization among blacks, coupled with the state's growing Hispanic and Asian American populations, could have formed the basis for an Obama victory.

Despite 2012 national polling showing a close race, the Obama campaign quickly decided not to invest in Georgia, and once the Democrats wrote off Georgia, Republicans also turned their attentions elsewhere. As has become common in recent years, Georgians sat on the sidelines as observers and were not aggressively courted during the 2012 election. To the extent that candidates came into the state during the summer and fall, they did nothing more than fly into Atlanta and make a hurried trip to a downtown hotel for a fund-raiser before speeding back to the airport. Except for those unfortunate Atlantans who got stuck in traffic because of the presidential candidate's motorcade rushing to or from the airport, voters in the state had no awareness of the candidate's visit. When in Georgia, the presidential candidates in 2012 made no speeches, shook no hands, and kissed no babies.

With Georgia not considered a swing state, relatively few polls were conducted during the election cycle. Of those taken during 2012, all but one Insider Advantage survey, which put Obama at 35 percent, had the president within a narrow range, hovering between 40 and 44 percent. Survey USA conducted one of the last polls prior to the election, asking 574 likely voters during the last week of October about their preferences. The Survey USA poll, portions of which appear in Table 4.2, show Mitt Romney with an 8-point advantage over the challenger with 52 percent of the vote. Romney led among males by 13 points and had a narrow 4-point lead among women. Support for the Republican correlated with age, as he beat Obama by 20 points among voters fifty and older. Giving hope to Democrats for the future, millennials favored the president by a margin of 48 to 43 percent. The survey showed Obama with 24 percent of the white vote, right in line with the share of the white vote that he received four years earlier and with what John Kerry got in 2004. According to the poll, Obama received 88 percent of the black vote, which was 10 points less than he received in the 2008 exit polls and probably was an underestimate of the actual share he received in 2012. Each candidate dominated his own partisans, and Romney took the independent vote by a margin of 52 to 36 percent. Evangelicals, who constituted 41 percent of the survey, supported Romney 67 to 28 percent, while nonevangelicals favored Obama 55 to 41 percent.

With the Obama campaign having starved Georgia of the resources shared four years earlier, it was not surprising that the president fared slightly worse. Romney ran 1 percent ahead of John McCain's 2008 performance and bested the president 53.3 to 45.5 percent. Despite slipping by 1.5 points, Obama nonetheless attracted a share of the vote larger than that of any Democrat competing for statewide constitutional office two years earlier.

In line with national findings, Obama did well in urban areas.[8] He actually outpolled Romney by almost 13,000 votes in the twenty-eight-county Atlanta metro area. The president rolled up a margin of 118,000 votes in Fulton County (city of Atlanta) and took neighboring and more heavily black DeKalb by an even larger margin of 174,000 votes. The president's highest percentage in metro Atlanta came in Clayton County, home to Atlanta's airport, where he took almost 85 percent of the vote. The president won only three other Atlanta-area counties.

Support for Romney in Atlanta's suburbs offset much of the incumbent's success in counties with large minority populations. Romney's largest vote margins came in Cobb, which he won by 38,000 votes, and Gwinnett, which he took by 27,000 votes. In terms of percentages, Romney had his biggest advantage in smaller counties on the edge of metro Atlanta—Dawson, which he won with 86 percent; Pickens, with 83 percent; Pike, with 82 percent; Haralson, with 81 percent; and Forsyth, with almost 81 percent. Of these counties that Romney won by more than a four-to-one margin, Forsyth with more than 81,000 voters was the only one with a large population.

Outside Atlanta the president won the major urban counties of Clarke (Athens), Richmond (Augusta), Bibb (Macon), Dougherty (Albany), and Chatham (Savannah). He also swept much of the rural Black Belt—the band of counties along and south of the fall line.

Romney did especially well in north Georgia, losing only Clarke County among counties north of Atlanta. Romney outpolled Obama in 125 counties and took majorities of the vote in all but one of them. The county vote for Romney tracked very closely with the vote received

Table 4.2. Georgia Voter Presidential Election Preferences, 2012

	Total	Obama	Romney	Other	Undecided
Total	100	44	*52*	2	2
Gender					
Male	46	41	*54*	2	2
Female	54	46	*50*	2	2
Age					
18–34	24	*48*	43	3	5
35–49	36	46	*51*	2	1
50–64	23	39	*58*	2	2
65 and over	17	39	*59*	0	1
Race					
White	65	24	*72*	3	2
Black	27	*88*	9	1	2
Tea Party Member					
Yes	6	19	*70*	9	3
No	92	46	*50*	2	1
Evangelical					
Yes	41	28	*67*	2	2
No	52	*55*	41	2	1
Education					
High school	18	44	*50*	2	3
Some college	33	40	*55*	3	2
College graduate	49	46	*50*	1	2
Income					
< $40,000	32	*52*	44	2	2
$40–80,000	33	37	*57*	3	3
> $80,000	35	43	*55*	2	2
Party identification					
Republican	39	3	*96*	0	1
Democrat	37	*91*	7	1	1
Independent	21	36	*52*	7	5

Source: Survey USA Election Poll #20026 of 574 actual and likely voters conducted October 25–28, 2012.
Note: Winning percentages are italicized.

by John McCain four years earlier. It also correlated strongly with the vote Nathan Deal won in his successful gubernatorial bid in 2010. Romney ran ahead of McCain in 99 of Georgia's 159 counties. For each additional 1 percent of the vote received by McCain, Romney gained 1.08 percent more of it. Romney's greatest improvement came in eleven mountain counties, where he won from 3.7 to 5.6 percent more of the vote than McCain. Romney also outperformed McCain in the state's most populous county, Fulton, running 2.4 percent ahead of the 2008 nominee despite losing the county by a large margin.

In 108 counties the 2012 Republican vote share was within 2 percent of the 2008 showing. Of the eleven counties in which Romney ran at least 2 points behind McCain, all but two were in south Georgia. The two exceptions were in the second ring out from the heart of Atlanta in counties where the population was becoming increasingly diverse. The biggest drop-off in Romney support compared with that for McCain came in Brooks County along the Florida border, where Romney ran 3.8 percent behind the Arizona senator.

The Obama vote correlated strongly with the percent black among registered voters in the county (b = 0.824). His two best counties were the two in which more than 70 percent of the registrants were African American. He took at least two-thirds of the vote in each of the counties with more than 60 percent black registrants. Obama carried every county in which blacks constituted the bulk of the registered voters, but only three in which blacks were less than 46 percent of the registrants. The one heavily white county in which Obama did especially well, Clarke, had less than 26 percent black registrants but was the home of the University of Georgia and continued its tradition of strong Democratic loyalties. Obama carried six of the state's eleven largest counties—those with at least 100,000 registrants. Using county data, the ecological inference estimate of white support for Obama is 22 percent, which is only slightly below the 23 percent of the white vote that exit polls showed Obama receiving in Georgia in 2008.

Other Elections

As a result of another decade of rapid growth, Georgia picked up a fourteenth congressional seat following the 2010 census. The 2011 redistricting for the first time gave Republicans the opportunity to redraw state legislative districts. Republicans had reconfigured the congressional districts in 2005 after taking control of both state legislative chambers.

As Republicans went about redrawing the congressional districts in 2011, they faced constraints imposed on the state by Section 5 of the Voting Rights Act. Georgia had four African American members of Congress, and the Republican map makers, recognizing that diminution of strength in these districts would undoubtedly result in federal authorities rejecting the plan, took care to craft districts likely to elect African Americans. The new plans gave all four districts with black representatives African American majorities in population, compared with three districts that had concentrations at that level previously. The number of districts with black majorities in their voting-age populations increased from two to three, and the number of districts in which most registered voters were black increased from two to four. Bolstering black concentrations in these districts that would surely elect Democrats left other districts whiter and, consequently, more inclined to elect Republicans. GOP legislators could respond to charges that they were packing African Americans into four districts by pointing to the nonretrogression standard used by federal authorities when conducting reviews pursuant to Section 5 of the Voting Rights Act and the requirement under Section 2 that blacks be able to elect their preferred candidates.

Having designed four districts with African American representatives for Democrats, the Republican legislators sought to make the other ten districts safe for the GOP. The new congressional district gained through reapportionment was drawn as arguably the most Republican in the state.[9] The chief GOP objective, however, involved reconfiguring the district of John Barrow, the last white Democrat in the Deep South.[10] Prior to 2010, Alabama, Louisiana, Mississippi, and South Carolina still had a white Democrat in Congress, but only Barrow survived that year's tidal wave. Barrow's district had extended along the South Carolina border from Augusta to Savannah. The old district had been competitive, as evidenced by Barrow's reelection in 2006 by a margin of fewer than nine hundred votes. The new district removed Savannah's black population and pushed Barrow into heavily Republican suburbs north of Augusta. Only 53 percent of the people in Barrow's new district had previously been represented by him. Not only would Barrow have to introduce himself to almost half of the district's population, but the new district included extensive new territories in rural Georgia, where many white voters were especially conservative. Barrow's new district was approximately 10 points more Republican than his former marginal district.

Republicans held a spirited primary to pick Barrow's challenger. With four candidates competing, the decision extended into a runoff won by state representative Lee Anderson. Augusta (Richmond County) had the district's largest population concentration, but Augusta voters could not control the Republican primary. Two factors weakened the Augusta influence. First, two of the four primary candidates claimed Augusta as their home and split the support in that city. Second, a heated primary and runoff to nominate the Democratic candidate for sheriff attracted a number of voters who otherwise would have asked for Republican ballots under Georgia's open primary arrangement. With the contest boiling down, however, to a choice between a black and a white candidate in the sheriff's runoff and with voters who participated in the Republican primary banned from the Democratic runoff, the Augusta vote on the Republican side was relatively modest.[11] Further helping the ultimate winner, Anderson made use of connections developed while serving in the state house to raise funds. He also engaged the services of one of the state's premier campaign consultants, Joel McElhannon.

Despite securing the GOP nomination, Anderson proved a flawed candidate. Public speaking was not his forte. Conservative blogger Eric Erickson said of Anderson, "The man has seemingly never met two syllables without tripping over them."[12] Barrow, a verbally talented Harvard-educated attorney, adopted a stance atypical for incumbents and baited Anderson to meet him in debates. Although incumbents usually avoid giving challengers an equal status by debating them, Barrow, aware of the advantage he would have in a debate and knowing that he had to attract thousands of Republican identifiers in order to win, longed for a chance to be seen side by side with his tongue-tied challenger. Anderson declined debate invitations, saying he wanted Barrow to first indicate for whom he would vote for president and whether he supported Nancy Pelosi for Speaker of the House. (In 2011, Barrow was one of a handful of moderate Democrats who refused to support Pelosi for Speaker.)

Challengers usually compare unfavorably with incumbents when it comes to substantive knowledge, since incumbents spend much of their time mastering the complex issues that come before Congress. Anderson showed little interest in the details of public policy, and therefore, his information gap was much wider than that of most challengers. In a debate among the four Republican candidates in Statesboro, Anderson demonstrated a total ignorance of the Federal Reserve. In response to a question from a high school student who asked whether Anderson would favor changing or abolishing the Federal Reserve, Anderson replied, "We must build our reserves even stronger than what it is now . . .

on the federal level. On the state level we are building back our reserves now."[13]

Barrow has the reputation of being an indefatigable campaigner, and he took on the challenge dealt him by Republicans as he went about introducing himself to the new district. He also crafted some of the best campaign videos of the year. One of these emphasized his support for the Second Amendment, an issue on which Republicans have often capitalized. In the ad Barrow brandished a pistol that his grandfather had used to stop a lynching and his father's rifle. Barrow boasted of his endorsement by the NRA and vowed that no one would ever take these guns from him. In other ads Barrow showed himself to be a fiscal hawk by telling constituents that he had voted to cut funding for the New York Ballet and for research on how to improve grapes. In yet another ad Barrow underscored his political independence, noting his stands on roll calls, some of which antagonized his fellow Democrats. Through his hard work and skill at crafting a diverse message, Barrow managed to connect with both the urban component of his district, centered in Augusta, and the more rural parts.

Barrow has always been an extraordinary fund-raiser, having amassed almost $1.9 million in his first race in 2004. In 2012, Barrow raised more than $2.5 million. The fund-raising advantage that incumbents have typically enjoyed was offset, however, by heavy expenditures by Super PACs supporting Anderson. The National Republican Congressional Committee (NRCC) spent $1,656,400 against Barrow. Also in Anderson's corner was Americans for Tax Reform, which spent more than $1 million, along with another $284,000 from the YG Action Fund and almost $200,000 from the Congressional Leadership Fund. Outsiders funded attack ads against Anderson, as well, but they spent far less than those groups that supported him, with the House Majority PAC dropping more than $500,000 and the Patriot Majority spending more than $200,000 on ads criticizing the challenger.

Key members of the campaign staffs of the two opposing candidates agree that the outside spending in the Twelfth District had relatively little impact. More important were the funds Barrow raised that allowed him to run positive ads that enhanced his appeal. Anderson raised relatively little money after the primary and could not compete in terms of positive ads. Unable to control the dominant message for which outside conservative groups paid, Anderson lacked the ability to create a favorable impression. The deluge of negative attack ads run by Super PACs and the NRCC against Barrow were more than offset by the incumbent's positive appeals. The bottom line appears to be that although attack ads can be helpful, by themselves, even in a district heavily tilted against an incumbent, they cannot engineer a defeat.

As word of Anderson's unwillingness to meet Barrow in a debate spread, the incumbent began encountering staunch Republicans who questioned the challenger's ability to represent them. Some of these voters told Barrow that he would be the first Democrat for which they had ever voted. Barrow's internal polls consistently showed him ahead by approximately 5 points. The one public poll released on the contest came out about one week before the election and confirmed what the Barrow polls had found. Barrow ended up winning by almost 20,000 votes, a margin that surprised most observers from outside the district. His success confirmed the old adage that "you can't beat somebody with nobody."

Despite failing to defeat Barrow, Republicans did increase their share of the Georgia congressional delegation from eight to five to nine to five, since they won the seat awarded Georgia through reapportionment. In addition to adding a ninth congressional seat, 2012 saw Republicans acquire near supermajority status in the state legislature. Adding two senate seats gave Republicans two-thirds of that chamber, as shown in Table 4.3. In the house, Republicans won 119 of 180 seats, with a potentially decisive seat held by an independent who at times supports Republican initiatives.

The results from the 2012 elections indicate only one competitive district in the congressional delegation and the state senate. The state house had seven seats won by less than 55 percent of the vote and another eight seats in which the victor took less than 60 percent of the vote. The vast bulk of the seats in both chambers went uncontested by the district's minority party.

The 2012 Election and the Future

Even Republican insiders acknowledge that 2012 may put the GOP near the maximum strength they can achieve in Georgia. While the state has gone from being sky blue to blood red, Republicans will never achieve the level of dominance that Democrats enjoyed for generations. The presence of a sizeable and growing minority population that is firmly committed to the Democratic Party ensures that today's minority party will have a substantial enclave anchored in the state's urban areas.

Table 4.3. Georgia General Assembly Partisan Makeup, 1963–2013

	House			Senate		
	Dem	GOP	% GOP	Dem	GOP	% GOP
1963	203	2	1.0	51	3	5.6
1965	182	23	11.2	45	9	16.7
1967	184	21	10.2	46	8	14.8
1969	168	27	13.8	49	7	12.5
1971	173	22	11.3	50	6	10.7
1973	151	29	16.1	48	8	14.3
1975	156	24	13.3	51	5	8.9
1977	156	24	13.3	52	4	7.1
1979	159	21	11.7	51	5	8.9
1981	156	24	13.3	51	5	8.9
1983	156	24	13.3	49	7	12.5
1985	156	24	13.3	47	9	16.1
1987	152	28	15.6	46	10	17.9
1989	144	36	20.0	45	11	19.6
1991	145	35	19.4	45	11	19.6
1993	128	52	28.9	41	15	26.9
1995	114	66	36.7	35	21	37.5
1997	106	74	41.1	34	22	39.3
1999	102	78	43.3	34	22	39.3
2001	105	74	41.1	32	24	42.9
2003	107	72	40.0	26	30	53.6
2005	81	99	55.0	22	34	60.7
2007	74	106	58.9	22	34	60.7
2009	75	105	58.3	22	34	60.7
2011	63	116	64.4	20	36	64.3
2013	60	119	66.1	18	38	67.9

Beneath today's placid red sea, waves of change are building. Republicans in Georgia, like elsewhere, succeed by attracting large majorities of white voters. In recent Republican primaries whites have cast about 95 percent of the votes.[14] Equally large numbers of African Americans vote for Democrats, along with majorities of the growing numbers of Hispanics and Asian Americans. In 1996, whites cast approximately 78 percent of all votes in the general election. By 2008, that number had dropped to 64 percent. The registration rolls for the 2012 election showed whites, for the first time, constituting less than 60 percent of the eligible voters. With Georgia projected to join Texas, California, and New Mexico as one of the states in which whites comprise a plurality and not a majority, it is only a matter of time before the number of whites becomes too few to propel statewide Republican victories. This change will not occur immediately but within the foreseeable future. Consequently, unless Republicans succeed in broadening their appeal, they are on a bobsled run headed for defeat. Currently, single white women constitute the keystone in the Republican arch of success. Nationally, single women supported Obama by a 67 to 31 percent margin. If Georgia's single white women become alienated from the GOP, they could expedite the realignment of the state back toward the Democratic Party.

The overwhelming majorities that Republicans command in the general assembly may actually hasten the arrival of the day on which their hegemony is challenged. If Republicans use their control to push through constitutional amendments that restrict access to abortion, it could alienate critical elements in the female electorate. Religious conservatives within the legislature have whittled away at abortion access in the past and may now be in a position to approve a personhood amendment and other further restrictions.

A second possible threat to Republican dominance comes from generational placement. Younger voters in Georgia, as in the rest of the nation, are less committed to the kinds of social issue positions that fueled GOP advances in the past. In 2004, Georgia incorporated a ban on gay marriage into its constitution by a margin of 76 to 24 percent. Milliennials, including many Republican enthusiasts, see no reason to restrict marriage to heterosexual couples. As younger voters who are less socially conservative replace their elders, if the leadership of the GOP does not adjust, it may see young voters, especially in urban areas, drifting away from the party.

Threats from within endanger Republican control. One of the problems that a large majority confronts is division within its own ranks. A minority party or even a narrow majority has substantial pressures to maintain unity, but as control expands, factionalism becomes a possibility. Already, Republicans in the state senate have fought one civil war. In 2010, the chamber's leadership stripped the Republican lieutenant governor of most of his powers. This resulted in two years of chaos and uncertainty. The two senators who led the coup against the lieutenant governor had lost their positions by the end of 2012. The final power distribution between senators and the lieutenant governor, who presides over their institution, remains unsettled, although the lieutenant governor will likely reacquire at least some of the influence that position has traditionally had over items such as appointing committee members and chairs.

Still further divisions may become apparent in 2014, when senior senator Saxby Chambliss comes up for reelection. In his previous reelection bid, he was pushed into a runoff when some conservatives defected to the Libertarian candidate.[15] Chambliss's participation with the bipartisan Gang of Six's efforts to resolve the national fiscal crisis and his willingness to see taxes increased along with cuts in entitlements alienates Tea Party enthusiasts. Conservatives have threatened to find an alternative, and several members of the congressional delegation have indicated an interest in leading the charge against the senator. Should one or more members of Congress enter the list against Chambliss, a costly and bitter campaign could leave the GOP in disarray going into November. It would also open up the congressional seats vacated by those who challenged Chambliss.

While 2014 may be too soon for the demographic changes to catch up with the GOP, Georgia may be in play in the 2016 presidential election. Of the twenty-four states won by Romney, Georgia saw his weakest performance save for North Carolina. In 2016, a Democratic nominee seeking to expand on the Obama coalition might well look to the Peach State as a possibility. A serious Democratic effort in 2016 might prime the pump for an even more aggressive effort in 2018.

Democratic fortunes for the 2020s rest heavily upon their ability to win the governorship in 2018. If Governor Nathan Deal serves two terms, he will have to vacate the office in 2018. Democrats may focus all of their resources on winning the governorship, since that will be the only way in which they will have a seat at the table when new congressional and state legislative districts are drawn following the release of the 2020 census. If Democrats do not have a veto over Republican maps, they will likely be consigned to minority status in the congressional delegation and the legislature for yet another decade, much as Florida Democrats have had little success winning legislative seats even as that state has become one of the most competitive in the nation and has given its Electoral College votes to the Democratic nominee in three of the five most recent presidential elections.[16]

The 2012 election found Georgians acting more as observers than as participants in determining the outcome, a situation that has characterized each presidential election of the new century. In all likelihood, the situation will change as the electorate changes, and perhaps as soon as 2016, candidates may be vying for Georgia support in October. If that situation does not occur by 2016, it will happen soon thereafter.

5

Louisiana

For Republicans and Obama, Second Verse, Same as the First

Robert E. Hogan
Joshua D. Hostetter

One of the most interesting aspects of the 2012 presidential election in Louisiana is its close resemblance to the election four years earlier. In an election marked by relatively high turnout, the Republican nominee, Mitt Romney, won the state with 57.78 percent of the vote, compared with President Obama's 40.58 percent. The two-party vote margin favoring the Republican nominee in 2012 (17.5 percent) was only slightly lower than John McCain's margin in 2008 (18.9 percent). Even the primary election among the Republican contenders resembled the contest four years earlier. The eventual Republican nominee lost to a favorite of the state's Christian conservatives. Thus, the 2012 presidential election in Louisiana was mostly a replay of the 2008 elections. While Louisiana may once have been a southern bellwether of national voting trends in presidential politics, the state is now a reliable Republican stronghold.[1]

Brief History

Similar to other southern states, early signs of Louisiana's shift from one-party politics began in the 1950s and 1960s as voters began supporting

Republican presidential candidates. Voters in 1956 helped reelect President Eisenhower and in 1964 backed Republican nominee Sen. Barry Goldwater. Even though less than 3 percent of Louisiana voters were registered Republicans in 1972, they strongly supported Nixon for reelection.[2] In that same year, Louisiana elected its first Republican to Congress since Reconstruction, David Treen. Seven years later, Treen went on to become the state's first Republican governor since Reconstruction. Despite these early successes, the rise of Republicans was slower and more erratic in Louisiana than in other southern states.[3] While Republican presidential candidates did well (Reagan won handily in 1980 and 1984), Republican registration did not reach double digits until the mid-1980s. In the meantime, Democrats continued to dominate most statewide and state legislative offices.

By the 1990s the state experienced sustained growth in Republican adherents and greater competition for congressional seats. Republican Mike Foster was elected governor in 1995 and then reelected four years later. During this period Republicans began contesting more statewide constitutional offices, and for the first time a majority of congressional seats went to the GOP. Of course, such changes in party offices did not occur for all offices in the state. While Republicans won many state legislative races, even by the mid-1990s they still held less than a quarter of the seats. During the 1990s Louisiana voters helped elect Democrat Bill Clinton both in 1992 and again in 1996. By the end of the 1990s, the political environment of the state was best characterized as competitive, as both parties had the potential to win statewide office.

In the first statewide elections of the new century, Democrat Kathleen Blanco defeated Bobby Jindal in the race for governor, and Democrats continued to hold nearly two-thirds of the seats in the legislature. The electoral fortunes of Democrats began to shift in the aftermath of Hurricane Katrina, however. With her public support weakened, Governor Blanco decided late in the 2007 election cycle not to seek reelection, and prominent Democrats such as former U.S. senator John Breaux passed on the opportunity to run. These decisions paved the way for an easy victory for Republican Bobby Jindal, who faced a field of lesser-known Democrats. Following his election and then reelection in 2011, the state witnessed rapid gains in Republican officeholders. A wave of party defections by statewide and legislative officials coupled with efforts by the GOP to ramp up their representation in state government resulted in a major shift in party control. Following the 2011 elections, all seven statewide constitutional officers, along with a majority of members in both legislative chambers, were Republican. Only one U.S. House seat remained in Democratic hands (Rep. Cedric Richmond), and Sen. Mary Landrieu stood as the sole Democrat elected from a statewide constituency.

From one perspective the ascendency of the Republican Party over the past decade appears rapid. While some have attributed these changes to the population displacements following Hurricane Katrina in 2005, several long-term changes have been at play for some time. For example, the continued alignment of voters' ideological and party allegiances has been a trend throughout the South since the 1960s. Another more significant change specific to Louisiana involves the state's large Catholic population, which makes up nearly one-third of the electorate. Whereas Catholic voters for many years were swing voters, today they increasingly support Republican candidates. By 2008, 70 percent of the state's Catholics cast ballots for John McCain.[4] What appears to be a rapid rise in electoral fortunes for Republicans is more likely the result of long-term changes that have come to a tipping point. Ambitious candidates now see greater electoral opportunities to run as Republicans. Whatever the source, the state's political environment is one where Republicans have a much easier time winning. As the 2012 election season approached, electoral conditions in Louisiana strongly favored the Republican Party.

Primary Elections

With such a wide field of candidates vying for the Republican nomination, many Louisiana Republicans hoped the state would have an opportunity to play a pivotal role in deciding on the nominee.[5] The state held a late place on the primary calendar (March 24), however, and only a small number of delegates were up for grabs in the primary (twenty of the state's forty-six delegates). Four years earlier in 2008, the presidential nominating contest in Louisiana had little consequence. In that campaign by the time the Republican nomination battle rolled around to Louisiana, John McCain's only major rival, Mitt Romney, had already dropped out. Those hoping to see an active Republican nomination battle waged in Louisiana in 2012 would get only some of their hopes realized. By mid-March many candidates had already suspended their campaigns, including Texas governor Rick Perry, who had been endorsed by Louisiana governor Bobby Jindal. By late March a sense of inevitability about Romney's nomination was starting to emerge. An increasing number of national polls showed voters believing Romney would ultimately win the nomination, and funding for many of the other contenders began to dry up. Still, three major contenders remained in the hunt for votes: Rick Santorum, Newt Gingrich, and Ron Paul.

In 2008, Mike Huckabee edged out a small plurality win over John McCain. His support came in large measure from the many social conservatives who typically participated in the state's Republican presidential primaries. The potential support from these types of voters drew particular attention in 2012 from Rick Santorum and Newt Gingrich, as well as from front-runner Mitt Romney. The economy and opposition to Obamacare were common issues emphasized during campaign stops by the candidates. Issues that had particular local resonance included freedom of church-run institutions to exclude insurance coverage for contraception and enhanced energy extraction efforts (facilitated by more federal drilling permits). Much of the campaign rhetoric centered on which candidate had credibility on these hot-button issues that were important to social conservative voters.[6]

When the votes were counted, Santorum won a huge victory over his competitors as the plurality winner (or majority winner) in all but one of the state's sixty-four parishes (see Table 5.1). Santorum received approximately 49 percent, while Romney came in at a distant second with 28 percent. Gingrich and Paul fell well behind with 16 and 6 percent, respectively (each of the other five candidates had 2 percent or less). It is interesting how closely these results mirror the primary results of 2008 and how well they display the division between conservative elements and more moderate elements of the Republican Party.

Table 5.1. Louisiana Republican Presidential Primary Results, 2012

Candidate	Votes	%
Rick Santorum	91,321	48.99
Mitt Romney	49,758	26.69
Newt Gingrich	29,656	15.91
Ron Paul	11,467	6.15

Source: Louisiana Secretary of State.
Note: The five additional candidates attracted less than 2 percent of the vote each and are not included in the table.

An examination of exit/entrance polling conducted in Louisiana shows that there were often sharp differences in support for candidates across categories of Republican voters. As Table 5.2 shows, these contrasts were particularly stark between Santorum and Romney. Whereas Santorum drew greater support from younger voters, those with lower levels of education and income, and rural voters, Romney supporters tended to be older, have higher levels of education and income, and reside in urban areas. Differences in support from ideological groups between the two men were quite large. For example, Romney received only 23 percent of support from very conservative voters, but 32 percent from somewhat conservative and 29 percent from moderate or liberal voters. By contrast, Santorum's support among the very conservative was 53 percent, while only 47 percent of somewhat conservative and 40 percent of moderate or liberal voters supported him. These ideological differences confirm what one voter told the *Los Angeles Times* when asked why they were voting for Rick Santorum: "This is what we stand for—good old conservative values."[7]

Religious differences among voters help to explain the support received by candidates, particularly between Romney and Santorum. Voters identifying themselves as born-again were almost three times as likely to support Santorum as they were Romney (56 percent for Santorum compared with 20 percent for Romney). Among those who were not born-again, support for the two candidates was similar (Romney, 38 percent; Santorum, 37 percent). Among voters who reported that the religious beliefs of the candidates mattered a great deal or somewhat, 57 percent supported Santorum, while only 23 percent supported Romney. For voters who said the candidates' religious beliefs mattered not much or not at all, 38 percent supported Romney, while only 26 percent supported Santorum. These findings demonstrate that religion had a role to play in the voting calculus of many Republican primary voters.

The Louisiana Republican electorate was primed for a social conservative candidate, and Santorum was well positioned to benefit from this situation. Santorum's decisive victory gave at least a brief lift to his flagging campaign. Shortly after his win in Louisiana, Santorum declared, "I am not running as a conservative candidate for president . . . I *am* the conservative candidate for president."[8] The victory also gave social conservatives in Louisiana, as well as across the nation, an opportunity to demonstrate their potency within the Republican Party. For Romney the loss was quickly brushed off as he moved on to prepare for other state contests.[9]

Table 5.2. Louisiana Republican Presidential Primary Exit and Entrance Poll Results, 2012

	Total	Santorum	Romney	Gingrich	Paul
Gender					
Male	49	48	26	17	8
Female	51	50	27	15	5
Age					
18–29	8	51	15	7	23
30–44	17	55	18	16	8
45–64	49	48	30	15	5
65 and over	26	46	29	20	3
Education					
Attended college	83	47	29	15	7
No college education	17	59	14	19	5
Income					
< $50,000	26	56	16	19	8
$50–100,000	33	51	25	14	8
> $100,000	42	42	34	17	5
Place					
Urban	40	45	31	14	6
Suburban	37	49	25	17	7
Rural	23	55	20	17	6
Ideology					
Very conservative	49	53	23	18	4
Somewhat conservative	28	47	32	14	6
Moderate or liberal	23	40	29	15	12
Evangelical					
Yes	61	56	20	17	6
No	39	37	38	15	8
Candidate religious beliefs matter					
Great deal/somewhat	73	57	23	16	4
Not much/not at all	26	26	38	19	11
Time of decision					
This year	86	53	25	15	6
Last year	13	24	30	25	17

Source: http://www.cnn.com/election/2012/primaries/epolls/la
Note: Percentages may not add to 100, because "other" and "no answer" responses are not included.

When the votes were counted, only Santorum and Romney reached the 25 percent threshold necessary for winning any of the twenty delegates up for grabs. Ron Paul's supporters continued their campaign, however, at the district caucuses held in April and at the state convention in June. A dispute over delegates emerged at the state convention that ultimately required a resolution by the Republican National Committee prior to the national convention.[10] When the floor votes were counted in Tampa, the delegate totals from Louisiana were as follows: thirty-two for Romney, twelve for Paul, and only one for Santorum.[11]

General Election Campaign

Louisiana was not viewed as a battleground, so little money or time was spent by either campaign in the state. The nominees for president and vice president did make a few stops in the state for speeches at interest group conventions (e.g., a National Urban League address by the president and an AARP convention speech by Paul Ryan) and for fund-raising events. Also, Hurricane Isaac gave both President Obama and Governor Romney the opportunity to visit the state to tour devastated areas. While neither candidate officially campaigned during these tours, the national media covered these visits in clearly political terms. Romney's visit in particular was viewed as a political gesture, and national news outlets and pundits gave it added scrutiny. Romney's visit received national attention when he told one resident in a devastated area that he should "go home and call 211" to find information on where to get help.[12] The quote made headlines as national pundits referenced it as an example of the emerging media narrative (and Obama campaign narrative) that Romney was out of touch with average Americans.

Because it was not a battleground, most Louisiana voters were relegated to watching the campaign unfold from afar. One resident of the state who was, however, very much in the thick of the campaign was Republican governor Bobby Jindal. Throughout the summer and into the fall, the Louisiana governor played an active role, traveling extensively as a surrogate for Romney in key battleground states. Having been mentioned as a potential vice presidential pick, Jindal traveled the country acting as Romney's attack dog and delivering the Republican campaign's talking points. Even after Romney announced that Paul Ryan, not Jindal, would be his vice presidential choice, Jindal continued to maintain an active schedule stumping for the nominee. Some viewed these efforts as part of a larger strategy by Jindal to lay the groundwork for his own future presidential campaign.

Louisiana citizens did play a supporting role in the presidential campaign by way of their monetary contributions to the national campaigns. FEC reports indicate that Louisiana contributions to presidential campaigns during the 2011–12 period amounted to approximately $9.2 million. Given the political predispositions of state voters and the lack of a competitive Democratic primary, it is not surprising to find that the contribution total to Republicans was nearly three times that to Democrats ($6.6 million to $2.4 million). Whereas Obama was the recipient of all the Democratic contributions, Romney received the lion's share of funding ($5.1 million).[13]

To the extent that rank-and-file voters were engaged in the actual campaign, it was mostly through the news media and some television ads broadcast through national network programming. President Obama was often the subject, however, of campaign advertisements by local politicians. Given the president's low popularity in many quarters throughout the state, a common practice among Republicans running in competitive races was to associate their Democratic opponents with the president. In a Baton Rouge mayoral election, for example, a mailer sent out by Republican supporters displayed the Democratic mayor's photograph alongside that of the president's. Thus, the presidential election played a part in several campaigns throughout the state.

As the election approached, the few polls that were conducted indicated a clear win for Republican Mitt Romney. A poll in early September by Southern Media Strategy showed Romney with less than a 6-point lead over Obama (44.5 to 38.8 percent, with 16.7 percent undecided).[14] Polls conducted in October, however, showed him with a more substantial lead. For example, a Magellan Strategies poll showed Romney with a 22-point lead over the president.[15]

On Election Day approximately two-thirds of registered voters in Louisiana turned out to cast ballots (68 percent). Table 5.3 shows the rate of participation by categories of race and political party. In 2012, turnout was higher among whites than among blacks or those citizens categorizing themselves as "other." Among party registrants, turnout was over 6 points higher for registered Republicans than it was for Democrats. Those registered as "other party" or "no party" had the lowest rates of voting. One of the most striking findings from this table is the great similarity between 2012 and 2008. The overall rate of par-

Table 5.3. Louisiana Voter Turnout in Presidential Elections, 2008, 2012

	2008	2012
Total	67.23	67.93
Race		
White	69.46	69.36
Black	64.64	67.19
Other	52.35	52.86
Party identification		
Democrat	68.91	69.75
Republican	75.08	76.43
Other/no party	54.34	54.70

Source: Louisiana Secretary of State.

ticipation in 2012 was only seven-tenths of a point higher than that it was four years earlier. These similarities are consistent across most of the categories. Indeed, the largest difference is the 2.5 percent–higher turnout for black registrants in 2012. Overall, turnout levels in 2012 were nearly identical to those in 2008.

Table 5.4 shows the number of votes received by both major party candidates, along with the percentage of the two-party vote won by Obama in 2008 and 2012. Looking first at the statewide vote totals, one can see that in 2012 Obama improved on his 2008 performance by 26,152 votes. Romney and the Republicans, however, picked up fewer than four thousand (3,987) in 2012 over their 2008 vote tally. With regard to the two-party vote percentages, Obama received approximately 41 percent to Romney's 59 percent. Within the four distinct regions of the state, however, some differences did emerge. Obama did best in the Greater New Orleans region, where he received a majority of the two-party vote. This area contains the heavily populated Orleans Parish, where over 59 percent of the registered voters are African American. Among the four regions, the Florida parishes were ranked second in terms of support for Obama at 43 percent. He won only 39 percent in the largest geographic portion of the state, the north-central parishes, often considered the most conservative region in Louisiana. Interestingly, his poorest showing was in the Acadiana. Once considered the swing region of the state, Obama received only 36 percent of the

Table 5.4. Louisiana Votes for President, 2008, 2012

	2008			2012		
	Obama	McCain	Obama %	Obama	Romney	Obama %
Parish Region						
Greater New Orleans	213,665	240,936	47.00	231,492	230,234	50.14
Acadiana	232,069	395,462	36.98	230,988	409,254	36.08
Florida	139,258	193,412	41.86	145,164	192,376	43.01
North-central	197,997	318,465	38.34	201,497	320,398	38.61
Statewide	782,989	1,148,275	40.54	809,141	1,152,262	41.25

Source: Louisiana Secretary of State.

vote there. Across the two time periods, one sees that Obama's performance improved somewhat in three of the four regions, while it declined in only one (Acadiana).[16]

Voter Support in General Elections

Because Louisiana was not a battleground state and because no U.S. Senate seat hung in the balance, national news organization excluded Louisiana from its exit/entrance polling. We therefore rely on survey results conducted in the weeks prior to the election for understanding voter behavior. While this limits the breadth of our analysis, it does provide us with insight on a few key variables of interest. Here, we consider the role of political party, race, and gender in affecting voter decisions.

We know from studies at the national level that political party is an important predictor of voting. For example, the 2012 exit polls conducted in thirty-one states showed that 92 percent of Democrats supported Obama and 93 percent supported McCain.[17] We also know that partisanship has generally been less useful in explaining votes in southern states. In particular, among Democratic identifiers there remains a considerable inconsistency between party affiliation and voting, as they cast ballots for Republicans nationally and Democrats on the local level. In Louisiana in 2008, 96 percent of Republicans supported McCain, but only 75 percent of Democrats supported Obama.[18] Heading into the 2012 election, the question was whether this pattern would hold.

A poll conducted about a month prior to the 2012 election showed considerable differences in the voting behavior by partisan registration.

The poll found that over 94 percent of registered Republicans supported Mitt Romney, whereas only about 59 percent of Democrats supported President Obama.[19] These results are not directly comparable with the 2008 Louisiana exit poll results, which divided voters by party identification instead of party registration, but they do demonstrate that Democrats are still splitting their votes, as they have done in the past.

Voters who consider themselves independents comprise a sizable portion of the electorate, and in Louisiana in 2008, independent identifiers supported the Republican nominee over the Democratic nominee by a nearly two-to-one margin (McCain, 62 percent; Obama, 32 percent).[20] In 2012, a nearly identical pattern emerged. Among voters registered as something other than Democrats or Republicans, support for Mitt Romney was little more than twice the support observed for President Obama (61 to 29 percent, with 10 percent undecided).[21] National exit polls in 2012 showed that among independent identifiers Romney edged out Obama by only about 5 percent (50 to 45 percent).[22] Thus, independents in Louisiana were a strong source of support for Romney.

In the past, support for presidential candidates has fallen along racial lines. In 2008, for example, African American support for Obama over McCain was 94 to 4 percent, while white support for McCain over Obama was 84 to 14 percent.[23] In 2012, poll results showed that in Louisiana race continues to be correlated with presidential vote choice. A few weeks prior to the general election, approximately 88 percent of African Americans reported a preference for Barack Obama, while 8 percent reported an intention to vote for Romney, with 4 percent for another candidate. White voters, however, supported Romney over Obama by a margin of 79 to 16 percent, with 5 percent for another candidate.[24]

Another way to understand the importance of race is to examine the combined effects of race and party. When the poll results are divided in this way, some interesting results are revealed. Earlier, it was noted that Democratic registrants supported Obama over Romney by a 59 to 35 percent margin. If one considers white registered Democrats only, however, then relative support for the candidates flips in the opposite direction. White registered Democrats were twice as likely to support Mitt Romney over Barack Obama, by a margin of 62 to 31 percent, with 7 percent for another candidate. Such findings demonstrate the crucial role that race continues to play in voting patterns in Louisiana.

Another factor often mentioned in assessing voting is gender. National exit polls in 2012 found a substantial gender gap, with women supporting Obama over Romney by a margin of 55 to 44 percent and men supporting Romney over Obama by a margin of 52 to 45 percent.[25] In Louisiana women were more supportive of Obama than were men, but overall, women still heavily favored Romney. In the poll from early October, women supported Romney over Obama by a margin of 56 to 39 percent, while for men the margin was 63 to 33 percent.[26] These results show that there was indeed a gender gap in Louisiana, but not one large enough to result in women favoring Obama.

Other Elections

State-level and legislative elections in Louisiana are held every four years and in odd-numbered years, so few important state offices were on the ballot in 2012. An open seat on the public service commission and one on the state supreme court were the only races that gained a significant amount of attention. Nine constitutional amendments were also put before voters, including one that sought to increase protections for gun rights in the state. While these offices and amendments garnered some voter interest, the level of money spent and media attention paid to them was quite minimal compared with what is often observed in other states where competitive statewide and legislative races appear on the ballot alongside the presidential contestants.

At the congressional level the degree of competition observed was quite minimal, as well. For the first time since 2000, there was no simultaneous U.S. Senate race on the ballot during a presidential election. In five of the state's six congressional districts, incumbents faced relatively unknown challengers who raised little funding. In fact, three Republican incumbents did not even face a Democratic challenger. The only major contest was in the Third District, located in the south-central and western portions of the state. Louisiana lost a seat in Congress following the most recent reapportionment, so two Republican incumbents faced each other, Charles Boustany and Jeff Landry. Given Louisiana's system of elections, all candidates regardless of party run in a first-round election. If no candidate receives a majority of the vote, then the top-two vote getters advance to a runoff.

Although both candidates benefited from their incumbency status, Boustany held a clear advantage over his rival. Boustany's greatest advantage was that 80 percent of the population in the newly drawn Third Congressional District's population came from his old district.[27] In addition, Boustany had far more seniority in Congress (four terms compared with Landry's one), which allowed him to claim credit for many more federal projects.[28] Moreover, this level of seniority gave Boustany clout among wealthy interests, which enabled him to far outpace Landry in fund-raising ($4.5 million to $2.3 million).[29] Landry did have the backing of some Tea Party activist groups, and this outsider status provided significant grassroots support, which made it possible for him to force Boustany into a runoff.[30] In the first round of elections, Boustany fell short of the majority vote, winning 45 percent to Landry's 30 percent (three other candidates, including one Democrat, split the remaining share).[31] In the runoff election held in early December, however, Boustany handily defeated Landry by a vote of 61 to 39 percent.[32] Both rounds of elections were characterized by their negative and often personal attacks.

Conclusion

Gone are the days when Louisiana was a reliable bellwether state in presidential politics. Louisiana voters as a whole are consistent supporters of Republican nominees for president. Indeed, in 2012 the state was never viewed by either party as a battleground—not likely to be lost by the Republicans and unlikely to be picked up by the Democrats. In the year leading up to the election, statewide polls showed President Obama consistently holding low levels of voter approval.[33] In early November 2012, the question was not which party nominee would prevail but by how wide a margin the Republican nominee would win. Most remarkable is how similar the results were to the presidential election four years earlier. While the Democratic primary was not contested this time around, the dynamics of the Republican primary were quite comparable. A moderate front-runner within striking distance of clinching the nomination lost to a less well-funded challenger with substantial voter support from the state's social conservatives. A general election campaign devoid of significant attention paid by either nominee to the state left voters with little meaningful role to play, although two-thirds turned out to vote. Factors such as party identification, race, and gender that have influenced patterns of voting in the past had a similar influence in the 2012 election. All in all, the 2012 election seemed very much like a replay of 2008.

The 2012 election results are part of a general pattern of strong support for Republican nominees for president that is matched by levels of support received by Republicans running for Congress, as well as for statewide and legislative offices. The GOP is clearly on the upswing in the state, and Democrats have their work cut out for them in coming years. The robust showing by Santorum in the primary fueled by support from social conservatives suggests that these voters will play a prominent role within the state's Republican Party for some time to come.

Louisiana's well-entrenched Republican Party, with deep conservative roots, will be the dominant force in state politics for the foreseeable future. Its influence will likely be felt in national politics as the Republican Party struggles to find its direction following its presidential defeat in 2012. As Republicans began to assess their November losses, Louisiana's ambitious governor, Bobby Jindal, was quoted as saying that Republicans needed to "stop being the stupid party." He went on to say that the GOP needed to "stop being simplistic." "We need to trust the intelligence of the American people and we need to stop insulting the intelligence of the voters."[34] It will be interesting to see what role Louisiana's brand of Republican Party politics will play as the party seeks to find a path to victory in national politics in the coming years.

6

Mississippi

Democrats Struggle in an Increasingly Dominant Republican State

Stephen D. Shaffer
David A. Breaux

Political Context

Democrats in Mississippi entered the 2012 federal election campaigns facing a political landscape that appeared bleaker than at any time since Reconstruction. The once dominant state party had grown used to their long string of consecutive losses in presidential elections, which began with Ronald Reagan's narrow victory in the Magnolia State in 1980. In 1989, they lost the second of the state's U.S. Senate seats to the Republicans, and the 2008 reelection of GOP senator Roger Wicker over former governor Ronnie Musgrove to fill departing senator Trent Lott's seat confirmed the party's dominance in Senate elections. Upsets of two moderate Democratic congressmen in the 2010 national GOP landslide reduced the party to holding only one of the state's four House seats. The 2011 state elections confirmed Republican Party dominance at the state level, as the GOP became the first party since the previously dominant Democrats in 1987 to win three consecutive gubernatorial elections when Phil Bryant succeeded two-termer Haley Barbour. Furthermore, for the second consecutive state election, Republicans won six of the seven nongubernatorial statewide offices. To add insult to injury, Republicans finally broke through to the state legislative level, following the leads of the GOP in seven other southern states by seizing control of both legislative chambers.

Democrats had entered their 2010 debacle with some high-quality candidates, such as twenty-two-year veteran and party maverick Gene Taylor representing the Fourth Congressional District and freshman congressman and long-time chancery clerk Travis Childers representing the First District. Both were members of the centrist Blue Dogs but faced the challenge of representing districts where President Obama had failed to win more than 37 percent of the vote two years earlier. Republicans proceeded to tie both Democratic incumbents to unpopular "liberal" Obama policies, such as the stimulus bill and the national health care act, and to unpopular national Democratic leaders, such as House Speaker Nancy Pelosi. Sixteen-year Republican state senator Alan Nunnelee blasted Childers for backing Obama's stimulus bill, arguing that "we don't like to borrow money from the government of China to be repaid by our grandchildren," while state GOP chairman Brad White accused Childers of playing "on the team of Nancy Pelosi."[1] In the Fourth District race, five-year GOP state representative Steven Palazzo argued that having been a marine in the Persian Gulf War gave him "the courage to take on people like Pelosi and Obama" and criticized "the government takeover of health care."[2] State political observers were stunned that veteran congressman Gene Taylor joined freshman Travis Childers as victims of the national GOP landslide.

Republicans in the near sweep of statewide offices in 2011 now benefited from a strong farm team of experienced officeholders in the lower-level positions that the once dominant Democratic Party had previously held. Lieutenant Governor Phil Bryant, who as former state auditor had aggressively recovered misspent funds from public officials, defeated three-term African American Hattiesburg mayor Johnny DuPree in the race for governor after touting his close work with popular governor Barbour recruiting new jobs to the state and "being responsible with taxpayers' dollars by not spending money we don't have."[3] Thirty-six-year-old Tate Reeves, a two-term treasurer who featured a fiscally conservative record and a reputation as a rising star in the state and national GOP, moved up to the lieutenant governorship without Democratic opposition.[4] Secretary of State Delbert Hosemann, praised by the *Clarion-Ledger* for having "admirably served the public" by "ensuring that public lands are managed for the benefit of the public," was reelected without general election opposition.⁵ Victorious agriculture commissioner candidate Cindy Hyde-Smith, a stockyard owner and cattle farmer, had two terms as chair of the state senate's agriculture committee, earning the Mississippi Farm Bureau's Agriculture Legislator of the Year award and its Agricultural Ambassador award, for her efforts to promote the state's catfish industry.⁶ Another GOP woman, Lynn Fitch, parlayed her executive directorship of the state personnel board, which had jurisdiction over 32,000 workers in 130 agencies, into the state treasurer's position while boasting that she had cut her budget while being able to do "more with less."⁷ Two other GOP officeholders reelected to their statewide offices were Auditor Stacey Pickering and Insurance Commissioner Mike Chaney. Attorney General Jim Hood remained the lone Democratic statewide officer, winning an easy reelection to a third term.

Conservatives across Mississippi had been increasingly flexing their muscles, even at the state legislative level. In 2007, a conservative Democratic challenger to Billy McCoy's reelection as Speaker won forty-seven Republican and thirteen Democratic votes, prompting McCoy, who was reelected by the slim margin of sixty-two house Democrats, to refuse to appoint any Republicans to committee chairs, a historic shutout of intrachamber power for the long-time minority party.⁸ Early in 2011, some conservatives created the website FireMcCoy.com, labeling the New Deal Democrat McCoy, who was pro-gun and pro-life, as "Mississippi's Nancy Pelosi," leader of a "band of liberal merry men" who were harmful "to the conservative cause in this state" and who should receive "their pink slips."⁹ The Mississippi Tea Party also focused on "replacing Billy McCoy and his liberal House leadership with conservatives," endorsing ten house candidates (five of whom won) and providing them with candidate training, television and talk radio publicity, and targeted ads and a sign blitz in each district.¹⁰ Republicans seized control of both legislative chambers in November, claiming sixty-four state representatives to the Democrats' fifty-eight and thirty-one state senators to the Democrats' twenty-one.

As the 2012 presidential race progressed, one hopeful note for Democrats was the statewide Mississippi Poll in April, which suggested the average Mississippian was not as conservative as political observers believed. That poll found that although Republicans comprised 44 percent of party identifiers among all adults, Democrats constituted a formidable 41 percent of the population, with 15 percent being independent. The potential electorate also appeared increasingly libertarian, with a historic high of 51 percent being pro-choice to 45 percent being pro-life; 49 percent favoring gay marriage or civil unions to 46 percent opposing any legal recognition of gay couples; and a historic low of 42 percent backing the death penalty to 48 percent favoring life without parole or a fixed jail term. Even among likely voters, Mitt Romney held a mere 10.4 percent edge, with 51.1 percent favoring Romney, 40.7 percent backing Obama, and 8.2 percent being undecided at this early point.[11] Clearly, the task for Democrats was to mobilize this potential liberal element among African Americans and among the young, the women, and the less religious of both races.

Mississippi's Moment in the Spotlight: The GOP Presidential Primaries

Mississippi first achieved some national attention with speculation that its governor, Haley Barbour, would enter the presidential race. Barbour possessed both campaign and governing strengths, having served as national GOP chair in 1994 during the tsunami that swept the party into control of both congressional chambers for the first time in forty years and earning *Governing* magazine's Public Official of the Year award for his leadership after Hurricane Katrina. Facing some political vulnerabilities, such as his very southern accent, his tobacco lobbyist past, and his controversial defense of his hometown, which seemed to praise the segregationist white Citizens' Council for keeping the violent Ku Klux Klan away during the civil rights era, Barbour decided that he didn't have the "fire in the belly" to run such an all-consuming campaign.[12] One declared presidential hopeful who did visit Mississippi early in the campaign in November 2011 was Texas governor Rick Perry, but his brief airport stop in Jackson, where he offered to debate Speaker Pelosi after blaming her for the "routine insider corruption on Capitol Hill," merely gave the Speaker and her spokesman opportunities to mock his inability to remember all three of the federal departments he wished to eliminate.[13] Rep. Ron Paul did not campaign in the Magnolia State, but his youthful libertarian supporters did distribute his campaign material on college campuses.

A more viable conservative presidential hopeful who also got an early start in Mississippi was former House Speaker Newt Gingrich. At a Real Jobs town hall meeting at Millsaps College in December 2009, on the same day President Obama hosted a White House jobs summit, Gingrich promoted a balanced budget, increased domestic energy production, and tax cuts for small businesses as ways of boosting private sector employment.[14] After Gingrich criticized President Obama's energy policies during a visit to the state in March 2012, right before its presidential primary, state Democratic Party chair Rickey Cole responded that the circus must be in town, as Gingrich was the "head clown," and that while the former GOP Speaker attacked Obama for bowing to the Saudi Arabian king, "he and the Republicans bow to the CEOs of the oil companies."[15] The twice-divorced Gingrich offered his most compelling argument at a speech the same month at the Tupelo Furniture Market, after an introduction by his third wife and by American Family Association founder Don Wildmon: "I can clearly articulate conservatism with conviction and can beat Obama in the debates."[16]

Meanwhile, state GOP leaders unified behind former Massachusetts governor Mitt Romney. In January 2012, Romney announced the support of Mississippi's lieutenant governor and a long list of other prominent GOP officials, pledging a "conservative message" that would help those hurt "by the failed policies of the Obama presidency."[17] At a town hall meeting at the Farmer's Market in Jackson in March, Romney dubbed Obama a failed president who was "out of ideas," warned that the nation was on the track of Greece, and argued that cutting programs was better than borrowing "money from China" that "our kids" would have to pay back.[18] His state chairman, Auditor Stacey Pickering, touted Romney as the "only candidate who can beat Barack Obama and take over the White House" and praised him for understanding that "our dollars are better spent by you and I, and that we can better stimulate the economy than the bureaucracy in Washington."[19]

A social conservative who emerged as a viable candidate somewhat later in the process was former Pennsylvania senator Rick Santorum, who in a March 2012 speech at Hawkeye Industries in Tupelo reminded the crowd that he "acted like the conservative," while another candidate merely "talks the conservative message, when it's popular to do so."[20] Prominent conservative blogger Matt Friedeman called him the "best of the lot" despite being a "big-government conservative," as he was the "dad of a large family, Christian, homeschooler, big pro-lifer."[21] A few days later, Santorum visited the Mississippi Agriculture and Forestry Museum in Jackson, praising America as a place where people had the "freedom to build something precious for you, for your family, for your neighbor, for your community, for your church, for your God."[22] The Sunday before the state's primary, Santorum visited Tupelo once again to worship at his supporter Rep. Nunnelee's Baptist church, to visit the

Catholic church of his own faith, and to shake hands with patrons at two restaurants.[23]

Mississippi's virtual three-way tie between Santorum (32.7 percent), Gingrich (31.1 percent), and Romney (30.7 percent) suggested that the eventual party nominee might encounter some electability problems in the rest of the nation, even if not so much in Mississippi. Santorum drew a plurality of exit poll voters among the very conservative, among those caring a great deal about the religious beliefs of the candidates, and among those believing that abortion should always be illegal. Romney drew a plurality of support among the less numerous moderate and liberal voters and the pro-choice group. Whereas 51 percent of voters viewed Santorum's issue positions as about right and only 24 percent claimed that they weren't conservative enough, only 32 percent of Republican primary voters viewed Romney's views as about right, and fully 52 percent saw him as not conservative enough. Santorum won a plurality in rural northeast Mississippi, where he had campaigned more, while Romney won a plurality in the Jackson/Delta area, where his prominent GOP supporters were based.[24]

Another Invisible Presidential Campaign

As in 2008, Mississippi was viewed by political observers as such a safe Republican state in the presidential election that both national campaigns virtually ignored the state. Romney returned once in July for a fund-raiser at River Hills Club, where he talked about how tough it was "being middle class in American right now," pointed to the "waiters and waitresses" as "not having a really good year," and accused Obama of sending jobs overseas by being an "outsourcer-in-chief."[25] State Democratic Party chair Cole blasted the "big money and elites" and the "special interests and donors" that were backing the Republican and reminded voters that "on Nov. 6, they won't count dollars. They'll count votes."[26]

Perhaps anticipating the forthcoming Justice Department refusal to approve the new voter ID law passed in a public referendum the previous November, Republican secretary of state Hosemann at a Neshoba County fair speech in August urged fairgoers to back Romney, claiming that working with the Obama administration on election measures was like dealing "with the real housewives of the Justice Department."[27] The next month, Attorney General Eric Holder spoke at a nonpartisan ceremony at the University of Mississippi commemorating the fiftieth anniversary of its integration, claiming that discrimination was not yet dead in America and citing recent incidents in Mississippi and Texas. Democratic attorney general Jim Hood agreed that federal preclearance of election law changes in such states was still necessary.[28] After the Justice Department delayed the new voter ID law until after the election by requesting considerable supporting evidence that it did not have discriminatory effects, Governor Bryant urged Mississippians to voluntarily show their identifications at the polls, prompting the chairman of the legislative black caucus to express the caucus's "disappointment" over his comments; to remind everyone to just "follow the law," which did not yet require presenting identification to vote; and to contact him if anyone at the polls requested their ID.[29]

Two national events generated some excitement in Mississippi. State Republicans praised Romney's selection of Rep. Paul Ryan as his running mate, with state GOP chairman Joe Nosef praising how Ryan had "vigorously defended conservative principles . . . in an appealing, uplifting way" and Governor Bryant concluding that the GOP ticket would "work to defeat the failed policies of the Obama administration and continue to put forward fresh ideas on how to grow the economy and get spending under control."[30] The first presidential debate, despite the general public's perception that Romney had won, generated intense partisan divisions. State Democratic chairman Cole praised Obama's phrase "economic patriotism" and agreed that "we have a civic duty to work together and rebuild our national economy," whereas state GOP chairman Nosef charged that Obama merely "offered the typical excuses for the failure of the last four years and absolutely no solutions for the future."[31] Democratic Senate candidate and retiree Albert Gore warned that Romney's threat to cut PBS funding would undercut early childhood education in Mississippi, as it provided a "window to a world" that kids in rural county schools did not have.[32] American Family Association president Wildmon concluded that Obama had lost the debate because "he has fewer bullets in his gun than Barney Fife. He's got nothing to offer . . . his economic plan just simply did not work."[33]

Republican issues resonated with many Mississippians. In an opinion article, Rep. Nunnelee related, in their own words, that three small business owners were being "taxed and regulated to death" and that taxes were "just draining us" and concluded that "hard-working people should be allowed to keep more of what they earn" so that they could "grow their businesses and create new jobs."[34] At a park gathering in Tupelo, Tea Party members denounced abortion and the effort at "redefining marriage from what God says it is."[35] Starkville columnist Daniel Gardner criticized Obama's "failed foreign policies," as shown by "Islamic extremists . . . whipping up anti-American riots and violence around the globe."[36]

Obama's positions on economic issues resonated with some older Mississippians, while civil liberty issues seemed to benefit Obama among many young people. Veteran state reporter Bill Minor warned that Romney's proposed budget cuts constituted a "fundamental threat to the safety net" inaugurated by FDR's "Life-saving New Deal."[37] In a column, Stennis Institute director Marty Wiseman reminded Mississippians that they received over two dollars of federal money "for every dollar sent north from the state" and that federal aid funded highways, agricultural commodity programs, Medicaid, Medicare, Pell Grants, and student loans.[38] Student opinion editor for MSU's *Reflector*, Mary Chase Breedlove, attacked Romney's 47 percent comment, pointing out that "having money does not make you any more deserving of life than someone who has none" and urging the Republican to worry more about people "who work overtime and live paycheck to paycheck."[39] On Election Day, in a front-page chart of four major issues dividing the presidential candidates, the *Reflector* highlighted that Obama was "pro-choice" and "pro gay marriage," whereas Romney was "pro-life" and "pro traditional marriage."[40]

Both parties' state and local organizations geared up for the presidential race. State Democrats had held their Jefferson-Jackson-Hamer Dinner in June, where civil rights veteran congressman John Lewis of Georgia praised the unity and diversity of the state party.[41] State Republicans maintained an impressive website announcing the openings of Romney/Ryan headquarters across the state and upcoming county dinners and rallies, soliciting campaign donations, and making available Romney television ads online. Well-organized county parties, such as those in Oktibbeha County (MSU's home), held Democratic Beans and Greens dinners and Republican Patriots dinners. The likelihood of an easy Romney victory in Mississippi led state GOP chairman Nosef at the Oktibbeha dinner to ask for volunteers to travel to Pensacola, Florida, to campaign for the party's ticket.[42] One week before the election, Governor Bryant found himself campaigning in North Carolina for Romney.

Congressional Incumbency Dominates Once Again

After the 2010 unseating of two congressional incumbents, political observers expected Mississippi to go back to its historic pattern of re-electing incumbents, especially in view of the reigning consistency between the incumbents' parties and their constituents, with Republicans representing the three districts that had voted for McCain with at least 61 percent of the vote and the sole Democrat being African American Bennie Thompson, who represented a majority-black district that had backed Obama by a two-to-one margin. Thompson's renomination conformed to that expectation, as he won 87.5 percent of the primary vote over Greenville mayor Heather McTeer. McTeer lamented the incumbent's inability to transform the poverty-stricken nature of his district, and Thompson countered that he had voted for the educational, agricultural, and health care interests of his district and had delivered federal money to the district's cities, counties, colleges, universities, and agricultural interests.[43]

For their part, freshmen Republicans Nunnelee and Palazzo had to overcome spirited challenges from the Tea Party. One challenger to Palazzo expressed dismay that Obama had gotten "everything he wanted and Mr. Palazzo has done nothing to slow him down," prompting the GOP congressman to retort that "they didn't send me to Washington to shut down government or to default on our national debt," as he breezed to a 73.9 percent renomination victory.[44] Nunnelee faced two Tea Party sympathizers, including attorney, former judge, and Eupora mayor Henry Ross, who accused the incumbent of having "a moderate record" that toed the line of the House GOP leadership by refusing to cut federal programs and voting to raise the debt ceiling.[45] A newspaper advertisement appearing the day before the election posed the question in stark terms, "You either vote for a Statesman, or for a Benedict!" and urged voters not to vote for "Benedict Alan Nunnelee."[46] Nunnelee, whose first-year voting record was rated as 83.33 percent correct by the respected American Conservative Union, gained a more narrow first primary victory with 57.4 percent of the vote.[47]

The general election campaigns were a return to the norm of incumbents scaring off strong challengers. Sen. Roger Wicker, enjoying a $2.3 million campaign war chest, faced retired minister, Army colonel, and former Oktibbeha County Democratic chair Albert N. Gore Jr., whose "travel budget is my back pocket. . . . I think I've been given about $3,200."[48] Gore pledged to be "a citizen legislator—not a career politician" and pledged to "fight to preserve Social Security, Medicare, and Medicaid."[49] Second District congressman Thompson, who spent over $1.4 million, with a message focused on the importance of health care, education, and agriculture, faced black Republican and Tea Party favorite businessman Bill Marcy of Vicksburg, who reported spending less than $26,000 through September 30 while pledging to "bring jobs" to the district.[50] Fourth District congressman Palazzo faced community college student Matthew Moore, treasurer of the Harrison County Democratic Party Executive Committee. Moore had replaced the party's nominee, who withdrew from the race for personal reasons, and he reported zero campaign money received and spent.[51] Third District congressman Gregg Harper, whose only general election opponent was a Reform Party candidate who also reported zero campaign money received and expended, spent the campaign season serving his constituents, speaking at events such as Starkville High School's Promote the Vote program, MSU's Morris W. H. Collins Speaker Series, and an MSU College Republicans meeting.[52]

One congressional contest that promised some suspense was in the First District, where GOP freshman Nunnelee, having fended off a Tea Party challenger from the right, now faced attorney Brad Morris, the former chief of staff for congressman Childers. The son of a teenage mother and raised by his grandparents, Morris explained how federal programs had helped him earn a good education and explained that federal education, health care, retirement, and home-ownership programs "helped build the middle class and allowed people to move up the ladder no matter where you started in life."[53] Nunnelee, who already boasted a spot on the powerful House Appropriations Committee, offered "a conservative view," defending his opposition to a federal program that benefited air service in four Mississippi rural communities, including his own hometown of Tupelo, by arguing that the GOP agenda he backed would provide low unemployment, a highly educated workforce, and a booming economy.[54]

Election Results and Analysis

The 2012 presidential election results confirmed the wisdom of the national parties in virtually writing off the state. Despite an Obama national victory, Romney easily carried Mississippi by winning the two-party vote 55.8 percent to Obama's 44.2 percent. Indeed, the preliminary two-party results indicated that the Magnolia State voted 1.7 percent more

Republican than did the South as a whole, marking the seventh presidential election in a row that Mississippi was more Republican than a region that had become the bastion of Republicanism. Indeed, Romney's percentage of the two-party vote in Mississippi was a sizable 7.5 percent greater than his vote in the rest of the nation, marking the eighth presidential election in a row that Mississippi was more Republican than the rest of the nation.[55] Republicans also easily reelected Sen. Wicker with 57.2 percent of the vote and easily reelected their three incumbent congressmen with over 60 percent landslides (see Table 6.1). Two of the few bright spots for Democrats were the over two-to-one landslide reelection of Rep. Bennie Thompson and a Romney victory that was narrower than that expected by most political observers, a somewhat closer GOP victory margin than in the three preceding presidential races.

As in 2008, as early as April the Mississippi Poll had demonstrated Barack Obama's major weakness: Mississippians' perceptions of his liberalism. In a state where 57 percent of likely voters labeled themselves as somewhat or very conservative and only 19 percent considered themselves liberal, Obama was viewed by 74 percent of voters as very or somewhat liberal. With the ideological self-identification scale in the poll ranging from a low of 1 for very liberal to a high of 5 for very conservative and 3 constituting the moderate category, Obama's mean score of 1.92, or somewhat liberal, was far removed from the average Mississippian's ideological mean of 3.61, slightly on the moderate side of somewhat conservative. Voters perceived Romney, however, to be their ideological soul mate, viewing his ideology, on average, as a 3.51 (see Table 6.2).

Further illustrating the comparative disadvantage that Democrats held on the ideological perception issue was that Obama was not only generally viewed as a liberal but also viewed as even more liberal than previous Democratic presidential nominees John Kerry (2.12 mean in the 2004 poll) and Michael Dukakis (2.20 mean in 1988), as well as very slightly more liberal than himself in 2008 (1.99 mean).[56] Mitt Romney's ideological consistency with Mississippians was shared with state Republican officials such as Governor Bryant, whose average score was 3.65, enhancing the credibility among voters of state GOP officials who aggressively backed Romney. The one bright light for Democrats was the success of their lone remaining statewide official, Attorney General Hood, in maintaining an acceptably moderate image of 3.0, which placed him much closer to the average Mississippi voter than it did to the image of the national Democrat.

Table 6.1. Mississippi Federal Election Results, 2012

Candidate (party)	%	Total votes
President		
Barack Obama/Joe Biden (Democrat)*	43.8	562,949
Mitt Romney/Paul Ryan (Republican)	55.3	710,746
Virgil Goode/Jim Clymer (Constitution)	0.2	2,609
Gary Johnson/James P. Gray (Libertarian)	0.5	6,676
Jill Stein/Cheri Honkala (Green)	0.1	1,588
Barbara Dale Washer/Cathy L. Toole (Reform)	0.1	1,016
Total	100.0	1,285,584
U.S. Senate		
Albert N. Gore Jr. (Democrat)	40.5	503,467
Robert F. Wicker (Republican)*	57.2	709,626
Thomas Cramer (Constitution)	1.2	15,281
Shawn O'Hara (Reform)	1.1	13,194
Total	100.0	1,241,568
U.S. House		
First District		
Brad Morris (Democrat)	36.9	114,076
Alan Nunnelee (Republican)*	60.4	186,760
Danny Bedwell (Libertarian)	1.1	3,584
Jim R. Bourland (Constitution)	0.8	2,390
Chris Potts (Reform)	0.8	2,367
Total	100.0	309,177
Second District		
Bill Marcy (Republican)	31.0	99,160
Bennie G. Thompson (Democrat)*	67.1	214,978
Cobby Mondale Williams (Independent)	1.4	4,605
Lajena Williams (Reform)	0.5	1,501
Total	100.0	320,244
Third District		
Gregg Harper (Republican)*	80.0	234,717
John "Luke" Pannell (Reform)	20.0	58,605
Total	100.0	293,322

Table 6.1. (continued)

Candidate (party)	%	Total votes
Fourth District		
Matt Moore (Democrat)	28.9	82,344
Steven M. Palazzo (Republican)*	64.1	182,998
Robert W. Claunch (Reform)	0.7	2,108
Ron Williams (Libertarian)	6.3	17,982
Total	100.0	285,432

Source: Mississippi Secretary of State, "Elections: 2012 General Election Certification," http://www.sos.ms.gov/elections_results_2012_certified.aspx.
Note: Results are complete and certified.
*incumbent

Table 6.2. Mississippi Voter Ideology and Perceptions of Candidate Ideology, 2012

	Voter ideology	Perception of Obama's	Perception of Romney's	Perception of Bryant's	Perception of Hood's
Very liberal	5%	52%	3%	2%	12%
Somewhat liberal	14	22	8	9	16
Moderate	18	8	27	20	18
Somewhat conservative	32	5	35	34	20
Very conservative	25	9	11	16	10
No opinion	6	4	16	19	24
Mean value	3.61	1.92	3.51	3.65	3.00

Source: 2012 Mississippi Poll, a telephone survey of 323 likely voters conducted April 2–25 by the Social Science Research Center at Mississippi State University.
Note: Cell entries above mean value total 100% down each column. Ideology was a self-identification question asking respondents whether their political beliefs were very liberal, somewhat liberal, moderate or middle of the road, somewhat conservative, or very conservative. Likely voters were those scoring in the highest three categories of an additive scale of the following three items: (1) likely voting in November, (2) interest in the presidential and congressional campaigns, and (3) recall of the congressional incumbent's name.

Exit polls further illustrated the importance of ideology in shaping Mississippians' general election votes. Both candidates received overwhelming support from their party's ideological core supporters, with Romney winning 81 percent of conservatives and Obama carrying 83 percent of liberals. Since conservatives outnumbered liberals among exit voters by an over three-to-one margin (51 to 15 percent), Romney was clearly advantaged by his ideology proximity to voters (see Table 6.3). Romney was also advantaged by the religious right factor, winning an overwhelming 95 percent of the votes of white born-again Christians.

Another factor that helped Romney was his narrow edge in party identification among voters. Republicans slightly outnumbered Democrats among actual voters (43 to 39 percent), and the 96 percent loyalty that Republicans gave to Romney slightly trumped the 92 percent loyalty of Democrats for Obama. Furthermore, 64 percent of the small band of independents backed Romney, thereby helping to counteract the 56 percent of self-identified moderates who favored Obama. Democrats were able, however, to claim a higher-than-expected turnout among their ranks, as their 4 percent deficit among actual voters was only 1 percent greater than the 3 percent deficit they faced among all adult Mississippians in the April Mississippi Poll.

Finally, as in 2008, Obama proved once again unable to move much beyond his African American and lower socioeconomic status base. The Democrat won a massive 96 percent of the African American vote, but only 10 percent of the white vote. Though Mississippi has the highest percentage of African Americans in the nation, whites nevertheless outnumbered blacks among voters by 59 to 36 percent. (One hopeful sign for Democrats, though, was that blacks comprised 3 percent more and whites 3 percent less of actual voters than in 2008.)[57] Whereas Obama won a 54 percent vote share of those with incomes under $50,000, Romney won an even greater 71 percent vote share of the sizable 48 percent of voters with incomes above $50,000. Furthermore, though a gender gap did emerge, Romney was able to win a majority of both men and women, though his 58 percent share of male voters was 4 percent less than McCain's in 2008, while his 53 percent of women was identical to McCain's (see Table 6.3).

There were two other bright spots for national Democrats besides the increased turnout of African Americans relative to that of whites. First, Obama was once again able to win a majority of those under thirty years old (55 percent, down 1 percent from 2008), but once again, as well, this group comprised only 19 percent of voters. Alternately, Romney's

Table 6.3. Mississippi Demographic and Attitudinal Sources, 2012

	Romney	Obama	Others	% of sample
Ideology				
Liberal	15%	83%	2%	15%
Moderate	42	56	2	34
Conservative	81	18	1	51
Party identification				
Democrat	8	92	0	39
Independent	64	30	6	18
Republican	96	4	0	43
Race				
White	89	10	1	59
African American	4	96	0	36
Income				
< $50,000	45	54	1	52
≥ $50,000	71	27	2	48
Gender				
Male	58	40	2	45
Female	53	46	1	55
Age				
18–29	43	55	2	19
30–44	54	44	2	29
45–64	55	45	0	39
65 and over	78	22	0	14
Most important issue				
Deficit	66	32	2	18
Economy	67	32	1	56
Health care	33	66	1	20
White evangelical				
Yes	95	5	0	50
No	25	73	2	50

Source: "Exit Polls: Mississippi," *CNN Politics,* June 26, 2012, http://www.cnn.com/election/2012/primaries/epolls/ms.

Note: The last column provides the demographic group's size of the sample. Groups that are too small to analyze, such as other races, are omitted from the analysis.

greatest strength was among the sixty-five-and-older category, a dying breed that comprised only 14 percent of the electorate. (The middle-aged groupings gave Romney a victory margin similar to the one he enjoyed statewide.) Second, Democrats, even national Democrats such as Obama, had the ability to benefit electorally from issues they tended to own, as Obama enjoyed a two-to-one advantage among voters citing health care as the most important issue, though only 20 percent of voters mentioned that issue. Romney enjoyed a similar lopsided advantage among the 74 percent of voters citing the economy or the deficit as the most important issue.

The Future of Party Politics in the Magnolia State

Mississippi Republicans in 2012 continued to maintain their post-Reconstruction high of electoral dominance. Republicans continued the unbroken streak of presidential election victories that began in 1980, maintained the control of both U.S. Senate seats that began in 1989, and for the second consecutive election retained control of every U.S. House seat except one. Such electoral dominance was presaged by GOP victories at the state level the previous year, as the party for the second consecutive election retained control of every statewide office except for attorney general and, for the first time since Reconstruction, seized control of both chambers of the state legislature. Democrats in the presidential election year of 2012 were once again hampered by a national ticket that was viewed as too liberal for Mississippians and that virtually ignored the state during the campaign season and by a state party organization that was not as well funded or as well organized as its GOP counterpart.

Lest political observers and national Democrats completely write off Mississippi, we should point to some isolated beacons of hope for the party. Many Mississippians, particularly the young, adhere to libertarian views, particularly civil liberty issues such as abortion and gay rights, as reflected in the majorities of those under thirty backing Obama for the second consecutive election. Democrats do own some important bread-and-butter issues, reflected in Obama's two-to-one margin among those rating health care as the most important issue. Some elected Democrats, such as Attorney General Hood, have crafted appealing centrist reputations, in Hood's case by cultivating a tough-on-crime image. Republicans in 2012 held only a narrow edge over the Democrats in party identification, illustrating the need for Democrats to fully mobilize their progressive supporters in the electorate on Election Day. Finally, Democrats continue to maintain an impressive biracial coalition consisting of African Americans and whites of modest means.

7

South Carolina

"It's Déjà Vu All Over Again"

Cole Blease Graham
Scott E. Buchanan

Electoral Traditions

Yogi Berra's playful description offers a helpful perspective on South Carolina politics. For significant periods one party has dominated state politics. First, it was the Democrats from the end of Reconstruction until the 1960s. After a period of transition from the 1960s to the early 1990s, it has been the Republicans since 1995. Political winners over time, regardless of party, have traditionally had agricultural roots (traditionally, cotton and tobacco; lately, soybeans and pine trees). One industry, textiles, was dominant until the transition to a more diversified manufacturing base, including automobile and aircraft assembly and distribution centers for consumer products. A politics of sameness has been reinforced by conservative social and fiscal values throughout the state's post–Civil War history.

Any political change has been triggered typically by white political rage. White reaction to post–Civil War Reconstruction presaged the installation of legalized, state-based racial segregation in the 1890s. Whites' negative reaction to national civil rights policies in the 1960s spurred the growth of the contemporary state Republican Party. After a period of some internal accommodation of national civil rights policies by Republicans, the Tea Party now rages against liberalism in Washington and, within the GOP, has helped promote conservative preferences in fiscal and social policy.

Changing Partisan Divisions

The transition from Democratic to Republican dominance in South Carolina took more than a century. After Reconstruction, Democrats saw back-to-back victories until the 1960s. Republicans had after all been the party of Lincoln, and the strife of Reconstruction led most white South Carolinians to favor Democratic presidential candidates, even if they were the necessary among undesirable choices. During this time African Americans, who would have favored the GOP as the party supporting their interests, and the few whites who opposed the Democrats were systematically excluded from the electorate. Consequently, white Democrats dominated state politics until the national civil rights revolution of the 1960s.

Except for the 1876 presidential election, the national Democratic Party tended to dismiss South Carolina's Electoral College votes. Large waves of immigrants in other parts of the country during the late nineteenth and early twentieth centuries became Democrats because of the party's support for labor unions, thus lessening Democratic dependence on the South. The growing opposition by national Democrats to racial segregation weakened the party's attractiveness to many South Carolinians, but national Democrats did not need South Carolina's votes to win presidential elections. Given the post–Civil War choice and repetitive politics, though, popular elections in South Carolina continued to be won by Democrats—at least in name—from statewide to local candidates.

South Carolina Democrats began to give way in their support for the national party by backing the Dixiecrat ticket in 1948. The Dixiecrats stridently opposed the national Democratic Party's support for civil rights policies. The Dixiecrats were led by South Carolina's J. Strom Thurmond, who was their candidate for president. Some evidence suggests that white South Carolinians' voting patterns were in flux throughout the 1950s and early 1960s.[1] Although not a Dixiecrat, favorite son James F. Byrnes added more energy to South Carolina's falling out with national Democrats. Byrnes served in the U.S. House and Senate and was "assistant president" to Franklin D. Roosevelt and, ultimately, secretary of state. He was also a U.S. Supreme Court justice for a time in the 1940s. Despite his extensive service and experience in all three branches of government, Byrnes found himself on the outs with national Democrats in 1944, as he opposed major party policies, especially on civil rights. When Byrnes's name was floated for nomination as FDR's running mate in 1944, nonsouthern delegates within the Democratic Party balked, resulting in Harry S Truman's nomination for the vice presidency.[2]

Late in his political career, Byrnes won election as governor and worked mightily in 1952 to get Dwight D. Eisenhower elected president. Byrnes invited Eisenhower to address a large crowd in front of the state capitol. Nevertheless, loyal Democrats continued to prevail in South Carolina. Illinois senator Adlai Stevenson won South Carolina's Electoral College slate in 1952 and 1956, and Massachusetts senator John F. Kennedy won them in 1960, albeit with a narrower margin, defeating Richard Nixon in the state by only 10,000 votes. Republican success in South Carolina began when Arizona senator Barry Goldwater carried the state in the 1964 presidential election. Only once since then, in 1976, has a Democrat, Georgia governor Jimmy Carter, won the state's electoral vote.[3]

In 1980, Governor Carroll Campbell and his political operative Lee Atwater supported Ronald Reagan and led the effort to stop former Texas governor John Connally's bid for the Republican presidential nomination early in the primary campaign. Despite spending millions, Connally lost the South Carolina primary convincingly, even though he had the support of Sen. Strom Thurmond and the first contemporary Republican governor, James Edwards. Reagan's primary victory in South Carolina and his successful national election gave rise to South Carolina's "First in the South" reputation. From 1980 until Newt Gingrich in 2012, the winner of South Carolina's First in the South primary went on to win the Republican Party nomination.

The Current Political Landscape

Statewide election results since 1980 reflect at least four distinct internal political regions with varying degrees of Republican interests and influence.[4] First is Upstate, representing about 30 percent of the state's population, where Republicans tend to emphasize social issues such as social services reform and freedom of religion. Republican support for independent, local decisions regarding schools or local determination of social policy is higher there than in other parts of the state. Greenville is the largest county in this region, with about 450,000 residents.

Next, Midlands Republicans tend to focus on national defense, especially the prospect of base closings. Major military facilities Fort Jackson and Shaw Air Force Base are in the area, as well as the Savannah River Project near Aiken and the headquarters of the national guard and many state law enforcement agencies around Columbia. Democrats compete more strongly with Republicans in the Midlands due to a larger African American population. About 22 percent of the state's residents live there. With 384,000 residents, Richland is the largest county in the Midlands.

Another 30 percent of the population lives in the Pee Dee and the Lowcountry, where Republicans are more libertarian than in other regions. They are attracted to the Republican agenda of lower taxes and smaller government. Charleston County's 350,000 citizens are the core there, followed by Horry County with 270,000, Beaufort County with 162,000, and Florence County with 137,000.

The last group of residents lives in rural counties, where Democrats are stronger. There are two crescent-shaped slices across the state, originating in Marlboro County in the northeastern border with North Carolina, that spread above and below Columbia to the Savannah River. About one-half of the state's counties are included in these slices, but only about 18 percent of the population. Many of these counties have large proportions of minority voters, and many lost population between 2000 and 2010.

Party Identification

Since the 1980s, party identification in the Palmetto State has become decidedly more Republican among whites, with blacks remaining overwhelmingly Democratic. The South Carolina State Survey included political identification questions in biannual surveys between fall 1989 and fall 2006. There were thirty-six survey periods, each with an average of 837 respondents, with partisan identification a research objective.[5] The average findings showed Republican support at 45.3 percent, including 19.5 percent strong Republican, 16.3 percent Republican, and 3.2 percent leaning Republican. By contrast, strong Democrats were 43.4 percent; Democrats were 21.4 percent; and leaning Democrats were 11.0 percent. Independent identifiers averaged 12.6 percent.

The April 2012 Winthrop Poll found similar results among registered voters' self-reported party identification. When leaners are counted as party members, Republicans tally 43.2 percent; Democrats, 39.4 percent; and independents, 13.6 percent. About 4 percent either did not answer or answered "something else."[6] Since neither party has a majority, the key is winning the independent vote. To account for margins of error in polls, a rule-of-thumb starting point is Republicans, 45 percent; Democrats, 45 percent; and independents, 10 percent. Election results suggest that Republicans have had more success in swaying independent voters than have Democrats. Based on past elections, the centuries-old social and fiscally conservative views of South Carolinians make the difference in statewide electoral outcomes.

The 2012 Presidential Nominating Primaries

There was no Democratic nominating primary for president in South Carolina in 2012. President Barack Obama was the only candidate who filed with the South Carolina Democratic Party to run in the primary. Compared with the lack of drama in the Democratic primary, the Republican nominating primary was a different story.

Republican candidates started campaigning and debating early in 2011, leading up to the January 2012 presidential preference primary. It was a long road for the contenders from the onset to the conclusion of the GOP nominating primary campaign. There were four major debate events. On May 5, 2011, Fox News and the state GOP sponsored the first debate in Greenville. Business leader Herman Cain, former New Mexico governor Gary Johnson, former Minnesota governor Tim Pawlenty, Rep. Ron Paul, and former Pennsylvania U.S. senator Rick Santorum participated. Former Massachusetts governor Mitt Romney was invited but did not attend. By the time of the second debate, held on November 12, 2011, Rep. Michelle Bachmann and former Speaker Newt Gingrich had joined the fray, along with Mitt Romney. Former Utah governor Jon Huntsman was invited but did not attend.

In November 2011, Clemson University's Palmetto Poll found that 68 percent of likely voters were undecided, and a similar percentage said they were likely to change their minds before the vote in January 2012. The top two in the field of candidates were Mitt Romney, with 22 percent, and Herman Cain, with 20 percent. Newt Gingrich, the eventual winner of the South Carolina GOP primary, scored only 10 percent at this point. Only about 12 percent said they were members of the Tea Party.[7] By January the Clemson Palmetto Poll had Newt Gingrich leading with 32 percent compared with Romney's 21 percent. An intermediate Palmetto Poll in December found Gingrich's lead at 38 percent. Romney polled roughly the same each time. The issues respondents cited in the survey as most important were federal spending, unemployment, corruption in politics, and partisan bickering. Clemson pollsters Bruce Ransom and Dave Woodard accurately foresaw that the closing margin between Gingrich and Romney would not be enough to deny Gingrich South Carolina's preference.[8]

In December 2011, Governor Nikki Haley endorsed Mitt Romney. Haley and Romney had traded endorsements in previous campaigns. Before her 2010 gubernatorial race, Haley as a sitting legislator had endorsed Romney in his 2008 presidential nomination bid. Romney was an early supporter of Haley's successful gubernatorial bid in 2010. Another significant Tea Party advocate, Sen. Jim DeMint, withheld an endorsement in 2012, even though he had endorsed Romney in 2008.[9]

On January 16, 2012, at Myrtle Beach, Fox News and the state GOP hosted the third debate. The field had narrowed to four: Gingrich, Paul, Romney, and Santorum. Gingrich's popularity surged among conservatives when he engaged in a verbal sparring match with Fox News contributor Juan Williams. A few days later, CNN and the Southern Republican Leadership Group hosted the fourth event, featuring Gingrich, Paul, Romney, and Santorum. When CNN's John King started the debate by asking Gingrich about comments made about him by his ex-wife, the former House Speaker responded by attacking King and the media. His comments drew raucous applause from the Charleston crowd. Based largely on his debate performances, Gingrich won the South Carolina nominating primary. Gingrich's win ended South Carolina's consistent First in the South prediction of the GOP nominee.

Exit poll results illustrate the dimensions of Gingrich's primary victory (see Table 7.1).[10] Gingrich led in virtually all categories. His closest competitor was Romney, who led him 32 to 19 percent among the 8 percent of GOP primary voters who opposed the Tea Party. Romney also led Gingrich 38 to 33 percent among the 35 percent of primary voters who did not identify themselves as born-again or evangelical Christians. In other categories, Gingrich led by convincing margins. Among males, Gingrich led Romney 42 to 26 percent and was 14 points ahead of Santorum and Paul. Among independents, the margin was closer, with

Table 7.1. South Carolina Republican Presidential Primary Exit Poll Results, 2012

	Total	Gingrich	Romney	Santorum	Paul	Perry
Gender						
Male	51%	42%	26%	14%	14%	1%
Female	49	38	29	20	12	0
Party identification						
Republican	71	45	28	18	10	0
Independent	25	31	25	17	23	0
Democrats	4	<1	<1	<1	<1	<1
Ideology						
Very conservative	36	48	19	23	9	1
Somewhat conservative	32	41	30	15	13	0
Moderate to liberal	32	31	34	13	18	0
Age						
18–29	9	28	16	21	31	1
30–44	19	37	19	21	19	0
45–64	45	40	29	19	11	0
65 and over	27	47	36	10	7	1
College degree						
Yes	47	37	31	16	12	0
No	53	43	24	18	14	0
Income						
< $50,000	36	40	25	16	17	1
$50,000–$100,000	37	41	25	20	13	0
> $100,000	27	39	34	14	10	0
Evangelical						
Yes	65	44	22	21	13	1
No	35	33	38	10	15	0
Tea Party						
Support	64	33	25	17	12	1
Neutral	27	35	30	18	21	0
Oppose	8	19	32	13	21	0

Source: CBS News, exit poll for South Carolina, http://www.cbsnews.com/primary-election-results-2012/exit.shtml?state=SC&race=P&jurisdiction=0&party=R&tag=contentMain;contentBody.

31 percent for Gingrich and 25 percent for Romney. Ron Paul had 23 percent support from independents. As a group, independents were 25 percent of the respondents in the exit poll. Gingrich polled over 40 percent support from conservative-identified voters in general and attracted 48 percent of very conservative voters. Non–college graduates (53 percent of voters) supported Gingrich (43 percent) about 19 percent over Romney (24 percent), his closest rival in that category. Voters over forty-five also preferred Gingrich. In sum, Gingrich's nominating primary victory was based on established South Carolina Republicans, who were generally conservative, born-again, and older.

When viewed at the county level, Gingrich's highest margins of victory were found in rural areas. Among these counties were Edgefield (60.3 percent), Williamsburg (56.7 percent), Barnwell (54.9 percent), and Dillon (54.4 percent). Many rural counties had high proportions of African American voters who did not participate in the GOP primary. As a group, the twenty-five rural counties contributed 13.5 percent of the total GOP primary vote, with a 2.9 percent turnout rate of registered voters.

Table 7.2 shows the county percentage totals for the three major urban county groups. Gingrich achieved a majority only in Florence County. By far the dominant county was Greenville in the Upstate, which accounted for almost 13 percent of the primary vote. Gingrich took almost 40 percent of the county. Romney won 25.4 percent of the vote, while Santorum won 17.6 percent and Ron Paul, 15.7 percent. The independent streak was evident across the seven Upstate counties. Independents as a group won 36.3 percent in the region—more than Gingrich's 34.5 percent and Romney's 29.1 percent.

The other urban groups showed overall support for Gingrich, as well. Yet Romney won pluralities in the Midlands' Richland County (38 percent) and the Lowcountry's Beaufort (43 percent), Charleston (36 percent), and Dorchester (41 percent) Counties. Collectively, the Midlands' counties gave Gingrich the most support, due to the influence of Aiken's (49.3 percent) and Newberry's (42.8 percent) votes for Gingrich. Gingrich's share was lower in the Lowcountry than it was in the Midlands or the Upstate. Beaufort (35.3 percent) and Charleston (32.6 percent) were the most lukewarm supporters of Gingrich. Perhaps the results in Richland, Beaufort, and Charleston were influenced by their large military base populations, who would not have been attracted to Gingrich's portrayal of himself as an independent or maverick candidate, thus making him an unpredictable supporter of military funding.

Table 7.2. South Carolina Republican Presidential Primary Vote by County, 2012

	Gingrich	Romney	Others	Total Vote	Turnout State %*	Rate**
Grand totals	44.8%	29.5%	29.5%	603,770	100%	18.6%
Region						
Upstate (Greenville-Spartanburg)						
Anderson	43.6	21.6	34.8	27,455	4.6	25.7
Greenville	39.7	25.4	34.9	77,270	12.8	27.8
Greenwood	42.6	23.7	33.7	9,060	1.5	23.3
Laurens	41.8	22.7	38.1	37,120	1.3	21.4
Pickens	42.0	21.0	37.0	18,787	3.1	29.4
Spartanburg	40.1	22.2	38.0	38,216	6.3	24.0
York	38.1	22.8	39.1	31,611	5.2	23.1
Totals	34.5	29.1	36.3	210,29	34.8	8.3
Midlands (Columbia)						
Aiken	49.3	25.5	25.2	24,377	4.0	4.5
Kershaw	37.9	30.1	31.2	8,653	1.4	22.5
Lexington	36.6	30.7	32.8	43,968	7.3	27.7
Newberry	42.8	28.5	28.7	4,813	0.8	21.8
Richland	31.5	38.0	30.5	15,358	5.9	23.6
Sumter	39.3	32.0	29.0	9,289	1.5	14.5
Totals	38.1	31.7	30.1	126,458	20.9	22.1
Lowcountry (Charleston) and Pee Dee						
Beaufort	35.3	43.0	21.7	27,317	4.5	26.7
Berkeley	36.7	26.8	36.6	20,973	3.5	21.3
Charleston	32.6	36.0	31.4	47,013	7.8	20.0
Darlington	48.9	24.0	27.2	6,930	1.1	16.9
Dorchester	36.8	41.0	35.8	17,931	3.0	21.7
Florence	51.3	23.7	24.9	14,880	2.4	18.4
Georgetown	45.6	33.7	20.8	9,633	1.6	23.6
Horry	45.7	30.0	24.4	40,671	6.7	24.6
Totals	30.0	24.5	2.0	185,348	30.7	21.8

continued >

Table 7.2. (continued)

	Gingrich	Romney	Others	Total Vote	Turnout State %*	Rate**
Totals for 46 Counties						
Urban counties (21)	*34.2*	24.7	27.6	522,097	86.5	18.6
Rural counties (25)	*6.2*	3.2	4.1	81,673	13.5	2.9

Source: South Carolina State Election Commission, "2012 Presidential Preference Primary: Results by County," http://www.enr-scvotes.org/SC/36831/67784/en/select-county.html.

Note: Winning percentages are italicized.

*Each percentage in this column represents the percentage of the total number of votes cast in the county or region as a proportion of all votes cast in the state. Totals have been rounded and may not always add to 100%.

**Percentage of registered voters. Total registered voters = 2,804,231.

Another dynamic at play was South Carolina's continued attraction of wealthy retirees from northern states, especially to the coastal counties.[11] According to the American Community Survey, nearly 21,000 citizens moved from the Northeast to South Carolina between 2001 and 2011, with most of that number coming from New York, New Jersey, and Pennsylvania.[12] Since the 1960s, northerners who moved to the South have been more likely to be Republican, which has helped to change the partisan composition of the South.[13] That migration has become much larger in recent years, as evidenced by the population explosion along the coast of South Carolina. Therefore, a significant component of Republican growth in South Carolina is from voters who are new to the state.

International corporations have been operating in the Upstate since the 1980s. The recent construction of the Boeing facility in Charleston and the corresponding move of workers from other portions of the country to South Carolina continue to add to the demographic diversity of the state. In large part this influx of new residents from other areas tends to be supportive of the Republican Party.[14]

The primary turnout of 603,770 voters (18.6 percent) showed general interest in the nominating process for president, although the turnout rate was down from 19.8 percent in 2008. The turnout rate across counties was higher in urban areas than in rural ones. Some Upstate counties had the highest turnout rates, including Pickens (29.4 percent), Greenville (27.8 percent), and Anderson (25.7 percent). Only Lexington (27.7 percent) in the Midlands and Beaufort in the Lowcountry (26.7 percent) had similarly high turnout rates.

The 2012 General Election Campaigns

In 2012, Republican candidate Mitt Romney defeated Democratic incumbent president Barack Obama in South Carolina by 10.47 percent. Given the slim-to-none chance of a South Carolina Democratic presidential victory in November, Obama did not campaign in the state. Many influential South Carolina Democrats campaigned in swing states, like neighboring North Carolina, to bolster Obama's support there.[15] Romney's challenge in the Palmetto State was to spend as little time there as possible and use surrogates, like Governor Nikki Haley, to remind the voters as often as necessary that Romney was the Republican candidate. This reduced his possible loss of supporters, especially among Tea Party fiscal and social conservatives. Obama's challenge was to remain positive about South Carolina and not waste political resources in a state he could not expect to win. Romney won South Carolina 54.6 percent to Obama's 44.1 percent.

Voter Registration and Turnout

South Carolina had a 2012 voting-age population (VAP) of 3,598,675.[16] The state had 2,820,774 registered voters, a registration rate of approximately 78 percent of VAP heading into the 2012 general election. State GOP officials and media pundits predicted a significant turnout in raw numbers of about 2.0 million. In fact, 1,963,876 ballots for president were cast on November 6, a turnout rate of 69.62 percent of registered voters.[17] Of the registered voters, 55 percent were female, and 69 percent were white. Nonwhite registration has been about 30 percent since 1990. Nonwhite registration includes African Americans and others who declare a category other than white when registering. By age, 74 percent of voters were between twenty-five and sixty-four. Younger voters, eighteen to twenty-four, made up about 4 percent of registered voters; voters over sixty-five comprised 21 percent.

Analysis: The Presidential Race

In late April 2012, based on fifty-state polling, Republican advocate Karl Rove considered South Carolina one of six "toss-up" states.[18] Newt

Gingrich's earlier primary success in South Carolina went no further toward a GOP nomination than did an additional victory in Georgia. The GOP primaries moved on to other states, and Mitt Romney was nominated at the national GOP convention in August. One outcome was clear. The winner of the South Carolina presidential primary would not be the eventual nominee of the national GOP for the first time since 1980.

Once he secured the nomination, Romney's victory in South Carolina was so anticipated that no postconvention Romney-Obama polling in South Carolina occurred.[19] In an effort to conserve resources, the national news services did not conduct any exit polls in South Carolina in November and called the race for Romney when the voting booths closed.

The firmness of the GOP grip on South Carolina was illustrated by results in the major political regions in the state. As seen in Table 7.3,

Table 7.3. South Carolina Presidential Election Vote by County, 2012

	Romney	Obama	Others	Total Vote	Turnout State %*	Rate**
Grand Totals	54.5%	44.0%	1.4%	1,963,876	100%	68.9%
Region						
Upstate (Greenville-Spartanburg)						
Anderson	67.5	31.0	1.5	72,212	3.7	67.5
Greenville	63.0	35.2	1.8	193,189	9.8	68.0
Greenwood	57.0	41.8	1.2	28,672	1.5	71.8
Laurens	58.0	40.6	1.4	25,416	1.4	69.8
Pickens	73.5	24.5	2.0	45,549	2.3	71.5
Spartanburg	60.9	37.7	1.3	109,906	5.6	69.5
York	59.4	39.0	1.5	100,210	5.1	70.3
Totals	62.8	35.7	1.5	575,154	29.3	69.8
Midlands (Columbia)						
Aiken	62.6	36.0	1.4	70,363	3.6	69.2
Kershaw	57.0	39.0	1.3	27,946	1.4	72.1
Lexington	68.1	30.3	1.6	112,623	5.7	69.6
Newberry	56.6	42.3	1.1	16,351	0.8	73.4
Richland	33.3	65.3	1.3	158,912	8.1	65.3
Sumter	40.7	58.3	1.0	47,309	2.4	70.8
Totals	53.1	45.2	1.7	433,504	22.1	70.1

the rural part of the state supported Obama 54 to 45 percent, though with only 18 percent of the total vote. The twenty-five counties in this group have small populations, large minority populations, and higher levels of unemployment and poverty.

Another way to think of Romney's margin of victory is to define any result approaching 60 percent of the vote as a landslide. A vote between 55 and 45 percent may be called marginal or competitive, with an outcome approaching 40 percent or less being noncompetitive.[20] By these standards Romney's 54.6 percent victory placed him in a virtually safe election. By comparison, George W. Bush's 2004 victory of 58 percent and 2000 victory of 57 percent were both comfortable margins, even close to landslides. The potentially competitive nature of Romney's victory suggests some challenges to GOP margins but consistent successes nonetheless.

Table 7.3. (continued)

	Romney	Obama	Others	Total Vote	Turnout State %*	Rate**
Lowcountry (Charleston) and Pee Dee						
Beaufort	*58.2*	40.7	1.0	73,297	3.7	69.3
Berkeley	*56.4*	41.9	1.7	68,195	3.5	67.5
Charleston	48.0	*50.4*	1.6	161,707	8.2	66.8
Darlington	47.9	*51.3*	0.8	30,150	1.5	72.2
Dorchester	*57.2*	41.2	1.5	56,855	3.0	65.5
Florence	*49.8*	49.2	0.9	58,122	3.0	70.1
Georgetown	*53.4*	45.7	0.9	30,965	1.6	76.1
Horry	*64.1*	34.6	1.2	112,393	5.7	66.4
Totals	*54.4*	44.4	1.2	591,684	30.1	69.2
Totals for 46 Counties						
Urban Counties (21)	*56.8*	41.8	1.5	1,601,342	81.5	69.7
Rural Counties (25)	44.8	*54.2*	1.0	362,534	18.4	68.1

Source: South Carolina State Election Commission, "2012 General Election: Results by County," http://www.enr-scvotes.org/SC/42513/116143/en/select-county.html.
Note: Winning percentages are italicized.
*Each percentage in this column represents the percentage of the total number of votes cast in the county or region as a proportion of all votes cast in the state. Totals have been rounded and may not always add to 100%.
**Percentage of Registered Voters. Total Registered Voters = 2,820,774

Romney's most significant margins were in the seven Upstate counties, where he topped Obama by 62.8 to 35.7 percent. In Pickens County the vote was three to one for Romney (73.5 to 24.5 percent). This is not surprising given the Upstate counties' dominant white majorities and expanding industrial and commercial activities. The region is also more fundamentalist in its religious perspective, which provided a basis for its support of Romney's socially conservative image and policies.

The Midlands and the Lowcountry/Pee Dee had similar degrees of Romney support (about 53 to 45 percent). President Obama took two Midlands counties (Richland by two to one and Sumter by 58 to 41 percent). Richland has a large minority population in its lower half bordering Sumter County, which also has a relatively large minority population. Obama barely took Charleston and Darlington counties with just over 50 percent of the vote, while Florence County was a virtual tie. Lexington County in the Midlands with 68.1 percent and Horry in the Lowcountry/Pee Dee with 64.1 percent were Romney's largest victory margins.

As illustrated in Table 7.4, Romney improved on the 2008 McCain/Palin ticket by less than 1 percent (0.69 percent). More specific comparison of 2008 with 2012 illustrates Romney's slightly better performance in urban areas (0.22 percent better) and in rural areas (0.26 percent better). The percentages are so close that "it's déjà vu all over again." In Upstate counties Romney did 1.5 percent better than McCain. Romney was less effective than McCain in the Midlands (1.8 percent less) and about a percentage point better in Lowcountry and Pee Dee counties. Romney showed the largest gain (5.4 percent) over McCain's total in York County, which borders Mecklenburg County, home of Charlotte, North Carolina. It is essentially a fast-growing bedroom county in the Charlotte metro area. Romney also improved on McCain's vote percentages in counties with expanding populations and economies, such as coastal Beaufort (3.32 percent), home of Hilton Head Island, Sun City, and large military facilities. Ever-growing coastal Charleston County (2.8 percent Romney gain) and Horry County (2.52 percent gain) also supported Romney's platform more than McCain's.

Notable was Romney's underperformance among Midlands counties. President Obama's popularity among black voters accounts for some of Romney's decline in Richland and Sumter Counties, due to their large minority populations. Fiercely conservative Lexington County was about breakeven. There was a slim improvement for Romney in traditionally conservative Aiken County, a county near the Savannah River

Table 7.4. South Carolina Federal Election Results, 2012

Candidate (party)	%	Total votes
President		
Mitt Romney/Paul Ryan (R)*	53.87	1,071,645
Barack Obama/Joe Biden (D)	44.09	865,941
Gary Johnson/James Gray (L)	0.83	16,321
Jill Stein/Cheri Honkala (G)	0.28	5,446
Virgil Goode/Jim Clymer (C)	0.24	4,765
Total		1,964,118
U.S. House		
First District		
Tim Scott (R)*	62.03	179,908
Bobbie Rose (D)	35.34	103,557
Keith Blanford (L)	2.18	6,334
Write-in	0.07	214
Total		290,013
Second District		
Joe Wilson (R)*	96.27	196,116
Write-in	3.73	7,602
Total		203,718
Third District		
Jeff Duncan (R)*	66.54	169,512
Brian Ryan B. Doyle (D)	33.26	84,735
Write-in	0.20	516
Total		254,763
Fourth District		
Trey Gowdy (R)*	64.90	173,201
Deb Morrow (D)	33.71	89,964
Jeff Sumerel (G)	1.27	3,390
Write-in	0.12	329
Total		266,884
Fifth District		
Mick Mulvaney (R)*	55.51	154,324
Joyce Knott (D)	44.40	123,443
Write-in	0.08	236
Total		278,003

continued >

Table 7.4. (continued)

Candidate (party)	%	Total votes
Sixth District		
James E. "Jim" Clyburn (D)*	93.62	218,717
Nammu Y. Muhammad (G)	5.53	12,920
Write-in	0.85	1,978
Total		233,615
Seventh District		
Tom Rice (R)*	55.51	153,068
Gloria Bromwell Tinbu (D)	44.39	122,389
Write-in	0.10	281
Total		275,738

Source: South Carolina State Election Commission, "2012 General Election: Statewide Results," http://www.enr-scvotes.org/SC/42513/116143/en/summary.html.

Note: R = Republican Party; D = Democratic Party; L = Libertarian Party; G = Green Party; C = Constitution Party. Columns for each contest may not add to 100%, due to rounding.
*incumbent

Site and the home of many horse farm operations owned by out-of-state investors.

Down ticket, Republicans continued their electoral successes. Even though there was no U.S. Senate seat up at the time of the general election, junior senator Jim DeMint resigned in early December 2012 to become the new head of the Heritage Foundation. Governor Haley appointed Rep. Tim Scott (First District Republican) in mid-December to replace DeMint. Under South Carolina law Scott will serve until the election in 2014, when a special election will determine the occupant of the term that ends in 2016. Scott has stated his intention to run in the 2014 election. Haley's appointment was historic. Tim Scott is the first black U.S. senator from a southern state since the Reconstruction Era. Scott was the only southern black Republican in the U.S. Senate when the new Congress met in January 2013. Given Scott's popularity in his congressional district, he is the odds-on favorite to win the 2014 special election.

In addition, senior senator Lindsey Graham's term is up in 2014, as well. In a rarity, South Carolina voters will have two U.S. Senate seats to fill. Given the Republican proclivities of white South Carolinians, the chances are extremely high that the GOP will retain both U.S. Senate seats into the foreseeable future. Depending on whoever inevitably runs for the Republican nomination in 2016, their fortunes will be helped enormously by friendly senators in the state.

The U.S. House delegation is similarly Republican. For the first time since the early 1930s, South Carolina has seven members of Congress. In the 2012 election the Republicans succeeded in winning the new Seventh District, which is centered on Myrtle Beach and the Pee Dee region of the state. Republicans control six districts in the state, with Jim Clyburn being the lone Democrat, representing the Sixth District, which has a majority-black voting population. The only real surprise in the 2012 House elections was Republican Mick Mulvaney's relatively narrow 55 to 44 percent margin of victory over his Democratic opponent, Joyce Knott. Since representatives normally improve their margin of victory in their first reelection bid, Mulvaney's performance raises some questions about his popularity within the reconfigured Fifth District. Mulvaney's chances for reelection in 2014 are favorable, however, given the enormous advantages incumbents enjoy.

In 2014, the race for governor will headline the state's midterm elections. Governor Nikki Haley is eligible to run for reelection, but she has played coy about her run, though she is all but certain to run. Should she run again, it will be an interesting contest, as Haley won a close election in 2010 with some vocal Republican opposition to her candidacy. Since taking office, Haley's approval rating among the state's voters has generally been in the mid–40 percent range. In many ways, Haley is more popular outside the state than within. Still, given how Republican the state has become, it would take a moderate to conservative Democrat to mount a serious challenge to Haley or any other Republican for the governor's mansion. In all likelihood, a Republican governor will be in place to help assist in the 2016 South Carolina Republican primary.

Conclusion

South Carolina has often been a key player in national politics, especially since 1980, with its First in the South presidential nominating primary. All national Republican presidential nominees between 1980 and 2008 won the South Carolina primary, but that streak ended in 2012 with Newt Gingrich's victory in the state's primary. It remains to be seen if 2012 was an aberration or if South Carolina's First in the South primary has lost its significance.

The future of South Carolina politics turns on whether South Carolina Republicans can maintain their dominance. With safe margins in virtually all elections, Republicans have a dominant slate with a majority in the general assembly, the governorship, all statewide elected officers, both U.S. senators, and the majority of the House delegation (six to one).

Democrats by comparison seem competitive in only a few select general assembly races. In most cases, Democratic success is assured only when legislative districts feature majority-black electorates. There was some hope for a statewide Democratic resurgence when Jim Hodges defeated incumbent Republican governor David Beasley in 1998 by over 87,000 votes, a 53 to 45 percent margin of victory. Mark Sanford soon reversed the Democrats' reawakening by taking the governorship away from the incumbent Hodges by 64,000 votes in 2002. Sanford ran without significant opposition in 2006. Nikki Haley's election as governor in 2010 continued Republican dominance in the state.

Today, there is only a thin statewide lineup of Democrats to challenge the Republicans. This lineup includes three Midlands legislators: state senators Vincent Sheheen (Kershaw) and Joel Lourie (Richland) and state member James Smith (Richland). In perspective, Midlands candidates have had tough sledding statewide. There seems to be a do-not-cross line for Democrats entering the Upstate. The Lowcountry has significant independent, conservative, and even libertarian leanings and does not offer an inherent advantage to a statewide Democratic candidate.

Republicans' tasks are to keep Democrats on the defensive and maintain as many noncompetitive races as possible. Barring any destructive state factions or third-party splinter groups, a future GOP November vote count for president may be projected to start at 50 percent and then slowly improve as votes are counted to a winning share of 55 percent or more. The governor's November tally may be closer to a fifty-fifty Republican victory, depending on how internally destructive the Republican Party nominating primary is. Currently, with Governor Nikki Haley as the potential incumbent, Republican prospects in 2014 seem encouraging. The strong Republican congressional delegation gives a broad statewide but locally focused Republican base. By comparison, the Democrats seem to have only a short list of gubernatorial candidates and do not claim to have a pipeline of potential statewide candidates under development. The unchanging levels of Republican representation in the state house and state senate seem as solid as the granite walls of the state capitol. Given these static conditions, for the political observer it seems future electoral results in South Carolina will be yesterday's results "all over again."

III

Elections in the Rim South

8

Arkansas

Another Anti-Obama Aftershock

Janine A. Parry
Jay Barth

The election of 2008 provided the first in a series of major jolts that have transformed Arkansas politics. Barack Obama's pronounced unpopularity in the state—driven by a combination of factors, including his defeat of the former first lady of Arkansas in an intense nomination battle—made Arkansas the state that had the most pronounced shift in the GOP direction between 2004 and 2008.[1] In rebuffing Barack Obama's Democratic Party, with its emphasis on an unfamiliar social diversity exemplified in the candidate himself, many Arkansas voters—particularly, white rural residents—showed through their votes a clear discomfort with the change Obama promised. Still, the inability of the traditionally hapless state GOP to field candidates outside northwest Arkansas and a few other pockets limited its 2008 successes down ticket even as John McCain ran up his numbers across the state.

Two years later, with antipathy toward Obama at its national peak, a second Obama-driven aftershock hit Arkansas hard, pulling Republican candidates (some from local Tea Party operations that the state party had not recruited and barely knew) into an array of offices up and down the ballot. Consequently, the GOP picked up a U.S. Senate seat, three additional statewide offices, and two new congressional seats and reached post-Reconstruction highs in bouncing numerous Democratic incumbents from the state house and senate. Polling in that cycle showed that the better-funded and better-known Democrats led their opponents when no party labels accompanied the names but that because of the Democratic brand's toxicity, the GOP candidates opened up leads when party names accompanied candidates' names.[2] Election Day 2010 provided confirmation of those polling patterns.

With respect to 2012, it was always clear to Arkansas partisans that with the deeply unpopular Democratic president at top of the ticket, it would no doubt provide a third consecutive jolt to Arkansas. The key question was whether that aftershock would be significant enough to have an impact at the lowest levels of Arkansas politics and, specifically, whether it would propel Republicans into control of the Arkansas state legislature for the first time since Reconstruction's end. While not as pronounced as it was in the 2010 cycle, the Obama effect remained significant enough to do exactly that.

The Primary Season

In 2008, the presence of a former Arkansas governor on the Republican primary ballot and a former Arkansas first lady on the Democratic slate meant that the state's Super Tuesday primary was lacking in drama on either side. The decision of the state legislature to hold the presidential nomination vote in 2012 at the traditional late-May date ensured that Arkansas voters would find themselves even more irrelevant to the 2012 nominating process than they were four years earlier. That said, the strikingly poor performance of President Obama against a protest candidate reiterated the depth of the president's electoral travails in the state.

On the GOP side there were numerous signs that Arkansas's Republicans were slow to warm to Mitt Romney. The greatest burst of enthusiasm was for Texas governor Rick Perry, who received the endorsement of twenty-six Arkansas GOP elected officials and party leaders in June 2011.[3] Late 2011 polling also showed Perry to be a stronger general election candidate in the state than Romney, although both led President Obama by large margins.[4] However, Perry's poor debate performances and his perceived moderation on immigration issues eventually pushed some GOP activists away from the Texas governor.[5] About that time, businessman Herman Cain headlined a sold-out Washington

County Lincoln Day Dinner in vote-rich northwest Arkansas, and state party loyalists still looking for their candidate expressed interest in backing Cain.[6] Although outnumbered, two high-profile Republicans, central Arkansas congressman Tim Griffin and Lieutenant Governor Mark Darr, did throw support to Romney early.[7] Griffin would become Romney's state campaign chair and gain a coveted speaking role at the Republican National Convention.[8]

If Arkansas's primary had been held earlier in the spring, Rick Santorum no doubt would have performed well, as he had in neighboring states with ideologically and religiously similar GOP electorates. The former Pennsylvania senator had suspended his campaign, however, by mid-April, weeks before the Arkansas primary. As a result the wealthy Mormon former Massachusetts governor—out of step with most Arkansas GOP voters in a host of key demographics—sailed to victory in the May 22 primary, winning the votes of nearly seven in ten primary voters.

Ironically, by the time of the primary it was the Democratic race that generated the most drama. Arkansans had voted consistently against Barack Obama throughout his national electoral career. In the days leading up to the Arkansas primary, political observers focused on the percentage of the vote that might be gained by Tennessee attorney John Wolfe, on the Democratic primary ballot along with Obama. Based on the strong performance of a protest candidate against Obama in West Virginia weeks earlier, some saw a path for Wolfe to a majority of the vote.[9] Despite the fact that Wolfe's failure to file a delegate selection plan with the state party led officials to announce that he would receive no delegates regardless of his vote percentage, a flurry of pro-Wolfe robocalls hit phones in the state in the days leading up to the primary. While falling short of a majority, Wolfe did gain the votes of over four in ten Arkansas Democratic primary voters. Following his strong showing, Wolfe filed suit in federal court to gain delegates, but the suit was quickly thrown out, and Obama received all of the state's Democratic National Convention delegates.[10]

Perhaps the most telling outcome in the Arkansas primary was that it showed a dramatic acceleration in two trends in recent primary elections in the state: the decline in primary voting in the state and the relative growth of participation in the GOP primary.[11] Table 8.1 shows Arkansas's primary turnout across time. In comparing 2012 with previous election cycles, the decline in the number of Arkansans participating is stunning. While it would be expected that turnout would decrease

Table 8.1. Arkansas Presidential Primary Voter Turnout, 1976–2008

Year	Democratic Primary	Republican Primary
1976	525,968	22,797
1980	415,406	8,177
1984	492,321	19,040
1988	497,506	68,305
1992	502,130	52,297
1996	300,389	42,814
2000	246,900	44,573
2004	256,848	38,363
2008*	315,322	229,665
2012	162,647	152,360

Source: Arkansas Secretary of State.
*In 2008 Arkansas, in an ultimately unsuccessful bid to increase its significance in the nominating process, moved its primary election from May to February. This was a significant shift for observers of state politics because it separated voters' national partisan preferences from the overwhelming number of local contests in which Republican candidates do not appear or are not competitive. The resulting surge in Republican identifiers is dramatic.

from 2008—when the nominations were still in question and candidates with deep ties to the state were participating in each primary—the sharp decrease in 2012, which unlike 2008 contained races up and down the ballot, showed a growing recognition on the part of Arkansans that in modern politics the sole election that matters is the general election. Even more striking, in light of the state's electoral history, was the near parity shown in participation in the Democratic and GOP primaries. Historically, because so many local elections were determined in the Democratic primary, many Arkansas voters who voted Republican in fall elections (especially at the federal level) continued to participate in Democratic primaries. These 2012 numbers indicate that the Arkansas GOP has strengthened remarkably compared with the historical majority party in the state.

The General Election Campaign

As the presidential election outcome in Arkansas was preordained, there were almost no signs of a presidential campaign in the state. That said, the dynamics at the presidential level—particularly, white Arkansans' persistently negative attitudes toward President Obama—did have ramifications for Arkansas politics. Most important, the president was central to Republicans' (ultimately successful) efforts to gain control of both houses of the state legislature for the first time since Reconstruction.

Polling throughout President Obama's first term provided evidence that if anything he had only become less popular in Arkansas since his overwhelming 2008 defeat in the state. White rural voters, in particular, showed deep electoral antipathy to a man with whom they could not relate culturally.[12] Obama's approval ratings in the state remained consistently low, and once head-to-head polling against potential 2012 Republican opponents was under way, it was clear there would be no legitimate contest for the state's six electoral votes.

Indeed, the only signs of a campaign by either team in the Natural State were fund-raising visits. In March, Obama campaign manager Jim Messina visited the state for a series of fund-raisers and a grand opening of the campaign's Arkansas headquarters.[13] As in 2008, that headquarters was focused on engaging Arkansans in campaign work in other swing states, especially North Carolina, rather than any Arkansas-oriented duties. In late August 2012, Romney attended a downtown Little Rock fund-raiser where just over $2 million was raised; the candidate himself made no other public appearances in the state.[14]

Absent a legitimate presidential race or competitive races for Congress or statewide constitutional offices, the key battle in Arkansas in 2012 was for control of the recently redistricted state legislature. Not only had Arkansas's general assembly been controlled by Democrats for 138 years, but—for two generations—Arkansas politics had been marked by a pragmatic progressivism that separated the state from others in the region and produced change on issues ranging from education to health care to fiscal policy.[15] For instance, prodded by state supreme court rulings, Arkansas developed a model early childhood program, upped teacher pay dramatically, and overhauled school facilities. The outcomes included rising test scores and a K–12 education system ranked fifth nationally by *Education Week*. The current poster child for this style of governing has been Mike Beebe, the Democratic governor, whose public approval has consistently topped 65 percent since his 2006 election and who won every one of the state's seventy-five counties during his 2010 reelection.

Democrats running for the legislature in 2012 attempted to latch themselves to the governor, and the party attempted to frame the election as a choice between "Beebe or backwards."[16] Arkansas Republicans promoted a platform they termed the "SIMPLE Plan" and represented modern conservative positions: smaller government, lower taxes, voter identification laws, and school vouchers. In reality, however, the Republican campaign was not about these issues.[17] Instead, it was about one man: President Obama. A billboard in a rural northeast Arkansas county summed it up as follows:

> Save America.
> Vote Republican.
> Every Democrat Elected Helps Obama.[18]

The Koch brothers–funded Americans for Prosperity (AFP) made expert use of this environment by inserting itself into the most competitive state legislative races. The effort started with a successful effort to knock out a handful of moderate Republicans with AFP-backed conservatives in the spring primary. The AFP mailers highlighted incumbents' votes for a Beebe tobacco tax program dedicated to a widely accepted effort to improve emergency trauma centers throughout the state. Still, the mailers were hard-hitting, and the Kochs went five for five in their campaign to speed the transformation of Arkansas's political landscape.[19] In the general election AFP invested around $1 million in mostly mail-based attacks on state Democrats in a state that remains fairly low budget at the legislative level.[20] The president was front and center in these attacks, as well. Mailers about Obamacare primed racial sentiments by using an image of an African American doctor. Recipients were asked to "thank [Republicans] for protecting our health care freedom."[21]

Democrats attempted to detach themselves from national political dynamics while emphasizing that the party's candidates were on the side of the popular governor. Beebe himself energetically and somewhat uncharacteristically joined the fray, bankrolling state Democrats' campaign efforts, appearing in TV spots attacking AFP for "trashing Arkansas," and making a last-minute campaign swing through counties in the northeast quadrant of the state, where many of the most competitive legislative races were found.[22] Late in the campaign, state Democrats began focusing on the extremist writings of three Republican state house candidates (two of whom were incumbents). One, Jonesboro representative Jon Hubbard, declared in a 2009 self-published work that "the institution of slavery . . . may actually have been a blessing in disguise" for African Americans. Democrats rarely spoke, however, of the history that would be made if the party retained control of the state house—the elevation of the state's first African American Speaker, Darrin Williams of Little Rock. At least one Republican incumbent stumping for other GOP candidates did make note of Williams's race.[23] In the end, all three Republicans were defeated. When the party that had been in the minority since the end of Reconstruction managed to deliver fifty-one other victories, however, Williams lost his leadership bid.

It is impossible to determine how much of the 2012 aftershock can be attributed to animosity toward the Democrat at the top of the ticket. The preliminary results of a priming experiment we put in the field the weekend prior to Election Day are revealing, however. Respondents who were asked whether they approved or disapproved of President Obama *before* they were asked about their vote choice in the relatively high-profile state senate races in their districts were more likely to prefer the Republican candidate than those who were asked to evaluate the president later in the interview. Exposure to a Beebe prime showed no effect in either direction. Although the results are only suggestive, they do offer evidence of the down-ballot depression of which Arkansas Democrats had long expressed fear and of which Arkansas Republicans—with national support—managed to take effective advantage.

The Outcome

Clearly, the fact that Arkansas again cast its six Electoral College votes for the Republican nominee in 2012 surprised no one. Even the immense magnitude of Romney's victory in the state failed to generate as much as a raised eyebrow among experienced observers of Arkansas's political climate. Indeed, every statewide poll conducted between September and November placed the state decidedly in the red column. The average projected margin of victory among these polls was fully 24 points, matching the actual outcome (see Table 8.2).

What is somewhat notable is that the final gap between the two major-party candidates was greater in Arkansas than in any other southern state. In fact, Romney earned stronger support only in Utah (73 percent), Wyoming (69 percent), Oklahoma (67 percent), Idaho (65 percent), and West Virginia (62 percent).[24] Even more, the gap was sizeable in almost every corner of the state. Romney earned almost two-thirds of the votes cast in the predominantly white, heavily Republican Third Congressional District in the state's northwest corner. Romney also picked up more than 60 percent of the vote in the eastern (First District) and southern (Fourth District) regions, both of which have heavier black populations but suffer from low turnout and declining

Table 8.2. Arkansas Presidential Election Polls, 2012

Poll, polling dates	Romney	Obama	Spread
The Arkansas Poll (University of Arkansas), 10/9–10/14	58%	31%	27%
Talk Business Poll, 9/17	56	35	21
Talk Business Poll, 3/26	57	33	24
Talk Business Poll, 9/15	50	34	16

Source: RealClearPolitics.com, "Arkansas: Romney vs. Obama," http://www.realclearpolitics.com/epolls/2012/president/ar/arkansas_romney_vs_obama-2918.html.

population density. Only in the Second Congressional District, with urban, educated, multicultural Little Rock at its heart, did Obama hold the Republican challenger to under 55 percent, a proportion closer to what he earned across the region (see Table 8.3).

Of course, most regional analyses of Arkansas voting patterns have employed not congressional districts but instead five different regions: two of these (northwest Arkansas and the suburbs around Pulaski County) skew heavily Republican, while two others (urban Pulaski County and the Arkansas Delta) skew Democratic. In modern election cycles statewide election outcomes have been decided by the fifth grouping, rural swing counties—mostly white, overwhelmingly rural counties on a diagonal from the southwest to the northeast of the state, skipping over the Little Rock metropolitan area—which have shown a propensity to alternate between Republican candidates (when cultural issues are front and center in campaigns) and Democratic candidates (when economic populism comes to the fore). In both 2004 and 2008, these counties emphatically swung Republican. We argued that the vote on a state constitutional amendment defining marriage as between one man and one woman helped shape the easy 2004 victory in Arkansas for George W. Bush, who overperformed in these counties. In 2008, we argued that the voters in these counties felt the greatest cultural disconnect from Barack Obama.

Analysis of these counties' voting patterns in 2012 (bolded in Table 8.4) reveals another significant pro-GOP jolt across them. Indeed, in 2012 these counties made up most of the heavily skewed counties in the state, with Romney consistently outpacing his support in northwest Arkansas and the Little Rock suburbs in places that traditionally have been up for grabs.

Table 8.3. Arkansas Federal Election Results, 2012

Candidate (party)	% (2008 party vote)	Total votes (2008 party vote)
President		
Mitt Romney/Paul Ryan (Rep)	60.6 (58.8)	647,744 (628,711)
Barack Obama/Joe Biden (Dem)	36.9 (38.8)	394,409 (414,828)
Gary Johnson/James P. Gray (Lib)	1.5 (0.4)	16,276 (4,633)
Jill Stein/Cheri Honkala (Grn)	0.9 (0.3)	9,305 (3,359)
Peta Lindsay/Yari Osorio (Soc)	0.2 (—)	1,734 (—)
U.S. House		
First District		
Rick Crawford (R)*	56.2	138,800
Scott Ellington (D)	39.1	96,601
Jacob Holloway (G)	2.0	5,015
Jessica Paxton (L)	2.6	6,427
Second District		
Tim Griffin (R)*	55.2	158,175
Herb Rule (D)	39.5	113,156
Barbara Ward (G)	3.0	8,566
Chris Hayes (L)	2.3	6,701
Third District		
Steve Womack (R)*	75.9	186,467
Rebekah Kennedy (G)	16.0	39,318
David Pangrac (L)	8.1	19,875
Fourth District		
Gene Jeffress (D)	36.7	95,013
Tom Cotton (R)	59.5	154,149
Joshua Drake (G)	1.9	4,807
Bobby Tullis (L)	1.9	4,984

Source: Arkansas Secretary of State, "2012 Elections," http://www.sos.arkansas.gov/electionresults/index.php?ac:show:choose_elec=1.

*incumbent

Table 8.4. Arkansas Presidential Election Republican Vote by County, 2004, 2008, 2012

County	2004	2008	2012	% change 2008 to 2012	% change 2004 to 2008	% change 2004 to 2012	2010 % black
Arkansas	54.6	60.0	60.0	0.0	5.4	5.4	24.5
Ashley	53.7	62.3	61.4	-0.9	8.6	7.7	27.8
Baxter	60.1	64.3	70.8	6.5	4.2	10.7	0.3
Benton	68.4	67.2	69.0	1.8	-1.2	0.6	1.1
Boone	66.3	68.3	72.5	4.2	2	6.2	0.3
Bradley	47.3	56.1	58.4	2.3	8.8	11.1	28.2
Calhoun	**58.2**	**65.9**	**67.1**	**1.2**	**7.7**	**8.9**	**23.2**
Carroll	59.0	57.5	60.2	2.7	-1.5	1.2	0.3
Chicot	36.3	40.3	38.3	-2.0	4	2.0	53.9
Clark	44.9	50.7	51.7	1.0	5.8	6.8	22.3
Clay	**45.3**	**55.0**	**63.1**	**8.1**	**9.7**	**17.8**	**0.3**
Cleburne	59.2	70.2	74.6	4.4	11	15.4	0.5
Cleveland	**57.5**	**69.9**	**70.8**	**0.9**	**12.4**	**13.3**	**13.5**
Columbia	57.8	61.1	61.2	0.2	3.3	3.5	36.6
Conway	**49.6**	**57.6**	**58.4**	**0.8**	**8**	**8.8**	**12.5**
Craighead	53.1	61.0	64.2	3.2	7.9	11.2	9.7
Crawford	65.6	71.5	73.6	2.1	5.9	8.0	1.1
Crittenden	45.3	41.9	41.9	0.0	-3.4	-3.4	49.4
Cross	54.6	61.6	63.9	2.3	7	9.3	23.4
Dallas	**50.2**	**53.0**	**54.0**	**1.0**	**2.8**	**3.8**	**40.7**
Desha	37.2	43.3	42.9	-0.4	6.1	5.7	46.8
Drew	52.2	58.4	58.6	0.2	6.2	6.4	27.5
Faulkner	58.6	62.9	64.5	2.6	4.3	6.9	9.3
Franklin	57.4	68.1	70.8	2.7	10.7	13.4	0.7
Fulton	50.9	57.8	65.2	7.4	6.9	14.3	0.3
Garland	54.1	61.2	63.9	2.7	7.1	9.8	7.9
Grant	**62.1**	**73.9**	**74.5**	**0.6**	**11.8**	**12.4**	**3.1**
Greene	**51.9**	**63.0**	**65.9**	**2.9**	**11.1**	**14.0**	**0.3**
Hempstead	48.0	58.1	61.9	3.8	10.1	13.9	29.1
Hot Spring	**49.4**	**60.3**	**63.0**	**2.7**	**10.9**	**13.6**	**10.2**
Howard	**55.4**	**61.1**	**64.8**	**3.7**	**5.7**	**9.4**	**20.7**
Independence	**57.1**	**67.1**	**70.4**	**3.3**	**10**	**13.3**	**2.1**
Izard	**51.8**	**61.2**	**67.7**	**6.5**	**9.4**	**15.9**	**1.5**
Jackson	**42.3**	**55.9**	**57.5**	**1.6**	**13.6**	**15.2**	**19.4**
Jefferson	33.5	36.0	34.8	-1.2	2.5	1.3	51.9
Johnson	53.6	60.1	62.5	2.4	6.5	8.9	1.8

Table 8.4. (continued)

County	2004	2008	2012	% change 2008 to 2012	% change 2004 to 2008	% change 2004 to 2012	2010 % black
Lafayette	50.3	58.1	58.5	0.4	7.8	8.2	36.1
Lawrence	44.6	57.6	63.8	6.2	13	19.2	0.7
Lee	36.6	38.7	37.4	-1.3	2.1	0.8	57.2
Lincoln	46.8	57.1	59.0	1.9	10.3	12.2	32.9
Little River	48.6	63.0	67.0	4.0	14.4	18.4	21.2
Logan	59.4	67.7	69.3	1.6	8.3	9.9	1.3
Lonoke	65.4	72.7	74.2	1.5	7.3	8.8	6.5
Madison	60.7	62.8	64.9	2.1	2.1	4.2	0.2
Marion	60.1	63.2	67.7	4.5	3.1	7.6	0.3
Miller	57.6	65.8	69.3	3.5	8.2	11.7	23.4
Mississippi	43.3	49.9	49.4	-0.5	6.6	6.1	34.1
Monroe	43.3	50.9	49.1	-1.8	7.6	5.8	39.3
Montgomery	**59.8**	**65.3**	**69.9**	**4.6**	**5.5**	**10.1**	**0.6**
Nevada	50.4	56.7	59.0	2.3	6.3	8.6	32.7
Newton	63.5	67.0	68.5	1.5	3.5	5.0	0.2
Ouachita	**50.2**	**53.9**	**53.5**	**-0.4**	**3.7**	**3.3**	**40.2**
Perry	**55.0**	**64.2**	**65.5**	**1.3**	**9.2**	**10.5**	**2.0**
Phillips	35.6	34.5	32.8	-1.7	-1.1	-2.8	61.4
Pike	**59.8**	**68.8**	**75.2**	**6.4**	**9**	**15.4**	**3.9**
Poinsett	**46.0**	**61.8**	**65.8**	**4.0**	**15.8**	**19.8**	**7.4**
Polk	66.6	71.3	77.0	5.7	4.7	10.4	0.3
Pope	65.1	70.9	72.2	1.3	5.8	7.1	3.0
Prairie	**56.0**	**65.8**	**68.6**	**2.8**	**9.8**	**12.6**	**14.5**
Pulaski	44.6	43.5	43.3	-0.2	-1.1	-1.3	34.0
Randolph	**47.4**	**57.2**	**62.1**	**4.9**	**9.8**	**14.7**	**1.2**
Saline	63.2	69.4	70.0	0.6	6.2	6.8	50.5
Scott	**62.3**	**69.9**	**72.3**	**2.4**	**7.6**	**10.0**	**3.2**
Searcy	64.3	70.9	73.1	2.2	6.6	8.8	0.5
Sebastian	61.8	66.3	67.3	1.0	4.5	5.5	0.2
Sevier	54.7	68.3	72.4	3.9	13.6	17.5	6.3
Sharp	54.9	62.5	67.6	5.1	7.6	12.7	4.4
St. Francis	39.8	41.7	40.3	-1.4	1.9	0.5	0.9
Stone	**57.5**	**66.4**	**70.5**	**4.1**	**8.9**	**13.0**	**0.3**
Union	58.9	62.2	62.3	0.1	3.3	3.4	33.0
Van Buren	54.1	63.8	67.9	4.1	9.7	13.8	0.5
Washington	55.7	55.5	56.3	0.8	-0.2	0.6	2.7

continued >

Table 8.4. (continued)

County	2004	2008	2012	% change 2008 to 2012	% change 2004 to 2008	% change 2004 to 2012	2010 % black
White	64.3	72.2	75.5	3.3	7.9	11.2	4.0
Woodruff	33.7	43.7	49.9	6.2	10	16.2	28.7
Yell	55.2	63.1	67.7	4.6	7.9	12.5	1.5
Avg. (all counties)	53.3	60.1	62.6	2.3	6.8	9.1	—
Avg. (RSC)	53.6	62.6	65.7	3.1	9.1	12.1	—
Statewide Vote	54.3	58.7	60.6	1.9	4.4	6.3	—

Source: Arkansas Secretary of State, "2012 Elections," http://www.sos.arkansas .gov/electionresults/index.php?ac:show:choose_elec=1; see also U.S. Census Bureau, "State & County Quickfacts: Arkansas," September 18, 2012, http:// quickfacts.census.gov/qfd/states/05000.html.
Note: Counties in bold are Diane D. Blair's "rural swing counties"; see Diane D. Blair, *Arkansas Politics and Government: Do the People Rule* (Lincoln: University of Nebraska Press, 1988).

Social/Demographic Factors

To better understand the dynamics of Arkansas's second presidential rout in a row—and one again out of step with the country (in terms of direction) and region (in terms of magnitude)—we turn to an examination of the only comprehensive election polling conducted in Arkansas after the disappointing announcement by the National Election Pool that it would not conduct separate exit polls in almost half the states, including Arkansas.[25] The results of the University of Arkansas's annual preelection Arkansas Poll together with the postelection findings of a Hendrix College/*Talk Business* poll are presented in Table 8.5.[26]

Overall, the GOP candidate maintained (or even saw some small upticks in) support from members of nearly every demographic category, although in keeping with nationwide patterns Arkansas women were somewhat less likely to support Romney than they were McCain. Still, the shift was not large enough to counter a tidal wave of opposition to President Obama.

Ethnicity, Income, and Age

As was widely reported, white voters nationwide preferred Romney in 2012, but a growing coalition of African American, Latino, Asian, and

Table 8.5. Arkansas Presidential Election Exit Poll Results, 2012

	Obama	Romney	GOP 2008
Party identification			
Democrat	85%	13%	21%
Republican	4	96	93
Independent	28	67	67
Most important problem			
Economy	32	65	—
Education	58	40	—
Health care	49	47	—
Drugs	40	56	—
Taxes	38	57	—
Immigration	13	83	—
White Evangelical			
Yes	32	65	77
No	44	55	34
Gender			
Male	32	66	58
Female	42	54	58
White male	27	71	67
White female	34	62	68
Racial/ethnic identity			
White	31	66	68
Black	93	3	5
Age			
18–29	52	44	49
30–44	31	61	60
45–64	37	61	57
65 and over	37	60	65

continued >

Table 8.5. (continued)

	Obama	Romney	GOP 2008
Income*			
< $7,500	60	28	—
$7,501–15,000	49	42	—
$15,001–25,000	42	57	—
$25,001–35,000	41	56	—
$35,001–50,000	32	65	—
$50,001–75,000	34	65	—
$75,001–100,000	42	58	—
> $100,000	23	77	—
Place*			
Urban	41	57	—
Suburban	35	63	—
Small town	37	58	—
Rural	33	61	—
Most important quality of candidate			
Cares about people like me	70	28	—
Is a strong leader	31	68	—
Shares my values	22	75	—
Has a vision for the future	31	67	—
Other	28	66	—
Was your vote . . .			
. . . for a candidate?	43	55	—
. . . against a candidate?	16	80	—
Don't know	41	47	—
Medical marijuana vote			
Yes	51	46	—
No	25	72	—

Sources: "2012 Arkansas Poll," http://plsc.uark.edu/7834.php; "Exit Polls: President: Arkansas," *CNN Politics,* 2008, http://www.cnn.com/ELECTION/2008/results/polls/#ARP00p1.

*National news organizations canceled exit polling in Arkansas in 2012. Some categories are consequently not comparable across election cycles.

multicultural voters proved large and cohesive enough to carry the day for President Obama. Arkansas voters proved no exception in that two-thirds of whites supported the Republican nominee as compared with only a negligible number of blacks. Earning more than 90 percent of the ballots cast by African Americans does not have as much purchase in Arkansas, however, as it does in the rest of the region, because black voters compose only about 10 percent of the electorate. Latinos, while growing in number, still barely register in public opinion polling or at the voting booth. The patterns prove equally predictable with respect to income and age. As revealed in Table 8.5, President Obama won the support of only the very poorest and youngest Arkansas voters. Governor Romney, in contrast, held a strong advantage in every other category.

Gender

The election of 2012 again saw males, particularly white males, prove an important source of support for the Republican candidate, and they were assisted by white females, although even in Arkansas this did not occur to the degree seen in the recent past. Specifically, nearly three-quarters of white male voters cast ballots for Romney (4 percent *more* than the proportion cast for McCain), as compared with nearly two-thirds of white females (6 percent *less* than that cast for McCain). The result was that although there was no gender gap in Arkansans' presidential votes in 2008, a significant gap emerged in 2012. White males preferred Romney by 9 points over the preference of white females, and when voter respondents from all ethnic backgrounds are considered, the margin between the sexes increases to 12 points.

Other Social/Demographic Factors

Other factors proved equally predictable in Arkansas's overwhelming rejection of the incumbent president. Although the analyses are not shown, in the interest of space, Romney earned strong support among likely voters at every level of education except for those with a high school diploma or less, among whom the two candidates were more equally matched. The marriage gap was significant, as well, with nearly 70 percent of married respondents preferring the Republican candidate. Support for Romney was robust among the 72 percent of Arkansans who consider themselves born-again, or evangelical, Christians; nearly two-thirds of this group reported support for the Republican.

Political Factors

Partisanship

Politically, Arkansas voters appear finally to be edging toward the partisan realignment most of their southern peers experienced decades ago, but the shift is subtle at the individual level. In the past decade the proportion of Arkansas Poll respondents identifying as either generically Republican or generically Democrat has not much changed, save a modest but relatively steady contraction in the size of the latter. The more important (if related) shift is among the state's always large, and growing, contingent of independents, who in recent years have begun to lean consistently and forcefully to the right.[27] This has bearing on the party identification data featured in Table 8.5. At first glance, one might assume that Democratic identifiers in Arkansas were less likely to defect to Mitt Romney in 2012 (13 percent) than they were John McCain in 2008 (21 percent). We strongly suspect it is more likely that the state's conservative Democrats—thanks to the Koch-backed nationalized messaging that made its way even into local election contests—have left their ancestral partisan home for categories more consistent with their actual ballot casting. Arkansas Republicans, in contrast, proved as stalwart as ever in support of their party's nominee.

Issues and Candidate Appraisals

With respect to specific issues, the economy again proved to be the "most pressing issue or problem in Arkansas today" among Arkansas Poll respondents, and Governor Romney earned the strong support of this group. President Obama was the favorite among those for whom education or health care was of greatest significance, but these groups composed a much smaller portion of the Arkansas electorate.

More telling, we think, are the broader candidate appraisals captured by the Hendrix/*Talk Business* postelection poll. Only the most affective respondents—the 22 percent desiring a president who "cares about people like me"—preferred Democrat Barack Obama. Those who instead wanted a president who "shares my values" (32 percent), "has a vision" (22 percent), or "is a strong leader" (14 percent) all showed strong support for his Republican challenger, patterns loosely in line with exit polls nationally.[28] Even more, when respondents were asked to consider whether their votes were "for a candidate" or "against a candidate," fully 80 percent of those in the latter group reported casting a ballot for Mitt Romney. Whatever the nuances of shifting partisanship and issue appraisals, for a significant portion of Arkansans the 2012 presidential election was a straight-up rejection of the incumbent.

Turnout

In 2012, the state's votes were concentrated, as in years past, in the state's ten largest counties, which together constitute about half of the state's total population (see Table 8.6). In keeping with years past, however, turnout and vote preference varied widely in these counties. The relatively affluent suburban communities of Benton and Saline Counties, for example, not only exceeded the statewide turnout average by 2 and 5 percent, respectively, but posted enormous margins for the Republican nominee. Ever-shrinking Jefferson County, in contrast, again threw most of its weight to the Democrat but managed only an average turnout rate, clinching its dwindling influence against the Republican tide in Arkansas's presidential contests.

Other Election Races

Just as there was no battle at the presidential level in Arkansas, there was similarly no true competitiveness as Republicans picked up yet another seat in the U.S. House of Representatives with the retirement of twelve-year incumbent Mike Ross in the newly drawn Fourth District (south and west Arkansas). With the addition of the Fourth District, the GOP now holds all four House seats in Arkansas. Party primaries on each side in that district were competitive, but once the dust from those events had settled, GOP nominee Tom Cotton, a Harvard-educated Iraq War veteran, maintained his momentum (and his impressive fund-raising abilities) and rolled over Democratic nominee Gene Jeffress, a term-limited state legislator whose grassroots campaign was no matched for Cotton. Democrats always felt their best hope was in the First District, where first-term congressman Rick Crawford had stumbled throughout his congressional term and was facing a dramatically redrawn district. After Jonesboro prosecuting attorney Scott Ellington exceeded expectations in winning the Democratic runoff over the establishment favorite, he was unable to raise the funds necessary to match the coffers of a Republican incumbent running in counties where Romney was posting huge margins.

Table 8.6. Arkansas Registered Voter Turnout and Presidential Vote in Ten Most-Populous Counties, 2012

County and population 2010 (2000)	% Population Change 2000 to 2010 (1990 to 2000)	% 2012 Turnout (2008)	Vote %	
			Republican (2008)	Democrat (2008)
Pulaski 373,911 (361,474)	3.4 (3.4)	67.5 (67.7)	43.3 (44.2)	54.8 (55.1)
Benton 203,107 (153,406)	50.0 (57.3)	68.7 (71.5)	69.0 (68.4)	28.6 (30.7)
Washington 191,292 (157,715)	21.3 (39.1)	66.2 (68.3)	56.3 (55.7)	40.1 (42.4)
Sebastian 121,766 (115,071)	5.8 (15.5)	63.8 (66.3)	67.3 (61.7)	30.2 (31.6)
Faulkner 104,865 (86,014)	21.9 (43.3)	61.8 (65.2)	64.5 (58.6)	32.9 (35.0)
Garland 96,371 (88,068)	9.4 (20.0)	65.5 (60.0)	63.9 (54.1)	33.9 (36.6)
Saline 96,212 (83,529)	15.5 (30.1)	71.3 (70.4)	70.0 (63.2)	27.3 (28.4)
Craighead 91,552 (82,148)	11.4 (19.1)	57.0 (57.9)	64.2 (53.1)	33.2 (36.5)
Jefferson 78,986 (84,278)	-6.3 (-1.4)	69.0 (58.8)	34.8 (33.5)	63.8 (62.1)
White 73,441 (67,410)	8.9 (22.6)	56.8 (60.2)	75.5 (64.3)	21.7 (25.0)

Source: Data compiled from the U.S. Census Bureau and the official website of the Arkansas Secretary of State, www.arelections.org; see also U.S. Census Bureau, "State & County Quickfacts: Arkansas," September 18, 2012, http://quickfacts.census.gov/qfd/states/05000.html.

Ironically (or, for Arkansas, typically), Arkansas's voters showed some contradictory behavior as they voted for a handful of higher-profile ballot items. While voting for a series of emphatically antitax elected officials up and down the ticket, voters placed a new tax on themselves in the form of a decade-long increase in the sales tax to fund a new road system for the state. Similarly, while voting for a host of socially conservative candidates at virtually every level of government, voters came within an eyelash of becoming the first state in the South to legalize the medical use of marijuana. Interestingly, polls both before and after the election found support for the measure (Issue 5) decidedly lower than the actual returns, suggesting some voter hesitancy to admit their support.

Conclusion

In our analysis of the 2008 election, we concluded that while "only time will tell for certain, the 2008 election had many attributes of a realigning election—an election that reveals dramatic, lasting shifts in the electorate. But in realigning elections of the past, while the vast majority of the country shifts toward the new majority party, other portions of the country rejected the change and shifted in the opposite direction."[29] Clearly, Arkansas's even more pronounced rejection of Democrat Barack Obama in 2012 places the state firmly in the latter camp. Indeed, as we demonstrate here, the rejection, facilitated by a robust effort by Americans for Prosperity and a state Republican Party finally positioned to recruit and support candidates at every level of governance, was so thorough that it appears to have altered the state's political landscape permanently. With that said, however, the election cycle of 2014 (when Democrat Mike Beebe will be replaced as governor and the still-small GOP majorities in the legislature must be defended) will be crucial to ascertaining whether Arkansas will join other southern states as a solidly one-party GOP state or whether a stable two-party system will be the norm in the new Arkansas politics.

9

Florida

Sí, Se Puede!

Jonathan Knuckey
Tyler Branz

Florida was at the forefront of the battle for the White House in 2012. It was the South's premier battleground state, which accounted for more spent on television advertising than in any other state in the nation, and it trailed only Ohio in terms of campaign appearances by both party's presidential and vice presidential nominees. The status of Florida as a political bellwether state was further affirmed as for the fifteenth time in the post–World War II period it cast its Electoral College votes for the national winner. The Sunshine State was also prominent in 2012 for reasons other than the attention devoted to it in the general election campaign: an early Republican primary election, speculation about one of its U.S. senators being selected as the GOP's vice presidential candidate, and its hosting of one of the national party conventions, as well as the third and final presidential debate. The closing weeks of the general election also saw Florida in the news, for the wrong reasons, as the process and mechanics of voting in the state came under intense scrutiny, with many voters standing in line for several hours to cast a vote during the early voting period or on Election Day.

This chapter places the 2012 election in Florida in the context of recent party development in the state.[1] While Barack Obama scored a narrow victory over Mitt Romney—only the disputed 2000 election resulted in a closer percentage-point difference between the two parties—it will be argued that Florida is emerging as a state that now leans Democratic in presidential elections and that this is a result of the profound demographic changes that are evident in the state—most consequentially, the growth of the Latino vote.[2] This is not to say a Republican cannot win Florida in the future. After all, following the 2012 election the GOP still held a majority of U.S. House seats and dominated both chambers of the state legislature. Moreover, as the 2010 midterm elections in Florida demonstrated, Republicans can win statewide if the Democrats fail to mobilize their electoral coalition. Both demographic change and generational replacement of the electorate suggest, however, that it will be the Democrats who are better positioned to forge a majority coalition in the Sunshine State. This has profound consequences for future presidential elections and the battle to win the White House. While Florida's Electoral College votes will be a luxury for the Democrats—Obama would have won the presidency in *both* 2008 and 2012 without Florida—realistically, they will be a necessity for the Republicans.

The 2010 Midterm Elections in Florida: Tea Party Defeats the Establishment

The 2010 midterm election was an electoral earthquake for Florida. There was, on the one hand, little surprise that in a pro-Republican year the party won both of the major statewide offices being contested, further consolidated its grip in both chambers of the state legislature, and added to its U.S. House delegation. The identities of the victorious GOP candidates for both governor and the U.S. Senate, on the other hand, not only reflected a midterm backlash against President Obama but also sharply rebuked the GOP establishment. Moreover, the elections of Rick Scott as governor and Marco Rubio to the U.S. Senate would see both playing roles—albeit for different reasons—in the presidential election two years later.

When one-term U.S. senator Mel Martinez decided to resign in August 2009, he set in motion a chain of political events that few observers of Florida politics could have predicted. Martinez had already announced in early December 2008 that he would not seek another term, in part because of a perception of vulnerability in 2010 caused by his association with former president George W. Bush and his specific support of immigration reform that would have created a path to legalized citizenship for undocumented workers.[3] The initial speculation was that former governor Jeb Bush would be a strong favorite to hold the seat for the GOP, but Bush quickly announced the following month that he was not running. This cleared the way for Governor Charlie Crist to announce in May 2009 that he would run for the Senate seat and not seek reelection as governor.[4] In doing so, this meant that Florida would have open-seat contests for both major statewide offices in the 2010 election.

Crist was initially viewed as the clear favorite to succeed Martinez. Indeed, he was almost immediately endorsed by National Republican Senatorial Committee chair John Cornyn.[5] Enthusiasm for Crist was lukewarm, however, among many in the activist conservative base of the party and became especially hostile after his embrace—figuratively and literally—of Barack Obama when the president was in Florida to tout his economic stimulus plan.[6] The image of Crist and Obama together was the opening used by state representative Marco Rubio, Crist's opponent for the GOP nomination, to portray Crist as being out of touch with conservatives. Rubio's rise in the polls, fueled by his association with the emerging Tea Party movement from the right wing of the GOP, was spectacular, as he built a 20 percent lead over Crist. Ultimately, Crist abandoned his effort to win the Republican nomination, announcing in April 2010 that he would run as an independent.

The three-way race between Rubio, Crist, and the Democratic nominee, U.S. representative Kendrick Meek, appeared at first to be close, with Crist holding a small advantage over Rubio until early September.[7] Meek, who had represented a majority-minority district in the U.S. House, largely had a lock on the black vote, however, meaning that Crist would find it difficult to overtake Rubio.[8] In fact, Rubio consolidated his support among Republicans and opened up a double-digit lead, which he held right through Election Day, winning 49 percent of the vote, sweeping all but five counties in the state, compared with 30 percent for Crist and 20 percent for Meek. Exit polls showed that Rubio absorbed most of the GOP base, winning 87 percent of self-identified Republicans. Democrats split with Meek, however, who won 47 percent of the party vote, compared with Crist's 44 percent, which in all likelihood reflected a split among black Democrats and white Democrats.[9] Rubio instantly attracted media attention as a rising star in the Republican Party who might reach out to Latino voters and was often mentioned as a possible running mate on the 2012 GOP ticket. Indeed, although ultimately not selected as the vice presidential nominee in 2012, Rubio would nonetheless play a prominent role in the general election campaign both in Florida and nationally.

Crist's decision to run for the Senate meant an open race for governor. The expectation was that the general election would see two elected state officials, Republican attorney general Bill McCollum and Democratic chief financial officer Alex Sink, face off in the general election. Sink easily won the Democratic primary and the party's nomination. McCollum was challenged by millionaire businessman Rick Scott, who had held no prior office and who would go on to spend an unprecedented $49.8 million of his own money in the primary.[10] Scott ultimately defeated McCollum in the GOP primary, tapping into the same insurgent mood among GOP activists as Rubio and unleashing a barrage of negative attacks against McCollum. Most damaging for McCollum was Scott's ability to identify him as the GOP's "establishment" candidate, an establishment that had suffered its share of recent scandals, such as spending scandals involving the state party and the arrest of former state party chair Jim Greer.[11] Indeed, such was the negative tone of the primary campaign that McCollum did not formally endorse Scott until two months until after the primary. Character questions lingered around Scott, most notably his role as CEO of the Columbia/HCA hospital chain in the 1990s at the time of investigations into the largest Medicare fraud case in U.S. history. This meant a closer gubernatorial election than might have been expected in such a pro-Republican year, especially in a southern state. In the end, Scott narrowly defeated Sink 49 to 48 percent. While Scott's margin of victory was close, he entered office with Republicans dominating the state legislature, the GOP having made gains in both chambers in order to hold over two-thirds of the seats in the state house and senate.

The Republican triumph in state politics was matched by results in elections for U.S. House seats. The GOP unseated four incumbent Democrats to hold a historic nineteen-to-six edge in the Florida delegation to the U.S. House. Two gains were in Central Florida districts. In the Orlando-based Eighth District, one-term incumbent Alan Grayson was defeated by Daniel Webster, while Sandy Adams defeated Suzanne Kosmas in the Twenty-Fourth District. The defeat of Kosmas in a district that encompassed Seminole, Orange, and Volusia Counties, as well as Florida's Space Coast, was not a surprise. Kosmas had originally won in 2008 by defeating scandal-plagued Republican Tom Feeney in an otherwise safe GOP district. The defeat of Grayson, in a district that had become more Democratic because of demographic changes, specifically an increasing Latino population, owed more perhaps to the one-term incumbent's polarizing political style. During the health care reform debate, Grayson gained notoriety from conservatives and plaudits from liberals when he took to the floor of the U.S. House and said, "If you get sick, America, the Republican health care plan is this: Die quickly."[12] A further Republican gain was in the Second District in the Panhandle, where Republican Steve Southerland defeated seven-term incumbent Allen Boyd. Up until that point, Boyd was one of an increasingly rare species of white southern Democrats who had been reelected despite the district voting Republican at the presidential level in 2000, 2004, and 2008. Finally, in the increasingly Democratic-leaning Twenty-Second District, which included parts of Broward and Palm Beach Counties, two-term incumbent Rob Klein was defeated by Republican challenger Allen West. A prominent Tea Party–endorsed candidate, West gained instant visibility by becoming the first black Republican elected from Florida since Reconstruction and one of only two black Republicans elected to the U.S. House.

Overall, the 2010 elections set the stage for 2012. The GOP sweep suggested that President Obama might find it difficult to repeat his 2008 victory, especially if his base of young and minority voters had lost some of their affect for him and were less enthusiastic about voting. In 2010, the eighteen-to-twenty-nine age group constituted just 8 percent of the electorate, compared with 15 percent in 2008.[13] The faltering economy in the Sunshine State, together with higher disapproval than approval numbers for the president, suggested that any election that turned on a retrospective evaluation of the Obama administration might favor the GOP. Democrats could take some solace, though, from the fact that in both 2010 statewide contests, the winning Republicans had been held to under 50 percent of the vote in an otherwise dismal midterm election year for Democrats, particularly throughout the rest of the South.

Voting Rights in Florida

A description of the political context of the 2012 election in Florida is not complete without noting the major changes in Florida's voting and registration laws passed by the Republican legislature in 2011. The law was needed, Republicans argued, to prevent widespread voter fraud. According to the Florida Department of State, however, there were only thirty-one cases of alleged voter fraud between 2008 and 2011, resulting in only two arrests.[14] Opponents charged that the new laws were tantamount to voter suppression, designed to target the coalition of young and minority voters that had helped Barack Obama win the state in 2008. In response, GOP state senator Mike Bennett noted, "How much more convenient do you want to make it? This is a hard-fought privilege, something people died for."[15] Jim Greer, former chair of the Republican Party of Florida, was even more candid, noting, "The Republican Party, the strategists, the consultants, they firmly believe that early voting is bad for Republican Party candidates. . . . They never came in to see me and tell me we had a (voter) fraud issue, it's all a marketing ploy."[16]

The new voting law had four primary aspects. First, it cut the number of early voting days from fourteen to eight. The fourteen-day early-voting requirement had been in place in 2008 in large measure to address voting issues that had arisen during the 2000 election. By ending early voting three days prior to Election Day, no early voting could take place on the Sunday before the election, a day when many minority voters cast a ballot in 2008 as part of the Souls to the Polls drive by black churches throughout the state. Second, the law eliminated the provision whereby voters could update their address on the day of the election. After the law passed, voters could do so only if they had moved within the same county. The only alternative was for a voter to cast a provisional ballot and later provide identification to the Supervisor of Elections, even though provisional ballots were frequently not counted. Third, absentee ballots would be declared illegal if the voter's signature on the certificate did not exactly match the signature on record. Finally, the ability of third-party voter groups to register voters was made more difficult by requiring these groups to turn in registration cards within forty-eight hours of signature or face fines. This led to the League of Women Voters temporarily halting its voter registration drive in the state, resuming in August 2012 only after a federal judge described the registration restrictions as "harsh and impractical."[17]

The perception of voter suppression was also evident when in May 2012 Governor Rick Scott launched a drive to clear the voter rolls of noncitizens, using information from the Department of Homeland Security's database to check an initial list of 182,000 voters suspected of not being citizens.[18] Eventually, nearly 2,700 voters considered "suspicious" were notified by Supervisor of Elections officers to produce proof of citizenship within thirty days if they wanted to vote. One analysis found that Latino and registered Democratic voters living in South Florida were most likely to be targeted, ultimately prompting the U.S. Department of Justice to intervene and order the Florida Division of Elections to stop the purge of voter rolls.[19] Overall, the issue of voting rights—and the perception of an effort at voter suppression—would loom large as a campaign issue in Florida all the way through to Election Day itself.

The Presidential Nomination: Frontloading Florida Again!

As it did in 2008, the Republican-controlled legislature planned to make Florida relevant in the presidential nomination process by holding an early primary election. As in 2008, as well, this early primary prompted threats of sanctions from the Republican National Committee. Indeed, the RNC had warned of severe consequences for states other than Iowa, New Hampshire, South Carolina, and Nevada that held nominating contests prior to March 6.[20] Ultimately, the primary election date was set for January 31, resulting in Iowa, New Hampshire, and South Carolina moving their primaries, originally scheduled for February, into January. While this meant Florida would be the fourth state to hold a nominating contest, it resulted—as it had in 2008—in the state being stripped of half of its delegates to the Republican National Convention, with RNC chair Riece Priebus noting: "There is no discretion. There is no coming back. There is no kumbaya that's going to happen. They're going to lose half of their delegates and that's a pretty serious penalty."[21] The RNC would later mull further sanctions such as less-than-visible seating for Florida's delegation on the convention floor, as well as revoking the privilege of allowing Florida officials to grant VIP guest passes.[22]

The Republican Primary Election

Polls showed large fluctuations in the identity of the leading Republican in Florida throughout 2011, a pattern that was reflected nationally. Mitt Romney held a lead until the summer, only to lose it once Rick Perry declared his candidacy. Perry's decline as a candidate led to Herman Cain taking a lead, which then evaporated. Finally, Newt Gingrich assumed the lead near the end of 2011. Throughout this change of leading candidates in Florida, Romney's support averaged around 30 percent, suggesting that a considerable number of Republican primary voters suspected the former Massachusetts governor's conservative credentials and were searching for an "anyone but Romney" candidate, a pattern again reflected in national polling.[23]

The move to hold Florida's primary early on in the nominating process proved to be important, with the first three nominating contests producing three different winners: Rick Santorum in Iowa, Mitt Romney in New Hampshire, and New Gingrich in South Carolina. In this sense, Florida attracted more candidate and media attention than in any other year. Indeed, over $20 million was spent by the Romney and Gingrich campaigns and their respective Super PACs, Restore Our Future and Winning Our Future, although the advantage was decisively with Romney and his group, which outspent Gingrich more than four to one. This was more than twice the total expenditure in the 2008 GOP primary.[24] Much of the campaign advertising by Romney was negative, with one spot suggesting Gingrich had "cashed in" with Freddie Mac and a Spanish-language radio ad accusing Gingrich of once saying that Spanish was the language of the "ghetto."

Romney's financial advantage coupled with a realization that he was the most electable candidate resulted in a clear victory for the former Massachusetts governor, who won 46 percent of the vote to Gingrich's 32 percent, with Santorum a distant third at 13 percent. Exit polls showed Romney winning virtually all demographic groups among the Republican primary electorate. Moreover, even among those groups in which he had underperformed in prior contests, Romney showed strength, winning self-identified conservatives over Gingrich 41 to 37 percent, Tea Party supporters, 41 to 37 percent, and born-again/evangelicals, 38 to 37 percent.[25] Geographically, Romney swept most of the vote-rich Central and South Florida counties while losing the panhandle to Gingrich, a portent of his weakness in the adjacent Deep South states in future primaries.

Ultimately, Florida proved consequential in the Republican nominating process. First, Romney's victory stalled the momentum Newt Gingrich had built after his victory in South Carolina. Second, by winning in the largest and most diverse state to hold a nominating contest up to that point, Romney could argue that he alone was the most electable Republican. The Florida primary did not settle the GOP nomination—that would have to wait until after Super Tuesday—but it garnered the state the attention it wanted. In all likelihood, an early Florida primary will become a fixture in the presidential nominating process.

The General Election Campaign

Florida was front and center to both the Obama and the Romney general election campaigns and the path to reach 270 Electoral College votes. More money was spent on TV advertising than in any other state by campaigns and their allied parties and interest groups, $78 million on behalf of the Obama campaign and $95 million for Romney. And Florida trailed only Ohio as the state most visited by the presidential and vice presidential nominees and their spouses, with fifty-nine appearances for the Democratic ticket and fifty-six for the Republican ticket from June to Election Day.[26]

For the Obama campaign the intent to compete in the Sunshine State was evident as early as mid-January 2012 when the president visited Disney World in Orlando to unveil a plan to boost tourism and travel in the state. This was clearly designed to coincide with a period when candidates for the Republican nomination were gearing up to contest the GOP presidential primary. Indeed, before the end of January, Florida had been visited by no fewer than four cabinet secretaries, in addition to Michelle Obama.[27] The issues of the economy, Medicare, college loans, and immigration were central themes that would come to shape the pitch of the Obama campaign through the rest of the year. At the same time, efforts were made to define Mitt Romney as being out of touch with "ordinary" Floridians, which was part of the national campaign strategy. One TV ad focused on how Bain Capital, Romney's private equity firm, had laid off hundreds of workers at Dade Behring in Miami.[28] Ironically, it was perhaps the words of Romney himself during a private $50,000-a-plate fund-raiser in Boca Raton in May that did more to cement this image. In remarks that were secretly taped and that received widespread coverage, he implied that almost half of the population believed they were "victims" who were entitled to government aid and, hence, were unreachable voters for the Romney campaign. Indeed, the "47 percent" gaffe became a major line of attack for Democrats both in the Sunshine State and nationally.

The fact that the Republican National Committee had chosen Tampa to host its convention in 2012 meant that the official start of the general election campaign would commence in Florida. Indeed, an ideal scenario for many Florida Republicans would have been for Sen. Marco Rubio to be nominated as Romney's running mate, thus giving Florida even more visibility on the national ticket. Rubio was seen as a desirable choice, bringing youth and conservative credentials to the ticket and an ability to court Latino voters both in Florida and nationally. Eventually, U.S. representative Paul Ryan was selected as Romney's running mate, which did present something of a problem in Florida, given Ryan's prior desire to turn Medicare into a voucher-based system for future retirees. Indeed, following the convention, Ryan would make his first campaign appearance in Florida at The Villages—a retirement community in Central Florida—along with his mother, who lived in Broward County. Although Rubio was not offered the vice presidential position, he nonetheless featured in a TV advertisement reassuring seniors that a Romney/Ryan administration would protect Medicare benefits and campaigned extensively on behalf of the GOP ticket throughout Florida and the nation. Romney's campaign strategy in Florida resembled his national strategy, convincing voters to attach blame to the Obama administration for the slow economic recovery and emphasizing economic issues designed to appeal to moderates and independents—especially in the critical and vote-rich I-4 corridor—over cultural issues that might have resonated more strongly with the GOP's base.

Latino voters were a key group targeted by both campaigns in Florida. In 2008, Latinos had been a critical part of Obama's winning coalition in the Sunshine State, and the campaign hoped to recapture that enthusiasm. In 2012, the Obama campaign sought to portray the president as more in touch with Latino voters not only on national issues such as the economy education, and health care but also on immigration, as evidenced by the president's support for the DREAM Act. The Romney campaign also realized that it needed to compete more effectively for the Latino vote than had McCain four years earlier. Its efforts to do so were hampered, however, by Romney taking a tough line on immigration reform during the Republican primaries—partly to outflank his then-rival Rick Perry on the issue—when he suggested that Latino immigrants might "self-deport" from the United States. Romney would later sound more moderate on the issue of immigration, using an appearance at the University of Miami in a forum broadcast live online by the Spanish-language Univision network. There, he said he supported Marco Rubio's plan to offer permanent residence to those who served in the military and noted, "I'm not going to be rounding people up and deporting them."[29]

An intriguing aspect of the 2012 campaign in Florida concerned the roles played by the current governor of the Sunshine State and his two predecessors. Rick Scott was notably absent for most of the general election campaign, appearing in public with Romney just once—the day before the election—at a campaign event in Sarasota. At the same event, however, it was not Scott but Jeb Bush who introduced Romney and Romney who lavished praise upon Bush with respect to his work on education reform. This largely reflected Scott's unpopularity in the state, with approval ratings below 40 percent.[30] In contrast, Scott's immediate predecessor, Charlie Crist, endorsed Obama and was given a speaking slot at the Democratic National Convention in Charlotte, North Carolina. Crist was a frequent campaign surrogate for the Obama campaign both in Florida and in other key swing states, leading to speculation that Crist might run as a Democrat against Scott in 2014.

Following both party conventions, polls showed Florida as a toss-up state, with Obama initially holding a narrow 2 to 3 percent advantage in polls, only for Romney to catch up following the first presidential debate.[31] Given that Florida was likely to remain an exceptionally tight race through Election Day, both campaigns devoted time and effort into registering voters. Registration figures showed Democrats leading Republicans by over half a million votes—most critically, having registered more new voters than the GOP.[32] Given that more-restrictive voting and registration laws had been pushed by the Republican legislature to combat "fraud," it was ironic that the one major documented case of fraud in 2012 involved the GOP. Strategic Allied Consulting, a firm hired by the Republican Party of Florida to register votes, submitted faked voter registration forms. The Palm Beach County elections supervisor initially pointed out problems with the forms, noting that over one hundred of the firm's registration forms had similar handwriting, incorrect addresses, and incomplete information.[33] The Republican Party of Florida would later cut all ties with the firm.

The final week of the campaign in Florida focused on voter mobilization by both campaigns, which was especially critical given the reduction in early voting days, ending in 2012 on the Saturday before Election Day. Some of the campaigning in Florida was put on hold as Hurricane Sandy made landfall in the Northeast. Obama cancelled a planned appearance at the University of Central Florida. Bill Clinton, who had proved an effective surrogate for the president, still attended, though, along with Joe Biden. The focus of the last few days of the campaign in Florida was, however, largely on the voting process itself, with long lines evident in many of the most densely populated counties, especially those in South Florida, caused by the shortened number of early voting days, as well as a lengthy ballot that featured no fewer than eleven constitutional amendments along with the various federal, state, and local offices up for election. Many voters in Miami-Dade faced long lines, waiting from an average of two to three to up to nine hours to vote.[34] Requests to Governor Rick Scott to extend voting hours went unheeded, unlike in 2008 when then-governor Charlie Crist extended early voting hours. To meet the demand, Miami-Dade permitted in-person absentee voting on the Sunday prior to Election Day. The long lines during early voting were also evident on Election Day itself, with voting continuing in Miami-Dade hours after the polls had officially closed. Asked afterward about the mechanics of the election, Scott said, "Well I'm very comfortable that the right thing happened."[35]

Results and Turnout

Voter turnout in Florida, based on the voting-eligible population (VEP), was 63.5 percent. It was down from 67.1 percent in 2008 and lower than the 64.4 percent rate in 2004 and was perhaps a symptom of the aforementioned efforts to make voter registration drives more difficult.[36] The total number of votes cast remained about the same as 2008, however, with 78,298 more votes cast in 2012 compared with four years earlier. The total votes cast for Barack Obama was virtually the same as in 2008, the president winning just 44,611 fewer votes. Although Mitt Romney increased the Republican vote by 117,228 votes over that received by John McCain four years earlier, it was not enough to deny Obama a second victory in the Sunshine State. That Obama had largely held on to his previous vote totals was somewhat surprising given Democratic charges of vote suppression and that Romney had not added substantially more votes from those won by McCain in 2008, an election for which Republicans felt its base had not been enthused.

As predicted by preelection polls, the contest for Florida's twenty-nine Electoral College votes was exceedingly close. Indeed, it was not until four days after election night—largely as a result of uncounted votes in Miami-Dade—that the Associated Press finally called Florida for Obama. Even on election night, though, Obama led, and it was apparent that Mitt Romney was unlikely to make up the vote deficit. At the same time, the prospect of a repeat of a 2000-style recount was rendered irrelevant because Obama had already reached in excess of 270 Electoral College votes without Florida. In the end, the Obama/Biden ticket defeated the Romney/Ryan ticket by less than 1 percent, 50.0 to 49.1, with a majority of just over 74,000 votes (see Table 9.1). This marked the first time since 1948 that Florida had been carried by the Democrats in two consecutive elections. With the exception of the virtual tie between Bush and Gore in 2000, this was the closet percentage-point margin of victory in Florida's electoral history. Indeed, Romney received the highest share of a losing candidate's percentage vote in the history of presidential elections in the state.[37] In terms of the winning vote margin, in only two other elections in the post–World War II period, 1960 and 1964, were the winning candidate's majority less than that of Obama's in 2012—two elections, of course, in which the total number of votes cast was fewer than two million.

Obama's victory in Florida in 2012 also meant that the Sunshine State's bellwether status remained intact, having now voted for the winning presidential candidate in all but two presidential elections—1960 and 1992—in the post–World War period. Indeed, the vote change in Florida resembled that of the nation. Compared with 2008, Obama's support was down 1 percent in Florida, while it was down 2 percent nationally. As was the case nationally, the result in Florida reflected the fact that both parties established core and reliable bases of voter support.

Table 9.1. Florida Federal Election Results, 2012

Candidate (Party)	% of vote	Vote totals
President		
Barack Obama/Joe Biden (D)*	50.0	4,237,756
Mitt Romney/Paul Ryan (R)	49.1	4,163,447
Total		8,474,179
U.S. Senate		
Bill Nelson (D)*	55.2	4,523,451
Connie Mack, IV (R)	42.2	3,458,267
Total		8,189,946
U.S. House		
Third District		
Ted Yoho (R)	64.7	204,331
Jacques Gaillot (D)	32.5	102,468
Total		315,669

continued >

Table 9.1. (continued)

Candidate (Party)	% of vote	Vote totals
Sixth District		
Ron Desantis (R)	57.2	195,962
Heather Beaven (D)	42.8	146,489
Total		342,451
Ninth District		
Alan Grayson (D)	62.5	164,891
Todd Long (R)	37.5	98,856
Total		263,747
Tenth District		
Daniel Webster (R)*	51.7	164,649
Val Demings (D)	48.2	153,574
Total		318,269
Eighteenth District		
Patrick Murphy (D)	50.3	166,257
Allen West (R)*	49.7	164,353
Total		330,665
Twenty-Second District		
Lois Frankel (D)	54.6	171,021
Adam Hasner (R)	45.4	142,050
Total		313,071
Twenty-Sixth District		
David Rivera (D)	53.6	135,694
Joe Garcia (R)*	43.0	108,820
Total		252,957

Source: Florida Division of Elections, "Florida Election Watch," http://election.dos.state.fl.us/elections/resultsarchive/Index.asp?ElectionDate=11/6/2012&DATAMODE=.
Note: Votes for third- and minor-party candidates are excluded.
*incumbent.

Structure and Political Geography of the Vote

Statewide elections in Florida have become fairly predictable contests, in structural terms, with each party sustained by discernible geographic bases of party support.[38] The result of the 2012 presidential election in Florida was no different, with Obama winning the Sunshine State in the same way he had four years earlier. There was an almost perfect relationship (Pearson's $r = 0.99$) between Obama's county-by-county vote across both elections. Obama carried thirteen of the fifteen counties he won in 2008, with only Flagler and Volusia Counties moving into the Romney column. Overall, there was minimal change in the Obama percentage share of the vote from 2008. For example, although Obama's support was down in fifty-seven counties, in no county did his support decline by over 5 percent, the largest decline being in Martin County (-4.6 percent). In the remaining ten counties, Obama actually increased his percentage of the vote, with the largest—and most consequential—increase coming in Miami-Dade (+3.7 percent).

To further demonstrate the continuity in the structure of the vote in Florida, weighted least squares (WLS) regression analysis was utilized to explain variation in the county-level Democratic vote in both the 2008 and the 2012 elections as well as the change in the vote across both elections (see Table 9.2).[39] Independent variables consist of a variety of socioeconomic and demographic predictors generally employed to explain variation in the county-level vote in statewide contests. In both elections counties that were more urban and had larger minority populations, more college-educated residents, and more residents over the age of sixty-five were likely to provide significantly more support for Obama. Across both elections Obama's vote held up better in counties that were more urban and had a higher nonwhite population. This suggests some preliminary evidence that Obama's strategy of mobilizing the vote in Democratic base counties offset losses elsewhere in the state.

The structure and continuity in the county-level vote suggested in these regression analyses can be further expounded upon by examining the presidential vote across Florida's six discrete regions (see Table 9.3). After all, regional differences in the vote across Florida are themselves largely attributable to variations in the same socioeconomic and demographic variables that explain county-level voting patterns.

Although Obama's vote was down in four of the six regions relative to his 2008 performance, it was not by the margins that were needed—and maybe even expected—by the Romney campaign. In the Republican strongholds of the Panhandle, the north, and the southwest, Obama's vote percentage still exceeded that of John Kerry in 2004. Indeed, much of the discussion in 2008 was how John McCain failed to ignite the conservative base in these regions. That Romney failed to increase his vote share substantially in these regions should be worrying for the GOP, given that short-term forces may have been more favorable to Romney than they were to McCain in 2008.

Table 9.2. Florida Presidential Vote Demographic Analysis, 2008, 2012

	Obama 2008	Obama 2012	Change in vote 2008–12
% black	0.739***	0.768***	0.029*
	(0.140)	(0.136)	(0.016)
% Latino	0.181***	0.263***	0.082***
	(0.047)	(0.046)	(0.005)
% college educated	0.671***	0.619***	-0.052**
	(0.179)	(0.174)	(0.020)
Median income (in thousands)	-0.212	-0.284	-0.072***
	(0.202)	(0.196)	(0.023)
Population density (in hundreds)	0.326***	0.371***	0.046***
	(0.116)	(0.113)	(0.013)
% 65 and over	0.533***	0.416**	-0.117***
	(0.174)	(0.169)	(0.020)
Constant	15.927	19.055*	3.128***
	(9.867)	(9.604)	(1.119)
Adjusted R^2	0.626	0.710	0.898

Source: County-level vote taken from Florida Division of Elections, http://election.dos.state.fl.us/elections/resultsarchive/downloadresults.asp?ElectionDate=11/6/2012&DATAMODE=. Demographic county data are taken from the U.S. Census Bureau, USA Counties database, http://censtats.census.gov/usa/usa.shtml.

Note: Unstandardized regression coefficients are reported, with standard errors in parentheses.

*$p < 0.10$
**$p < 0.05$
***$p < 0.01$

More troubling for the GOP was that fewer total votes were cast in the Panhandle in 2012 compared with 2008 and that there were only negligible increases in the north and the southwest. If there was a conservative vote in these regions of the state that did not make it to the polls in 2008, it also largely failed to materialize in 2012. As in 2008, the two Central Florida regions were again the swing regions of the state, with Obama losing some support in the east-central region but actually gaining in the west-central region. It was in the east-central region that Obama had his largest percentage-point gain in 2008 (+5.4 percent), which was largely attributable to winning Orange and Osceola Counties by landslide margins, 19 and 20 percent, respectively.

While there was a drop in Obama's support above the statewide average in seven of the east-central counties (Indian River, Lake, Martin,

Table 9.3. Florida Presidential Election Vote by Region, 2012

	Obama	Romney	Change in Democratic vote from 2008	Total votes cast	Change in total votes cast from 2008	% of statewide vote
Panhandle	38.3%	60.6%	-1.2%	684,053	-7,773	8.0%
North	41.0	57.7	-2.3	1,160,560	+1,486	13.7
East central	48.8	50.2	-1.5	2,037,109	+26,059	24.0
West central	50.3	48.5	+1.1	1,370,979	+15,460	16.2
Southwest	41.8	57.3	-3.1	986,021	+631	11.6
Gold Coast	62.6	36.8	+0.7	2,235,457	45,572	26.4
Statewide	50.1	49.1	-0.9	8,474,179	83,435	100.0

Source: Florida Division of Elections, http://election.dos.state.fl.us/elections/resultsarchive/downloadresults.asp?ElectionDate=11/6/2012&DATAMODE=.

Note: The Panhandle includes the counties of Bay, Calhoun, Escambia, Franklin, Gadsden, Gulf, Holmes, Jackson, Jefferson, Leon, Liberty, Okaloosa, Santa Rosa, Wakulla, Walton, and Washington. The north includes the counties of Alachua, Baker, Bradford, Clay, Columbia, Dixie, Duval, Flagler, Gilchrist, Hamilton, Lafayette, Levy, Madison, Marion, Nassau, Putnam, St. Johns, Suwannee, Taylor, and Union. East central includes the counties of Brevard, Indian River, Lake, Martin, Orange, Osceola, Polk, Seminole, St. Lucie, Sumter, and Volusia. The west central includes the counties of Citrus, Hernando, Hillsborough, Pasco, and Pinellas. The southwest includes the counties of Charlotte, Collier, DeSoto, Glades, Hardee, Hendry, Highlands, Lee, Manatee, Monroe, Okeechobee, and Sarasota. The Gold Coast includes the counties of Broward, Miami-Dade, and Palm Beach.

Seminole, St. Lucie, Sumter, and Volusia), this was offset by a negligible drop in Orange County. Indeed, because more votes were cast in Orange County compared with 2008, Obama won just over six hundred more votes there in 2012. He also increased both his percentage and actual vote in Osceola County relative to his performance in 2008. In Orange and Osceola Counties alone, Obama received a majority of 111,723 votes over Romney, which reflected the changing demographics of both counties—most notably, their Latino populations, which were 26 percent in Orange and 43 percent in Osceola.

Finally, Obama again swept the Democratic base of the Gold Coast, actually increasing both his vote share and total votes from his 2008 performance. While the Obama campaign might have been concerned that the reduction in early voting hours would hurt it most in this region, there was actually an increase of 45,572 total votes cast, which accounted for over half of the statewide increase in total votes from 2008 to 2012. Indeed, it is plausible that efforts by Republicans to make voting more difficult actually backfired and made Democratic voters even more determined to vote.

Social Group Determinants of the Vote

Exit poll data examining some key demographic voting groups helps in understanding the individual-level dynamics underlying the aggregate data analysis presented in the previous sections (see Table 9.4).[40] Race has always been central to vote choice in Florida, as in the rest of the South. However, the long-term dynamics at work, in terms of the racial composition of Florida's electorate, were dramatically demonstrated in the 2012 election. Obama saw a 5 percent drop in his share of vote among whites to 37 percent. Had the white share of the electorate remained at or above 70 percent, it would have been impossible for Obama—or any Democratic candidate—to carry the Sunshine State. Likewise, historically, a Republican winning in excess of 60 percent of the white vote in Florida would have been a sure bet to win a statewide election. In 2012, however, whites accounted for 67 percent of the electorate, and Obama was able to overcome his deficit among whites by again sweeping the black vote, winning 95 percent of their vote, and, most crucially, by winning 60 percent of the Latino vote. Obama exceeded his share of the Latino vote in 2008 by 3 percent—the 57 percent he received in 2008 already a record high for a Democratic presidential candidate in Florida. Indeed, since George W. Bush carried the Latino vote in Florida in 2004, there has been a 17 percent decline in Latino support for the GOP. Of great significance was Obama's carrying the Cuban American vote 49 to 47 percent, which helped explain, in part, his increased support in Miami-Dade County.[41] The inability of Romney to reach beyond the GOP's white voter base was clearly a liability in 2012, and failure to do so in future elections will make it increasingly difficult—if not impossible—to reach over 50 percent of the vote.

Unlike 2008, a gender gap was evident in 2012, with Obama ahead of Romney by 7 percent among women and Romney leading among men by 6 percent. When examining the effects of gender while controlling for race, however, it is evident that two groups contributed to this gender gap. Among white men Obama saw a drop of 9 percent compared with his 2008 showing. This drop in support was diminished somewhat by white men constituting only 30 percent of the electorate in Florida, compared with 37 percent in 2008. It was also offset by a 6 percent increase in support among Latino women, suggesting an important interactive

Table 9.4. Florida Presidential Election Exit Poll Results, 2012

Voter characteristics/attitude	Obama	Romney	% of category
Race			
White	37%	61%	67%
Black	95	4	13
Latino	60	39	17
Gender			
Male	46	52	45
Female	53	46	55
Race and gender			
White male	33	65	30
White female	41	58	37
Black male	94	5	6
Black female	96	4	8
Latino male	58	40	7
Latino female	61	38	9
Age			
18–29	66	32	16
30–44	52	46	23
45–64	48	52	37
65 and over	41	58	24
Income			
< $30,000	61	37	21
$30–49,999	57	43	25
$50–99,999	44	54	31
$100–200,000	45	55	16
> $200,000	40	59	7
Party identification			
Democratic	90	9	35
Republican	8	92	33
Independent	50	47	33
Ideology			
Liberal	86	13	22
Moderate	53	46	43
Conservative	20	78	35

continued >

Table 9.4. (continued)

Voter characteristics/attitude	Obama	Romney	% of category
Most important issue			
Economy	46	53	62
Health care	78	20	17
Federal budget deficit	30	66	13
Foreign policy	53	45	5
National economic conditions			
Excellent/good	91	8	24
Not so good/poor	33	66	75
Economic problem facing people like you			
Rising prices	50	48	38
Unemployment	53	46	36
Housing market	57	43	11
Taxes	40	60	11
Who is to blame for current economic problems?			
Barack Obama	8	92	42
George W. Bush	83	15	51
Opinion of Obama administration			
Enthusiastic/satisfied	90	9	51
Angry/dissatisfied	5	95	47
Most important candidate quality			
Vision for future	46	53	32
Shares my values	40	59	23
Strong leader	40	59	22
Cares about people	83	15	19

Source: National Election Pool-Edison/Mitofsky Exit Poll (Florida), November 6, 2012.
Note: Obama and Romney totals may not add up to 100%, as other party candidates are omitted.

effect for race and gender. Possibly, the national salience of gender issues in the election affected vote choice, most notably the backlash caused after Republican U.S. Senate candidates in Missouri and Indiana made contentious remarks about the right of a woman to choose an abortion in the instance of rape. This is also suggested by the fact that even though Romney carried the vote of white women by 17 percent, Obama's support among them was virtually unchanged from 2008, declining by just 1 percent. Moreover, among single women Obama led Romney by a large margin, 63 to 36 percent.

A generational gap was again evident in Florida, with Obama increasing his support among the eighteen to twenty-nine and the thirty to forty-four age groups, winning 66 and 52 percent of the vote, respectively. Crucially, these two age groups constituted 39 percent of the electorate, just 1 percent less than in 2008. Clearly, the hope of the Romney campaign that there would be a lack of enthusiasm among younger voters was not realized. That Obama was able to increase his support among the two youngest age groups was also vital, given that he lost support among the forty-five to sixty-four and the over sixty-five age groups. While no exit poll data in Florida examines the vote among age groups by race, national exit poll data indicate that younger minority groups, especially Latinos, drove the generational gap. Nationally, for example, Obama won almost three-quarters of the vote among Latinos in the eighteen to twenty-nine age group.[42] This pattern was reflected also in Florida, suggesting that both the changing racial composition of the electorate and generational replacement worked together to advantage Democrats in the state. It might also offer a partial explanation for the aforementioned realignment of the Cuban American vote in Miami-Dade, with younger, more Democratically inclined cohorts replacing older Republican loyalists.

As in 2008, social-class voting was evident in Florida in 2012. Obama carried income groups below $50,000 per year, even though his support was down slightly compared with 2008. Obama increased his support among those with household incomes between $50,000 and $100,000 per year, even though Romney won a majority of the vote from this group. Only among those with a household income of over $200,000 was the drop in Obama's vote sharp (11 percent). Indeed, this was an income group Obama carried in 2008. Romney's inability to substantially improve the Republican share of the vote among other income groups perhaps demonstrated that the effort by the Obama campaign to portray

Romney as out of touch with many Americans was important to the final outcome in Florida.

Party Identification and Ideology

The stability demonstrated by the aggregate-level analysis appears to be the product of the strong effects of both party identification and ideology (see Table 9.4). Even more so than in 2008, the election in Florida came down to base mobilization. Obama won 90 percent of the vote among Democrats, while Romney won 92 percent of the vote among Republicans. Critically, Obama was able to win among independents, even though his support was down by 2 percent compared with 2008. Indeed, Obama's support among independents in Florida (50 percent) exceeded his share of the vote from them nationally (48 percent). Ideology also structured vote choice, with 86 percent of liberals voting for Obama and 78 percent of conservatives voting for Romney, with Obama retaining a 7 percent lead, albeit a reduced one compared with 2008, among moderates. Interestingly, Romney increased his support among conservatives by only 1 percent compared with the vote received by McCain in 2008. Given Obama's drop in support among both liberals and moderates, a more cohesive vote among conservatives for Romney—something approaching 80 to 85 percent, for example—would have likely produced a victory for the GOP.

Issues and Candidate Image

Just as was the case in 2008, the economy was by far the most important issue cited by voters in Florida in 2012. This was exactly what the Romney campaign had hoped for, that the election in Florida, and the nation, would allow voters to engage in retrospective voting and blame Obama for the previous four years of uneven economic growth. Given that 74 percent of Floridians viewed the economy as either "not so good" or "poor," Romney should have been advantaged by such voting. Why did this not produce an advantage for Romney in Florida? First, when voters were asked more specifically about which economic problem was being faced by people like themselves, voters who said rising prices, unemployment, and the housing market all favored Obama over Romney. Romney held an advantage among only those voters who cited taxes as the most salient economic problem. Second, a majority of voters had a positive approval of the Obama administration, with 51 percent saying they were "enthusiastic" or "satisfied" compared with 47 percent who were "angry" or "dissatisfied." Third and, perhaps, most telling, a majority of voters did not blame Obama for the current economic conditions, with 51 percent blaming George W. Bush. Thus, a vital condition for economic-based retrospective voting—attaching blame to the incumbent—was not met for many voters in Florida.

Table 9.4 shows that Obama's personal popularity may have also helped him win Florida despite the pessimism about the economy. A majority of Floridians had a favorable impression of Obama. The favorable/unfavorable numbers for Romney were much closer, however, with 49 percent viewing him favorably and 47 percent, unfavorably. Indeed, while Romney won more support from those who said that the most important candidate qualities were "vision for future," "shares my values" and "strong leader," Obama won among those who said "cares about people" by a massive 88 to 15 percent. Again, the strategy of the Obama campaign to make Romney appear out of touch with ordinary voters diminished any structural advantage Romney had in running against an incumbent president in a far from prosperous economy.

U.S. Senate, U.S. House, and State Legislative Elections

While the presidential election was clearly the main event in Florida in 2012, the undercard should not be ignored, as there were several interesting down-ballot races. In the election for U.S. Senate, incumbent Democratic senator Bill Nelson easily defeated his Republican challenger, U.S. representative Connie Mack IV, whose father had held the seat until retiring in 2000. As one of a dwindling number of southern Democrats in the U.S. Senate, Nelson had been viewed as vulnerable in 2012, especially had there been a strong pro-Republican tide combined with a quality GOP challenger. Fortunately for Nelson, neither condition was met in 2012. Mack never really dispelled character questions pertaining to his college days, which included two road rage incidents and an arrest over a Jacksonville barroom brawl with a Major League Baseball star. Indeed, during the Republican primary for the Senate nomination, Mack's opponent, George LeMieux, referred to Mack as the "Charlie Sheen of Florida politics."[43] Nelson easily won reelection, carrying twenty-nine counties and winning 55 percent of the vote compared with Mack's 42 percent. Generally, Nelson performed well where Obama exhibited strength, as evidenced by the very high correlation in the county-by-county vote between the two (Pearson's r = .96).

However, Nelson ran ahead of Obama in every county in the state. While this might be attributable to Nelson's incumbency advantage and the quality of his Republican opponent, it is interesting that in nineteen counties, Nelson ran ahead of Obama by 10 percent or more. All but two of these counties were in either the Panhandle or the north, suggesting racial backlash was most evident in these regions, with some white voters evidently willing to support a white Democrat for the Senate but not a black Democrat for president.

Although the Republicans held a seventeen-to-ten advantage in U.S. House seats over the Democrats after 2012, this amounted to an effective gain of four seats by the Democrats in the Sunshine State. The elections for U.S. House seats were the first to take place after the 2010 round of redistricting, and as such there was somewhat more volatility than normal, even for incumbents. Incumbent Clifford Stearns was defeated in the Republican primary by Ted Yoho in the Third District after Stearns's hometown of Ocala was placed in the newly drawn Eleventh District. Yoho was easily elected in the general election. In the Seventh District one Republican incumbent, Sandy Adams, was defeated in the primary election by another incumbent Republican, John Mica. Mica had switched from the Sixth District after his home in Winter Park was drawn into the new district. Mica won a decisive 59 to 41 percent victory in the general election. The now open Sixth District was retained by the Republicans, with Ron Desantis defeating Heather Beaven. Two Republican incumbents were defeated for reelection. In the Twenty-Sixth District, Republican David Rivera was easily defeated by Joe Garcia. This was not a surprise given a variety of scandals involving Rivera, including allegations of funneling at least $40,000 to the campaign of a candidate running against Garcia in the Democratic primary.[44] The other Republican incumbent to lose was Allen West in the Eighteenth District. West had gained visibility as one of only two black Republican members of Congress and as a leading figure within the Tea Party movement. He had also gained notoriety for his remarks in April 2012 that "there's about 78 to 81 members of the Democrat [sic] Party that are members of the Communist Party."[45] Despite raising $17 million and outspending his Democratic challenger, Patrick Murphy, by more than five to one—the only U.S. House candidate to raise more money in 2012 was Speaker John Boehner—West was narrowly defeated by Murphy.[46] It took two weeks until after the election, however, for West to finally concede, after claiming voting irregularities. Making matters worse for the Republicans was that the Twenty-Second District was an open-seat contest, as West had vacated it to run in the Eighteenth. The Democrats won that district, too, with Lois Frankel defeating Adam Hasner. Finally, two Central Florida districts featured notable contests. In the Ninth District, Alan Grayson returned to Congress after having been defeated in 2010. Grayson easily won the newly created district based on Osceola County and parts of Orange and Polk Counties, defeating his Republican challenger, Todd Long. In the Tenth District, Republican Daniel Webster, who had defeated Grayson in 2010 when running in the old Eighth District, narrowly defeated Val Demings. Webster's 4 percent margin of victory was the narrowest of any winning incumbent's in Florida. Given the changing demographics of Central Florida, especially of Orange County, this district is likely to remain competitive.

Finally, at the state legislative level, Republicans continued to dominate, holding seventy-four state house seats (62 percent) and twenty-six state senate seats (65 percent). The Democrats did, however, deprive the GOP of its post-2010 election supermajorities in both chambers of the state legislature. Moreover, Florida was the only southern state where the Democrats made net seat gains in both the state house and the state senate. Still, Republican control of the legislature seems assured for the foreseeable future.

Conclusions: Florida and the Newest Southern Politics

The 2012 election in Florida demonstrated that the Sunshine State was a microcosm of the nation. At the presidential level, Florida gave its twenty-nine electoral votes to Barack Obama and, in doing so, continued its record of picking the national winner in all but two elections in the post–World War II period. As in 2008, Florida was not the decisive state for Obama, but by winning in the Sunshine State, any path to victory for Romney was shut off. Moreover, Florida served a strategic purpose in another sense. Since 1992, Republicans have been forced to spend time and money in a state that was once part of the GOP's lock on the Electoral College, resources that the Romney campaign may have preferred putting in battleground states such as Iowa, Ohio, Pennsylvania, or Wisconsin.

Florida will almost certainly feature prominently in political discourse in future election cycles. In 2014, Governor Rick Scott will seek reelection, and it is possible that he will face former governor Charlie Crist, whose political evolution toward the Democratic Party continued in 2012. Given Scott's role in refusing to extend early voting hours, prompting generally unfavorable media coverage in the last weekend of the campaign, the 2014 gubernatorial election promises to be one of the most hotly contested and watched races of the cycle. Looking ahead further to the next presidential election, Florida will likely continue to exert a powerful voice in national politics. An early primary election will provide even more influence, as both parties will have open presidential contests. Of course, on the Republican side, both Jeb Bush and Marco Rubio are already being mentioned as possible presidential candidates. Irrespective of who both parties nominate as their presidential candidates in 2016, Florida will continue to be a hotly contested state. Indeed, a national Republican victory in 2016 would almost certainly have to include Florida in any Electoral College strategy to reach the needed 270 votes.

Perhaps the most striking aspect of the 2012 presidential election was the manner in which Barack Obama assembled a winning coalition in Florida and what this suggests about Florida's political future. Figure 9.1 shows the racial composition of both Obama's and Romney's vote in Florida. In many respects, it illustrates what might be thought of as Newest South and Old South electoral coalitions and strategies. While the term Old South is frequently associated with the old one-party Democratic Solid South, the Republican Party's successes in Florida and the rest of the South rested on the same formula Democrats once relied upon: winning landslide margins of victory among white voters. Had the racial composition of the electorate in Florida in 2012 resembled any prior election, then Romney would have likely eked out a narrow victory. However, the changing demographics of Florida meant that Obama reached 50 percent of the vote by winning less than 40 percent of the white vote. Indeed, 2012 may have been the last election in which a Republican strategy of assembling a coalition based on 60 percent of the white vote could have had a chance of winning.

Related to the changing racial composition of Florida's electorate is Democratic dominance in the seven largest counties in Florida. Table 9.5 shows the political evolution of these counties in the past twenty years. The Democrats have not only consolidated their vote in their South Florida strongholds of Broward, Miami-Dade, and Palm Beach but started to hold an advantage in Central Florida. Specifically, Orange County has moved from a swing county to one that in 2012 was more Democratic in its presidential voting behavior than was Palm Beach, while Hillsborough and Pinellas Counties have also started to lean in a more Democratic direction. Even in Duval County, which had been the

Figure 9.1. Florida Presidential Vote by Race, 2012

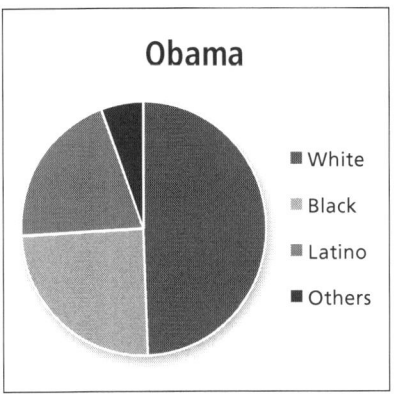

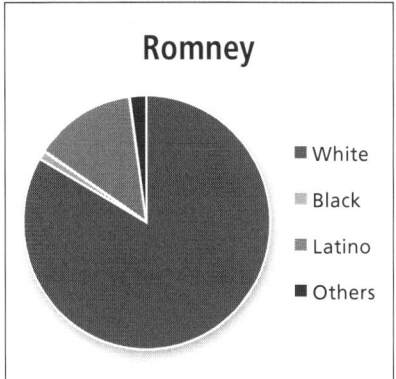

Source: National Election Pool-Edison/Mitofsky Exit Poll (Florida), November 6, 2012.
Note: Segments in charts show the contribution of each racial group to the vote total of each candidate.

only Republican stronghold among the largest urban counties, moved in a Democratic direction. In these seven counties Barack Obama garnered a 700,000 vote net advantage over Romney. To place that in perspective, that was 300,000 votes more than the net margin Bill Clinton achieved in these same counties on his way to winning the Sunshine State in 1996. Even if these margins remained constant in future elections—and both generational and racial compositional changes in the electorate suggest that the Democratic advantage might continue to grow—it makes it exceedingly difficult for any future Republican presidential candidate to reach 50 percent of the vote. Certainly, a Jeb Bush or a Marco Rubio candidacy in 2016 may be beneficial for competing in Florida, but it would also require a rebranding of the entire GOP image in the eyes of many of the voters the party would need to win. Indeed, as Rubio himself noted: "We have to earn [the Latino] vote. You don't earn it through mariachi bands or Spanish-language television or even promoting candidates of Hispanic descent. You do it by having policies that speak to the real hopes, the real dreams of real people."[47]

Obama gave the Republicans the blues by turning Florida blue in 2008. Republicans might have believed that this was merely the result of short-term forces in 2008 that favored the Democrats. If anything, 2012 may have been even worse for the GOP in Florida, since it provided evidence of a Democratic victory that was fuelled by major demographic

Table 9.5. Florida Megacounty Partisan Change in Presidential Elections, 1992–2012

	1992	1996	2000	2004	2008	2012
Miami-Dade	D +4%	D +19%	D +7%	D +6%	D +16%	D +24%
Broward	D +21	D +35	D +36	D +35	D +35	D +35
Palm Beach	D +11	D +24	D +27	D +21	D +23	D +17
Hillsborough	R +5	D +3	R +3	R +7	D +7	D +7
Pinellas	D +0.4	D +9	D +4	R +0.1	D +8	D +5
Orange	R +11	R +0.2	D +2	D +0.2	D +19	D +19
Duval	R +13	R +6	R +16	R +16	R +2	R +3
Net Democratic vote advantage	+106,752	+407,652	+331,928	+281,400	+682,524	+707,248
% statewide vote by megacounties	50.9%	49.5%	49.3%	48.8%	48.2%	48.5%

Source: Florida Division of Elections, http://election.dos.state.fl.us/elections/resultsarchive/downloadresults.asp?electionDate=11/6/2012&DATAMODE=.
Note: Cell entries show the winning party and the percentage-point margin of victory.

changes, led most dramatically by a growing Latino population in the state's urban centers. Indeed, just as demographic changes in the 1950s and the 1960s meant that Florida was an early leader in the rise of southern Republican voting in the region, so too demographic changes in the early twenty-first century will likely see Florida once again at the forefront of the region's newest southern politics.

10

North Carolina

No Longer Federal Red and State Blue?

Charles Prysby

Rob Christensen titled his recent book on North Carolina politics *The Paradox of Tar Heel Politics*.[1] In the five years since he wrote that book, the title has become even more appropriate. The 2012 elections certainly illustrated the unpredictable nature of politics in North Carolina. The Republicans won control of the state government—the governorship and both houses of the legislature—for the first time in modern history. At the same time, the Democrats did rather well in the popular vote for president, even though Romney carried the state. Whereas North Carolina appears to be trending Republican for state government, it also appears to becoming more competitive in presidential elections, exactly the opposite of the situation from 1992 through 2004.

The results of the four presidential election years from 1992 through 2004 were clear and consistent, as the data in Table 10.1 show: Republicans won each presidential election, usually by a wide margin, and all three U.S. Senate elections held in these years; Democrats won the governorship, a majority of seats in both houses of the state legislature (with one exception), and most of the Council of State offices in every year.[2] Even though North Carolina has continued to hold its major state elections in presidential election years, the only southern state to do so, Republican success in top federal elections did not produce victories in state government elections during this time period.[3] Thus, one could color North Carolina federal red and state blue.[4]

The 2008 elections fractured this pattern. Democrats continued to dominate state government, keeping control of the governorship and the state legislature, but they also won the presidential election (albeit by a narrow margin), the U.S. Senate election, and eight of the thirteen U.S. House seats, making North Carolina bluer than it had been in three decades.[5] The 2008 results suggested an emerging Democratic trend in the state, perhaps due to fundamental changes in the electorate. This interpretation was subsequently contradicted, however, by the 2010 and 2012 elections. In 2010, Republicans gained a majority of seats in both houses of the state legislature for the first time in modern history, and in 2012, Republicans won the presidential election, expanded their control of the state legislature, elected a governor and lieutenant governor, and won nine of thirteen U.S. House seats. These most recent election results seem to suggest that the state has suddenly taken a sharp turn to the right. A closer look at the 2012 election results suggests a more nuanced interpretation, however.

Table 10.1. North Carolina Election Results, 1992–2012

	1992	1996	2000	2004	2008	2012
National elections						
President	50.5	52.5	56.5	56.2	49.8	51.0
U.S. Senate	52.2	53.4	—	52.3	45.6	—
U.S. House	48.4	54.4	60.0	51.2	45.3	49.1
U.S. House seats won	33.3	50.0	58.3	53.8	38.5	69.2
State elections						
Governor	45.1	43.3	47.1	43.5	48.3	55.8
State senate seats won	22.0	42.0	30.0	42.0	40.0	64.0
State house seats won	34.4	50.8	48.3	47.5	43.3	64.2

Source: Computed from data obtained from the North Carolina Board of Elections.

Note: Vote percentages are the Republican percentage of the major-party vote. Other figures are the Republican percentage of seats won. No U.S. Senate election occurred in 2000 or 2012.

The Presidential Election

Having captured North Carolina in 2008, President Barack Obama believed that he could win the state in 2012. Scheduling the Democratic campaign for Charlotte was one indication that his campaign intended to compete in the state. The Obama campaign developed a strong and active organization, as it had in 2008, with over fifty field offices, a sizable paid staff, and thousands of volunteers.[6] The Obama campaign spent over $9 million on televised advertisements in the state through mid-October, and the Democratic National Committee added over $2 million.[7] Mitt Romney spent less, only about $5 million, but there was far more spending by the Republican National Committee and by outside groups for Romney; these organizations combined to spend around $24 million on ads.[8] Although the Republican get-out-the-vote effort was more limited than the Democratic effort, it was stronger than what the GOP had in 2008.[9] The Democratic advantage in the get-out-the-vote effort is supported by the exit poll data, which show that 30 percent of the voters reported being contacted by the Obama campaign and 25 percent, by the Romney campaign.[10] The Democratic advantage may have been larger than these figures suggest, as the Obama campaign probably made more individual contacts with each targeted voter because their organization was active for a longer time before the election. In sum, Romney was unable to match the grassroots effort of the Obama campaign, but he had a big edge in spending on televised ads.

While Obama put forth a strong effort in North Carolina, this was not an essential state for him. He could easily lose the state but win a majority of the Electoral College votes. For Romney the state was critical. Almost every scenario for a Romney victory included winning North Carolina, simply because if Romney failed to carry North Carolina, he would need to make up the fifteen Electoral College votes by carrying another state (or pair of states) that was projected as more difficult to win. Reflecting this difference in the value of the state to the candidates, Obama did not make any personal visits to after appearing at the Democratic convention in early September, relying on campaign surrogates to provide local enthusiasm and attention. This contrasted with 2008, when Obama visited the state six times during the general election campaign. Romney did visit the state, although he reserved most of his campaign time for the more critical battleground states, such as Ohio and Florida.

Public opinion polling in the state showed that Obama was at least even with Romney during September. One well-regarded polling organization, Public Policy Polling, found Obama and Romney even in late September, and another, the NBC/*Washington Post*/Marist poll, found Obama ahead by two points.[11] After the first presidential debate, widely regarded as a strong victory for Romney, polls began to show a small advantage for Romney. A mid-October Public Policy Polling poll found that Romney had a 2-point advantage, for example.[12] In the end, this was a very accurate prediction. Romney won 51 percent of the two-party vote, his most narrow margin of victory in the nation.

Table 10.2 presents the results of presidential elections in North Carolina from 1980 through 2012, along with the results for the nation, in order to provide a basis for comparison. The state appeared fairly solidly Republican through 2000. In both 1996 and 2000, North Carolina was about 7 points more Republican than the nation in its presidential vote, and it was even more Republican than the South as a whole. In 2004, the state was less than 5 points more Republican than the nation, and in 2008, the state dropped to about 3 points more Republican than the nation. In 2012, North Carolina was only 2.5 points more Republican than the nation, making it the third-most-Democratic state in the South, behind Virginia and Florida. Should this trend continue, North Carolina could soon have a vote division that equals the national vote, making the state a true bellwether and battleground state.

Viewed from this perspective, the Romney victory in 2012 does not represent a fundamental shift in the underlying political orientations of the state. Tar Heel voters are not becoming more conservative and more Republican. Rather, national political conditions in 2012 were more favorable to the Republicans. An economy that was widely perceived to be sluggish at best led to mediocre approval ratings for the president. Obama barely won North Carolina in 2008, a year in which the short-term forces were very favorable to Democrats, so it was hardly surprising that he failed to carry the state in a year when the short-term forces were less favorable. These data indicate that Obama probably would have won North Carolina if he had won about 53 percent of the national two-party vote, something that might well have happened had he given a much stronger and Romney a weaker performance in the first debate.

A frequent explanation for the increased competitiveness of Democrats in the state's presidential election is that the population of the state is changing. Some of the high-growth areas in the state, such as the Re-

Table 10.2. North Carolina versus U.S. Republican Presidential Vote, 1988–2008

	1988	1992	1996	2000	2004	2008	2012
North Carolina	58.2	50.5	52.5	56.5	56.2	49.8	51.0
United States	53.9	46.5	45.4	49.7	51.4	46.6	48.5
Difference	+4.3	+4.0	+7.1	+6.8	+4.8	+3.2	+2.5

Source: Computed from data in *America Votes*, various editions, the North Carolina Board of Elections website, and CNN's 2012 elections website.
Note: Entries are the Republican percentage of the two-party vote for president. The last row gives the difference between the Republican vote in North Caronia and in the nation.

search Triangle (Raleigh-Durham) area, appear to have attracted new migrants from other states who are younger and more liberal.[13] The urban areas of the state, which once were disproportionately Republican, are now areas of Democratic strength. The six largest counties, which account for over one-third of all votes in the state, were all easily carried by Obama in 2012.[14] A look at the two most heavily populated counties illustrates the Democratic advantage: Obama won Wake County (home to Raleigh) with 55 percent of the vote and Mecklenburg County (home to Charlotte) with 60 percent of the vote.

Other demographic changes are contributing to political change in the state, as well. The Hispanic population has increased substantially, and while it still represents less than 5 percent of the electorate, it is a growing source of Democratic votes.[15] Generational change also seems to be contributing to the Democratic trend in the state. Older, more conservative voters are being replaced by younger voters, who currently are more liberal and more likely to vote for Democrats. Of course, the relatively strong Democratic vote in 2008 and 2012 may have been also due to the strong Obama campaign effort in the state, which was substantially greater than previous Democratic efforts. To fully sort out the effect of population change on the vote from the effect of Democratic organizational efforts may require analyzing data from 2016 and 2020.

Exit poll data for the presidential election are presented in Tables 10.3 and 10.4. As we can see from Table 10.3, voting was very strongly related to partisanship and ideology. Romney did extremely well among Republicans, and Obama did almost as well among Democrats. Romney did win 57 percent of the vote from independents, a significant change from 2008, when independents leaned toward Obama. Romney also did very well among those with conservative orientations, either overall or on specific issues, such as health care or abortion, while Obama did well among those with more liberal orientations. Since the condition of the economy was an important topic in the campaign, it is not surprising that Obama did poorly among those who thought that he was to blame for the nation's bad economy, whereas he did well among those who did not place most of the blame on him. It is clear that the North Carolina electorate was highly polarized ideologically, reflecting what has been a national trend.[16]

The relationship of a number of demographic factors to the vote are shown in Table 10.4. First of all, race was an important factor, as usual. Like other Republican candidates, Romney won a large majority of the white vote but a minority of the Hispanic vote and very little of the black vote. In 2012, however, whites accounted for only 70 percent of the electorate, compared with 78 percent in 2000. The growing minority vote is one of the demographic trends that observers identify as a source of political change in the state. Nevertheless, Democratic support among whites remains a critical factor in election outcomes. Although Obama failed to win a majority of the white vote in either 2008 or 2012, he won a greater share of white voters in North Carolina than in most other southern states, which contributed to his competitiveness in the state.[17] Even if the minority vote continues to increase and Democrats continue to appeal disproportionately to minority voters, Democratic candidates will still need to attract a substantial percentage of the white vote to win statewide elections.

Presidential voting in North Carolina was also related to religion. Romney did better among those who regularly attended church and among whites who identified themselves as evangelical or born-again, a familiar pattern in North Carolina and in the South overall.[18] Again, the trends appear to be working against the Republicans. In 2012, 35 percent of the voters were white evangelicals, and in 2000, the comparable figure was 44 percent. Some of this decline simply reflects the decline in white voters, but even among whites, the proportion of voters who identify as evangelical has declined in recent years, due partly to generational change and partly to the more secular character of migrants from other states.

Finally, Obama did better among younger voters, as he did in 2008 and as Kerry did in 2004. This could also be a relationship that benefits

Table 10.3. North Carolina Vote by Political Orientation, 2012

	% Romney	% McCrory
Party identification		
Democrat (39)	8	15
Independent (29)	57	62
Republican (33)	96	96
Ideology		
Liberal (22)	14	19
Moderate (38)	42	49
Conservative (40)	82	82
Size of government		
Government should do more (41)	21	27
Government does too much (53)	77	78
Affordable Health Care Act		
Should repeal (55)	83	81
Should not repeal (40)	9	17
Abortion		
Legal in most or all cases (53)	30	38
Illegal in most or all cases (40)	79	76
Gay marriage		
Favor allowing (35)	20	28
Oppose allowing (57)	70	74
Blame for economy		
Obama (40)	94	92
Bush (49)	15	22

Source: National Election Pool 2012 North Carolina Exit Poll.

Note: Entries are the percentage of voters in the specified category who voted for the Republican presidential and gubernatorial candidates (Romney and McCrory). The figures in parentheses indicate the percentage of all respondents in that category. For example, the data for party identification indicate that 42% of the voters were Democrats in 2012 and that 8% of Democrats voted for Romney. Only the percentages for the Republican candidates are shown; these were essentially two-candidate races, so the proportion of the vote not going to the Republican candidate went almost entirely to the Democratic candidate.

Table 10.4. North Carolina Vote by Demographic and Social Variables, 2012

	% Romney	% McCrory
Race		
White (70)	68	70
Black (23)	4	13
Hispanic (4)	31	46
Religion		
White evangelical (35)	79	79
Other (65)	35	44
Church attendance		
Weekly (48)	56	60
Occasionally (38)	48	55
Never (13)	35	46
Income		
< $50,000 (46)	44	50
≥ $50,000 (54)	55	58
Gender		
Male (44)	54	58
Female (56)	49	54
Marital status		
Married (60)	60	63
Not married (40)	37	43
Age		
18–29 (16)	32	40
30–44 (25)	48	53
45–64 (39)	53	57
65 and over (21)	64	64

Source: National Election Pool 2012 North Carolina Exit Poll.

Note: Entries are the percentage of voters in the specified category who voted for the Republican presidential and gubernatorial candidates (Romney and McCrory). The figures in parentheses indicate the percentage of all respondents in that category. For example, the data for race indicate that 70% of the voters were whites in 2012 and that 68% of whites voted for Romney. Only the percentages for the Republican candidates are shown; these were essentially two-candidate races, so the proportion of the vote not going to the Republican candidate went almost entirely to the Democratic candidate.

the Democrats. If the attachment of younger voters to the Democratic Party remains intact as these voters age, the process of generational replacement should increase support for Democrats. There are many uncertainties here, of course. Younger voters might shift their political allegiances as they age. The next generation of young voters could prove to be disproportionately Republican. Still, the conservative stance of Republicans on controversial social issues, such as abortion and gay rights, may be appealing to a declining segment of the population. As the data in Table 10.4 show, Romney won 64 percent of the vote from those over sixty-five but just 32 percent from those under thirty. The strong support for Democrats among young voters is a fairly recent development. In 1996, for example, President Bill Clinton did only slightly better among voters under thirty than he did among older voters.[19] Also, North Carolina is not typical of the South in this regard. In many southern states younger white voters are not much more likely to vote for Democrats than are older voters.[20]

Congressional Elections

If the presidential election was a narrow victory for Republicans, only slightly different from the 2008 outcome, the congressional elections seemed just the opposite. In 2008, Democrats won eight of the thirteen U.S. House seats in the state, and they captured the U.S. Senate seat held by Republican Elizabeth Dole. In 2012, Republicans were the big winners, capturing nine of the House seats and almost winning a tenth (there was no Senate election in 2012). If North Carolina is becoming more competitive for presidential elections, how can the huge Republican success in congressional elections in 2012 be explained? The answer largely comes down to one word: redistricting. Republicans did increase their share of the congressional vote, from about 45 percent in 2008 to about 49 percent in 2012—not surprising given that 2012 was generally a better year for Republicans across the country—but this moderate increase in the vote normally would not produce such a dramatic shift in seats. However, the district lines for 2012 were drastically altered. Republicans won control of the state legislature in 2010, and they subsequently used their majority to craft a redistricting plan that was extremely favorable to Republicans.

Three very heavily Democratic districts (the First, Fourth, and Twelfth) were created, each of which was easily won by the incumbent Democrat. All three of these districts were solidly Democratic already, and the redistricting made them even more so. The remaining ten districts were constructed to lean Republican, but not too much so, to ensure that Republican votes were used more efficiently. Faced with less-hospitable districts, two Democratic incumbents, Heath Shuler (Eleventh District) and Brad Miller (Thirteenth District), chose not to seek reelection. One Democratic incumbent, Larry Kissel (Eighth District), was defeated. One Democratic incumbent, Mike McIntyre (Seventh District), barely won reelection. McIntyre was a six-term incumbent and the most conservative Democratic congressman in the state, so he had the best chance of winning reelection in a district that leaned Republican.

Table 10.5 shows the results of the U.S. House races for 2008 and 2012 by district. In the three districts that were drawn to be heavily Democratic (the First, Fourth, and Twelfth), the Republican share of the vote decreased from 2008 to 2012, and in none of these districts did the 2012 Republican exceed 26 percent of the vote. In the four districts that contained Democratic congressmen targeted by Republicans (the Seventh, Eighth, Eleventh, and Thirteenth), the Republican vote increased between 2008 and 2012 by an average of about 16 percent. In

Table 10.5. North Carolina U.S. House Election Results, 2008, 2012

	Republican % two-party vote		2012 election outcome
	2008	2012	
First District	29.7	23.4	Democratic incumbent reelected
Second District	31.8	57.5	Republican incumbent reelected
Third District	65.9	63.2	Republican incumbent reelected
Fourth District	36.7	25.5	Democratic incumbent reelected
Fifth District	58.4	57.6	Republican incumbent reelected
Sixth District	67.0	60.9	Republican incumbent reelected
Seventh District	31.2	49.9	Democratic incumbent reelected
Eighth District	44.6	54.1	Democratic incumbent defeated
Ninth District	63.5	53.1	Republican open seat won by Republican
Tenth District	57.6	57.0	Republican incumbent reelected
Eleventh District	36.6	57.4	Democratic open seat won by Republican
Twelfth District	28.4	20.3	Democratic incumbent reelected
Thirteenth District	34.1	56.8	Democratic open seat won by Republican

Source: Computed from data obtained from the North Carolina Board of Elections.
Note: Figures are the Republican percentage of the two-party vote.

the districts that had been already captured by Republicans in 2008, the Republican vote declined by an average of about 4 percent. These figures illustrate how the redistricting pulled Republican voters out of both safe Republican and safe Democratic seats and placed them in the districts of vulnerable Democratic incumbents.[21]

State Elections

Republicans also won the gubernatorial election for the first time since 1988. This would seem to be more evidence of a Republican resurgence in the state. Unlike the congressional elections, this Republican victory obviously cannot be attributed to redistricting. The Republican candidate, Pat McCrory, won almost 56 percent of the vote, a decisive victory. Republicans also added to their majority in the state legislature, which they first achieved in 2010. Few if any observers predicted in 2008 that the Republicans would gain full control of state government by 2012. Although the Republicans' success in the 2012 state elections may not have represented a fundamental shift in the political orientations of the North Carolina electorate, it undoubtedly reflected dissatisfaction with Democrats in Raleigh. Republicans did so well because many voters felt that it was finally time for a change in state government.

The gubernatorial election seemed uncompetitive from the beginning. The Republicans ran a particularly strong candidate, former Charlotte mayor Pat McCrory. McCrory was the GOP gubernatorial candidate in 2008, when he narrowly lost to Democrat Bev Purdue in a year that was very favorable to Democrats, both nationally and in the state. McCrory was considered a moderate Republican, increasing his appeal to independent voters, and in 2012 he had the experience and name recognition from his 2008 campaign. On the Democratic side, Governor Purdue decided in late 2011 not to run for reelection, a decision prompted by her low approval ratings. Lieutenant Governor Walter Dalton won the Democratic primary for governor, but he lacked name recognition (the office of lieutenant governor is not particularly important or visible in North Carolina), and he had difficulty raising campaign funds.

Dalton undoubtedly suffered because of growing voter disenchantment with Democrats in state government. Governor Purdue had some publicized scandals involving campaign finance and patronage in state government, which was one source of her low approval ratings. The previous Democratic governor, Mike Easley, left office under a cloud of scandals and was subsequently prosecuted and convicted for violations of campaign finance laws after his second term ended. During Easley's second term, the Democratic Speaker of the House, Jim Black, was the subject of well-publicized financial scandals, which led to his being prosecuted and convicted. Although Dalton was not directly connected to these scandals, he undoubtedly suffered from a general public feeling that Democrats had been in power for too long. In fact, such feelings surely contributed to Republican success in the 2010 state legislative elections, when they parlayed both the national and the state mood into control of both houses of the state legislature, the first time that the GOP had been able to do so in the modern era.

Tables 10.3 and 10.4 show that McCrory's electoral support was similar to Romney's, but McCrory did better than Romney among several groups of voters. For example, McCrory did better than Romney among Democrats and independents and among liberals and moderates, something that can be attributed to McCrory's moderate image and to the general dissatisfaction with past Democratic control of state government. McCrory did fairly well among Hispanics, winning 46 percent of their vote, and among those who did not attend church, also winning 46 percent of their vote. While he did better among older than younger voters, he did win 40 percent of the vote of those under thirty. In general, McCrory did considerably better among the groups that were the least favorable to Romney. By increasing support among the Democratic-leaning groups and maintaining support among the Republican-leaning groups, McCrory was able to win about 56 percent of the two-party vote, a higher winning percentage than any of the past three Democratic governors secured in their first election. McCrory is only the third Republican governor in the modern history of North Carolina politics, and he is the first one to have the pleasure of a state legislature under GOP control.

Conclusion

The first impression one might have of the 2012 election results in North Carolina is that the state has taken a hard political turn to the right. Republicans won the presidential election, 70 percent of the House seats, the gubernatorial election, and a substantial majority of seats in both houses of the state legislature. Never before has the GOP had so much success in one election. While the results of the 2012 elections might seem to indicate that the Republicans have become the majority party in the state, a careful examination of the data reveals a more complex picture.

First of all, an underlying trend in the state toward the Democrats seems to be present over the past decade, and this trend continued into 2012. This movement is slow, and it easily is outweighed by more powerful election-specific factors. Nevertheless, North Carolina is inching toward the national average in its presidential vote, which is a good measure of underlying partisanship in the state. This trend is produced by the cumulative impact of migration into the state, the growth of the minority population, and generational change. This suggests that North Carolina will be a competitive state in presidential elections, at least when the national vote is close. A Democratic presidential candidate who is winning nationally should now have a reasonable chance of carrying North Carolina, which was not the case a decade or so ago. In 1996, for example, Clinton did not even attempt to compete in the state, despite the fact that he was winning nationally by a comfortable margin. He was also a southern Democrat who presumably would be more appealing than a northern Democrat to Tar Heel voters. Republicans may still have an advantage in North Carolina in presidential elections, but they will most likely have to invest resources in the state to keep it in the GOP column.

The 2012 election results also demonstrate that election outcomes are greatly affected by election-specific variables. At the national level such factors as the state of the economy create conditions that are favorable to one party or another, sometimes strongly so. The pattern of recent elections demonstrates that North Carolina moves according to these national short-term forces. In years when the political winds are blowing in a Republican direction, Republicans in North Carolina benefit, just as they suffer when the winds blow the other way. The difference between the outcomes of the presidential elections in 2008 and 2012 is best explained by the change in national short-term forces, not by change in underlying political dispositions among voters in the state. Presidential and congressional elections are most affected by these national forces, but state elections are influenced, as well.[22] For this reason, it is difficult to predict the outcome of future elections in the state without knowing the national outcomes for presidential and congressional elections. It does appear, however, that the state is sufficiently competitive that election outcomes are likely to be altered as national conditions change. This stands in contrast with some southern states, which are sufficiently Republican so that the party can win even in a bad year for the GOP.

Finally, the 2012 election results indicate that state-specific forces play a significant role in election outcomes. These forces are separate from national short-term forces, and they seem to have played a significant role in state elections in North Carolina. While the presidential and congressional vote in the state shifted only modestly to the Republicans between 2008 and 2012, the gubernatorial vote shifted substantially, and the Republicans gained a large number of seats in the state legislature. The result was that North Carolina was more Republican in state elections than in federal elections, just the opposite of how it had been for two decades. That change is best explained by disapproval of the performance of Democrats in state government over the past several years. For a long time, Democrats benefitted from popular governors and general satisfaction with the performance of the Democratic-controlled state legislature, but the recent combination of political scandals, budgetary problems, and economic difficulties led voters to feel that it was time for a change in state government. Now that Republicans have control of state government, they have the opportunity to build the public support needed to keep them in power for several elections. Time will tell whether they accomplish that goal.

In sum, the political future of North Carolina politics is likely to be volatile. Both parties appear capable of winning major statewide races. North Carolina politics had been relatively competitive already, especially in comparison with many other southern states, but Republicans had a clear edge in elections to federal office, while Democrats possessed an advantage in elections to state government. The Republican advantage in federal elections has been reduced to the point that both presidential and U.S. Senate elections are less predictable than in the past. Similarly, gubernatorial elections may be more competitive, with more party switches in control of the governorship than Tar Heel voters have been used to. While the top statewide elections may be more competitive, the new district lines for congressional seats and the state legislature seem likely to reduce competition lower down the ballot. U.S. House elections in North Carolina have been quite competitive over the past two decades, much more so than in many other southern states. Many elections have been close, and a number of seats have changed hands, some more than once. The next decade will probably not be so competitive.

11

Tennessee

Republican Ascendency Affirmed

J. David Woodard

Tennessee's political culture is different from its rebel cousins' for two reasons. First, it has historically had a reputation for moderation on matters of race. The Volunteer State was the first one to be readmitted to the Union after the Civil War and to accept the Fourteenth Amendment and, later, desegregation when the *Brown v. Board* decision was announced. Nashville pioneered a Pulitzer Prize–winning school integration plan in accord with the "all deliberate speed" spirit of the ruling, and the state's U.S. senators and congressmen refused to sign the Southern Manifesto protest, breaking allegiance with the rest of the South. None of the state's cities bear scars of a dramatic racial protest, with death from assembled white racists in an unprovoked attack. Part of this legacy lies in demography. Tennessee has never had a large black population—17 percent in the 2010 census, half of whom live in or around Memphis in the western part of the state. The state's reputation for moderation on matters of civil rights is enviable.

The second cultural characteristic of Tennessee is, to quote V. O. Key in 1949, "two one-party systems. History, settlement patterns, and the earth's features left eastern Republicans opposite middle and west Tennessee Democrats."[1] These so-called Mountain Republicans had the potential to bring two-party competition to the state, since they had a geographic base and the elected officials to build a competitive organization. The territorial unevenness in the distribution of strength with the Democrats made this unlikely, however. Decades after this geographic prognosis, Republicans marginally improved their position in the state but were always in the minority.

Then, in the twinkling of an eye, everything changed. In 2012, voters ratified the GOP as the dominant political authority in Tennessee. The Republican conquest characterized every level of government in the state: legislative, congressional, gubernatorial, senatorial, and presidential. In advance of the presidential election, the National Election Pool, a consortium of news organizations that sponsors exit polls for each election cycle, decided not to include Tennessee in their sample. Their reason was simple: the state "was no longer competitive."[2] Although the Democratic Party remains a relevant and active force in state politics, their once-dominant roar has been reduced to a whisper. The reasons for this change are many, but the basic explanation for it was foreseen by V. O. Key himself when he wrote: "The growth of the cities contains the seeds of political change for the South."[3]

The Grand Divisions

Tennessee's uniqueness lies in its geography, one border anchored in the eastern Appalachian Mountains and the other in the western flatlands along the Mississippi River. The state's political culture is explained by this distance, rooted in Civil War loyalties for which east Tennessee counties voted heavily for the Union in 1861 and stayed Republican ever since. Middle and west Tennessee were secessionist and Democratic. Political strategy was once expressed in the refrain: "The Republicans had to 'come over the mountains of east Tennessee with a 100,000 vote lead' or risk losing the election to Democratic loyalty in the rest of the state." Such was the formula in 1960 when Richard Nixon won thirty-three of thirty-four east Tennessee counties and had an 118,000-vote margin over John Kennedy when the polls closed in Nashville. A decade later, Memphis dentist Winfield Dunn followed the same pattern, with a 100,000-vote Republican lead in east Tennessee in an off-year election, to become the first Republican governor since Reconstruction.

Urbanization changed the culture, and the adage about 100,000 votes coming over the mountains was superseded by the metropolises V. O. Key predicted to be change agents in the culture. To this day the distinctiveness of the three state divisions remains. The urban areas of Chattanooga, Knoxville, and the Tri-Cities (Bristol, Kingsport, and Johnson City) are mountain cities in the same time zone and are geographically and culturally similar. East Tennessee today has more than one-third of the state's population and stands as the Republican base for any statewide political campaign.

Middle Tennessee, with the multicounty Nashville metropolitan area at its heart, is the largest media market in the state, as well as the center of government, business, entertainment, and manufacturing. The suburbs around the city are home to enterprising businesses attracted to the state because it has no income tax. They are conservative at heart but can switch votes in support of a familiar Democrat or a libertarian plea for independence. Maybe it's the Music City legacy of pursuing dreams, the hope of national celebrity, or its spirit of creativity that make Nashville recalcitrant. For whatever reason, the city is different, and while the downtown is Democratic, the necklace suburbs bleed "red" Republican.

The third area of the state is Memphis, a place more like Mississippi than Tennessee, once called the "most rural-minded city in the South" by H. L. Mencken.[4] The label came from the cotton and other crops grown in the rich soil of the lowlands. It was in Memphis that rhythm and blues became popular with white audiences. As the major city in the Mississippi Delta, Memphis has always been a haven for black residents from the Mississippi backwaters trying to get away from their lives on the farm. The city is home to Democrats of both black and white lineages, as well as blues music, agriculture, and African American culture. It has a flavor of the Old South like no other city in the state.

Interstate 40 connects the east, middle, and west regions of the state. Figure 11.1 shows Tennessee's tripartite divisions, with the largest number of cities in east Tennessee, Nashville in the middle, and Memphis in the west. Memphis is the city with the largest one-county population in the state; the Nashville metropolitan area is the largest media market; and the populous cities of east Tennessee (Knoxville, Chattanooga, and the Tri-Cities) make it the growing and vigorous political base of the state.

Tennessee has no coastal lowland area. Instead, it has an unusual mountain heritage wedded to a Mississippi slaveholding legacy. Half the population of the state is in the ten counties shaded on the map, which reflects the concentrated growth in the state. In east Tennessee the population is scattered among four media markets, whereas Nashville in the

188 ★ J. David Woodard

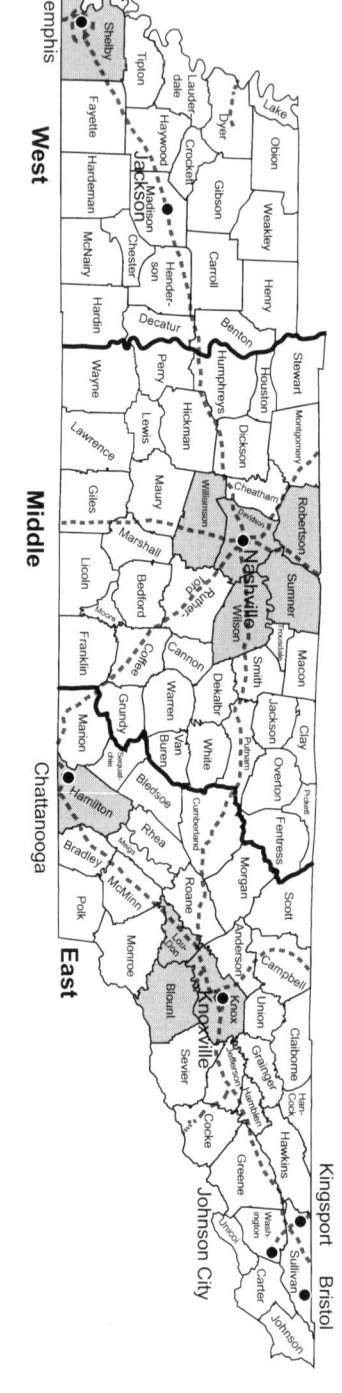

Figure 11.1. Tennessee Population Distribution

Population Distribution 2010

	Counties	Population	Percentage
East	34	2,341,656	36.8%
Middle	40	2,441,799	38.5%
West	21	1,562,650	24.6%
Total	95	6,346,105	100%

middle and Memphis in the west are each a single urban area and media market. A kind of harmony is apparent here. East Tennessee has diverse cities and a growing population. Nashville is the dominant metropolitan area and the seat of government—middle Tennessee is a kind of balance to the other two regions. West Tennessee is shrinking in population relative to the other two areas and is a throwback to the Old South.

Political Attitudes in 2012

This geography and past history make Tennessee a bit more moderate in its attitudes than its Confederate relatives, but it's not quite the same as its Yankee neighbors. Its natural border features and urbanization combine to give the state a mixture of commonly accepted southern opinions that live comfortably with their opposite. Tennessee fits the ideal of a border state in that it is less headstrong than are the Deep South states and more sympathetic to the siren song of national trends, novel ideas, and politicians selling the politics of accommodation. In Tennessee's case the state itself is often the originator of new ideas and styles.

Some of this cultural insubordination is evident in the voting history of the state. In 1952 and 1956, Tennessee broke with the Solid South Democratic Party and voted narrowly for Dwight Eisenhower. Then, Tennessee voted for Nixon in 1960 and for Reagan in 1980, after being Jimmy Carter's fourth-best state four years earlier. Of course, the most memorable unruliness came in 2000 when voters rejected Al Gore's presidential bid after he represented them first as a congressman and then as a senator for a total of sixteen years. In advance of the 2012 elections, the mood of the state was measured by a number of polls. Table 11.1 shows how the attitudes of Tennesseans compared with those of Americans generally on a number of issues.

Vanderbilt University began regular statewide polling in 2011 to measure citizen and voter opinions on a number of public matters. With a little poetic license, we can use several polls to compare the attitudes of respondents in the state with those of others across the nation. True to the state's history, the figures show a consistent but moderate conservatism on most issues. The question on immigration was asked in 2011, well before the issue became a central focus in the second Obama administration. Respondents in Tennessee evinced a wish to have illegal immigrants incorporated into the fabric of the society, but at the same time, they were quite critical of employers who knowingly hired such employees.[5] Given that the state was fifth nationally in a survey of church attendance, it came as no surprise that residents opposed gay

Table 11.1. Tennessee versus U.S. Attitudes on Political Issues

	Tennessee	United States
Government should deport illegal immigrants	35%	17%
Favor government creating a way for illegal immigrants to become citizens	61	51
Consider themselves pro-life	60	50
Believe handguns should be carried in public	73	69
Oppose gay marriage	69	50
Oppose tax on junk food	43	47
Approve the job Obama is doing as president	43	49

Source: Vanderbilt Poll, January 2011, June 2011, and November 2011; *National Journal* Poll, November 2012; Gallup Poll, November 2011, May 2010; *Washington Post* Poll, June 2011; Quinnipiac Poll, December 2012.

marriage and abortion in numbers greater than the national survey.[6] The presidential approval ranking, taken in May 2011, was prescient and signified an ill wind for the Democrats in 2012. In sum, the figures in Table 11.1 show a state that is conservative for the most part, with deep southern roots, especially on social issues, but not that far from the rest of the country on other questions.

Tennessee's mixed legacy in voting and contradictory geography mean that it has been designated as a toss-up or battleground state by pundits in presidential elections. That is what it was in 2000 when the voter turnout and the percentages in a few counties resulted in Al Gore's defeat. A look back at the returns from that year shows that the *battleground* designation may have been unmerited, given that the state's former senator did not get much help from his party at the grassroots level. Republican Bill Frist defeated his opponent by a two-to-one margin that election night, and the anemic state of the Democratic Party's downticket offices played a role in the downfall of Gore as large as that of the George W. Bush campaign. Conservatism descended on Tennessee like a wrecking crew, and it dismantled the Democratic platform plank by plank. The right to bear arms, pro-life legislation, and opposition to stem cell research, taxation, and gay marriage were constant topics on drive-home talk radio shows. A billboard in the city of Nashville flashed, "Where is the birth certificate?" in defiance of the Obama administration. Tennessee bristled in antagonism, and it was into this cultural windstorm that in 2012 Barack Obama, a multicultural candidate with ties to liberal causes, brought his reelection plea for more government spending and taxing the rich.

Partisanship

In advance of the presidential election, Tennessee turned latent red Republican sentiment into institutional supremacy in the 2010 midterm elections. Republican Bill Haslam, a native-born son and former mayor of Knoxville, won the governor's race. His victory meant that both U.S. senators, along with seven of the nine members of the congressional delegation, were in the GOP. The state's presidential primary should have been a referendum on the depth of GOP allegiance, but observers were in for a Democratic distraction before Republicans even came to town.

The expectation of Democratic Party regulars was that President Obama would have no opposition in national primaries. That speculation proved incorrect when in 2012 an oddball candidate who perennially ran for office became the second-highest vote getter, behind the incumbent. John Wolfe Jr., an attorney who lived in Chattanooga, presented himself as an alternative to the president. His website declared that he was a "man of peace and prosperity, not war and austerity."[7] He had few other credentials, unless you count losing races for Congress (1998), mayor of Chattanooga (2001), again for Congress (2002 and 2004), and the state senate (2007) as qualifications. To make matters worse, he was fined $10,000 for failing to file his campaign finance report properly. Wolfe was not on the ballot in Tennessee, because there was no Democratic primary, but he represented party malcontents nationwide. He garnered press attention but only microscopic support in New Hampshire, a little more in Texas and Louisiana, and a lot in Arkansas.[8] The Democratic National Committee subsequently disqualified Wolfe for not following rules and procedures in various states after the fact, but for a season he represented dissidents who wanted to register their displeasure with the president. In a sense, Wolfe's eccentric personality fit the model for Tennessee, but it did little for the party he represented.

The Republican primary was more conventional by comparison. After thirteen primaries in the first two months of 2012, the field of GOP candidates arrived at the month of March with no clear frontrunner. Tennessee, along with nine other states, hosted the Super Tuesday extravaganza, a contest designed to winnow the field to a manageable two or three candidates. The Vanderbilt poll of 1,500 registered voters came out on February 23, and the results foreshadowed the outcome (see Table 11.2).

Speculation in advance of the election showed a tussle among Romney, former U.S. senator Rick Santorum, and former U.S. House Speaker Newt Gingrich from next-door Georgia, a dark horse possibility. Speaker Gingrich hoped for an upset of the leaders reminiscent of his victory in South Carolina in January. State legislators Tony Shipley of Kingsport and Stacey Campfield of Knoxville declared that another upset was in the making in Tennessee and that only Gingrich "could really rally the Republican base."[9] Romney ran a nationwide campaign and did not worry much about Tennessee as a benchmark state. Favorite Rick Santorum opened his campaign in a Chattanooga church, declaring, "Family is the foundation of our country and I know where you stand Tennessee."[10] He did, too. On Election Day, Santorum won by 9 points over Romney, with Gingrich 4 points back in third.

Santorum carried ninety-one of Tennessee's ninety-five counties and led his competition by winning a majority of both men and women, as well as nearly half of the voters who described themselves as very conservative.[11] That philosophy characterized the makeup of the primary electorate. Exit polls found that GOP voters preferred the embrace of a Catholic pro-life evangelist to those of a Mormon governor or a libertarian doctor. Ron Paul did not live up to expectations, whereas Newt Gingrich exceeded his. Mitt Romney won Nashville and suburban Williamson County, as well as one east Tennessee county. Gingrich won Chattanooga, but the rest went to Santorum. The outcome had little effect on the Republican selection process. Romney walked away with the most wins on that Super Tuesday, taking six states. Santorum's solid

Table 11.2. Tennessee Republican Primary Poll Results and Actual Vote, 2012

Candidate	Vanderbilt Poll	Actual Result
Rick Santorum	33%	37%
Mitt Romney	17	28
Ron Paul	13	9
Newt Gingrich	10	24
Others/undecided	27	2

Source: Vanderbilt Poll, February 23, 2012; Tennessee Department of State, Division of Elections, Official Results.

victory enabled him to stay in the race and guaranteed that the battle for the GOP banner would drag on for a few more weeks.

Historically, the geography of Tennessee meant a wide range of opinions and conflict among opposing regions that all shared a common border. But that had changed by 2012, and the only thing that remained from the past was the disagreeable part. In the 1950s, U.S. senator and native son Estes Kefauver garnered national attention and a place on the Democratic presidential ticket as a liberal, yet Tennessee was implacably conservative at the time and has been since. It rejected him and voted for Eisenhower twice, the second time when Kefauver himself was on the ticket as vice president. In fact, Tennessee may be the only state to vote against native sons for vice president, with Kefauver, and president, with Al Gore. Had Gore received his home state's eleven electoral votes, he would have been president. In the statewide presidential vote that year, Bush won by a margin of 79,421 votes out of two million cast. Gore's defeat was the high-water mark of two-party state competition in presidential elections. Table 11.3 shows the deterioration of Democratic allegiance since that marathon election.

The table shows that Tennessee's reputation as a battleground state is obsolete. From a less-than-majority high in 2000, the Democratic vote has shriveled to barely more than one-third of the ballot. The presidential defeat was only the beginning. Incumbent senator Bob Corker defeated Democrat Mark Clayton on election night in 2012, receiving two-thirds of the vote. Before the election, Clayton, a part-time floor installer, gave an interview in which he said that the federal government was building a massive four-football-field-wide superhighway from Mexico City to Toronto as part of a secret plot to establish a new North American Union that would bring an end to America.[12] Two weeks before the election, he had a war chest of $278 and one yard sign, and on election night he received 30.4 percent of the vote.[13] The failure of

Table 11.3. Tennessee Presidential Election Partisanship, 2000–2012

Year	% Democratic	% Republican
2000	47.3%	51.2%
2004	42.5	56.8
2008	41.8	56.9
2012	39.1	59.5

Source: Tennessee Department of State, Division of Elections, Official Results.

Mark Clayton was noteworthy not for his shortcomings but for those of the political party that disowned him—one purpose of a political party is to field viable candidates at election time. Needless to say, President Obama had no coattails to help him in Tennessee, and even if he did, they would not have helped. The die was cast, and the state was red Republican at its core.

Figure 11.2 shows the allegiance of all Tennessee counties to the GOP in the decade of the new millennium through the 2012 presidential election. The analysis includes elections when Gore was on the national Democratic ticket (2000), as well as other statewide and presidential contests (four presidential, one senatorial, and one gubernatorial). Over one-third of the state's population lived in the forty counties that voted Republican every time in this twelve-year period, and only four counties had a similar Democratic allegiance. The map shows the GOP bastion in east Tennessee, which was as dependably Republican in 2012 as it was during Reconstruction and virtually every period since. The map also shows that the Republican base has grown to include Chattanooga and suburban Nashville, along with occasional counties in middle and west Tennessee. Memphis anchors traditionally Democratic west Tennessee, and the Nashville metropolitan area is Democratic downtown but solidly Republican in the suburbs. In 2000, Bush and Gore tied in eight county totals for Memphis, Nashville, Chattanooga, Knoxville, and the Tri-Cities, but Bush carried the nonmetro counties, and that vote ensured his victory in the state. The margin in 2004 was substantial for George W. Bush, who carried the east Tennessee base, suburban middle Tennessee, and the west Tennessee city of Jackson, along with the Memphis suburbs. This pattern was repeated in 2008 and 2012, but by larger margins, as Tennessee abandoned its Democratic heritage.

In the nine congressional races across the state, every incumbent won. The only pyrotechnics were in the Ninth Congressional District, in Memphis, where a Republican challenger outspent Democrat Steve Cohen by a two-a-one margin and lost by a three-to-one vote on election night in the majority-black district.[14] The Republicans carried thirteen of the fifteen most-populous counties in the state versus two for the Democrats. In the U.S. Senate and House races, the Republicans outraised their opponents $26.5 to $2.5 million, a ten-to-one advantage.[15] If one totals all the votes for national office recorded for president, the Senate, and the House on election night, the Republicans garnered 64 percent of the Tennessee vote versus 36 percent for the Democrats. That is a rout by any definition of the term.

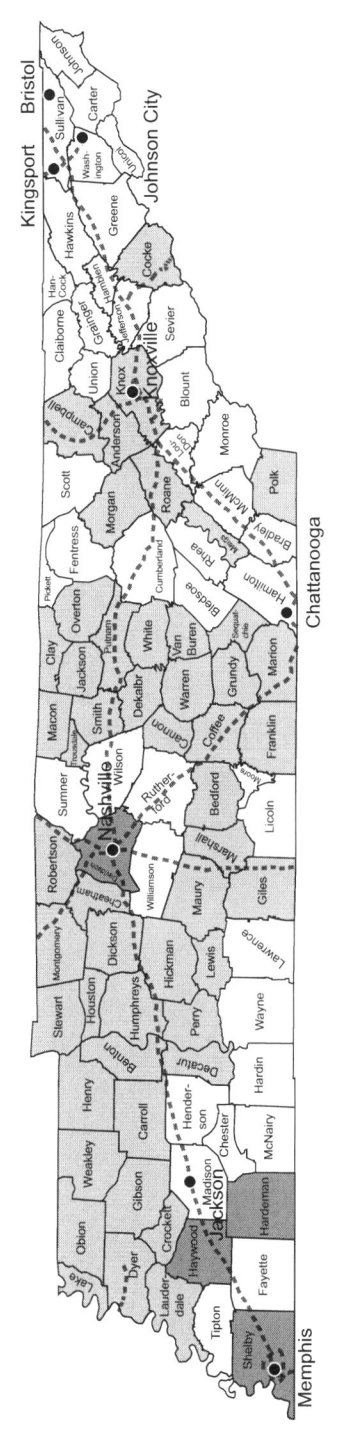

Figure 11.2. Tennessee Democrat / Republican Division

Democrat / Republican Division

	Counties	Population
Republican	41	2,747,690
Democrat	4	1,600,365
Mixed	50	1,998,050

State Elections

The partisan winds that buffet candidates for national office in the state have historically had little to no effect on grassroots state legislative contests. Democrats dominated the leadership of both houses from 1973 until 2007 and worked calmly with an occasional Republican governor, believing all the while that a return to united power was inevitable. After the state constitution was altered in 1978 to allow two consecutive four-year terms, the two parties alternated winning the governor's mansion—and each victor served two consecutive terms.

That seesaw of competition may have ended in 2010 when Bill Haslam won the gubernatorial election. Haslam campaigned by emphasizing his business background and executive experience. In the 2010 Republican primary, he bested second-place candidate and former GOP congressman Zach Wamp by nearly 20 points. Then, in the general election, Haslam effortlessly defeated Mike McWherter, the son of a former Democratic governor, by a two-to-one margin.[16] In the December 2012 Vanderbilt Poll, Governor Haslam registered a 68 percent approval rating, some 14 points better than that after his first year in office.[17] The same poll showed comfortable approval ratings for U.S. senators Lamar Alexander and Bob Corker.

The end of Democratic legislative rule in Tennessee came when Speaker Jimmy Naifeh gave up the reins of power in 2008 after Republicans won fifty of the ninety-nine seats in the state house of representatives. His counterpart, Lieutenant Governor John Wilder (the Tennessee constitution gives the title to the majority-party leader in the state senate), was removed one year earlier. Both Naifeh and Wilder were the longest-serving leaders of their respective houses in the history of the state. Republicans evinced no nostalgia for their opponent's accomplishments and, once in power, wasted little time in expanding their advantage in both houses when the Democratic warhorses retired. In the 108th General Assembly, which convened in January 2013, Republicans have a twenty-six-to-seven advantage in the state senate and a sixty-five-to-thirty-four lead in the lower house. Current Speaker of the House Beth Harwell has a doctorate in political science from Vanderbilt University and has crafted a legislative majority that shows a command of both the theory and the practice of politics. Ron Ramsey, the new lieutenant governor, is a businessman from east Tennessee.

On election night 2012, the grassroots GOP activists exulted in a walkover win. With half the state senate up for election in the cycle, meaning sixteen seats, the Democrats could seriously contest only five.

In six seats the incumbent Republicans were unchallenged, and in four others they coasted to a convincing victory over only token opposition.[18] This pattern was repeated in the Tennessee House of Representatives. Fully 40 percent of the Republicans won uncontested elections. Only five races were closely contested, and thirty-six others in which the Democrats offered opposition were one-sided victories for the GOP.[19]

Summary

The question can be asked, is Tennessee a typical southern state? On the one hand, it has its exceptions: an African American population smaller than its neighbors', a Mountain Republican history in its eastern provinces, an elected senator as a recent standard-bearer for the Democratic Party for the office of President of the United States, and a history of moderation instead of defiance on matters of race. On the other hand, it follows the southern rules: head-to-toe Republican voting in elections, a fierce antitax mood, a conservative allegiance to social policies, and 60 percent support for the Republican presidential candidate. One thing is for sure: the arrival of Tennessee as a red Republican state is a recent occurrence, not a long-standing tradition.

Noteworthy milestones along the way to realignment include Howard Baker's election and successful terms as a Republican U.S. senator (1967–1985), Winfield Dunn's election and term as the first Republican governor since Reconstruction (1971–1975), Lamar Alexander's career as both governor (1979–1987) and U.S. senator (2003 to the present), and the end of Democratic rule in the state senate (2007) and the state house (2008). No one can say what the future holds, but the political culture that brought the GOP to power in the state seems substantial enough to keep Tennessee in the Republican column for some time to come.

12

Texas

Big Red in the 2012 Elections

Brian Arbour

The 2012 elections in Texas only further solidified Texas's position as a deep-red state. Mitt Romney took the state easily, winning 57.2 percent of the vote, while former state solicitor general Ted Cruz easily won the state's open U.S. Senate seat with 56.6 percent of the vote. In state government Republicans continued their dominance, maintaining strong majorities in the state legislature and continuing to win every statewide election.[1]

Texas occupies a unique place in American politics. All of the other large states in the country either are dominated by Democrats (California, New York, Illinois, and Michigan) or are swing states up for grabs by each party (Ohio, Florida, and North Carolina). In addition, most other states with large Hispanic populations are either solid blue (again, California, New York, and Illinois) or swing states trending toward the Democrats (New Mexico, Colorado, Nevada, and Florida). Only Arizona joins Texas as a state that both is solidly Republican and has a significant Hispanic population.

Thus, Texas does not vote as a large state or a state featuring diverse multiracial politics. Instead, Texas votes similarly to small states, which are dominated by small-town and rural voters and in which, as in southern states, a majority of the voters are white and seem to vote as a unified racial block.

Nationally, the 2012 election demonstrated the declining significance of the white vote and the increased importance of the growing and solidly Democratic bloc of minority voters. In the wake of Obama's reelection and Democratic gains in the U.S. House and Senate, the Republican hold on Texas prompted two questions about the political future of the Lone Star State. First, does Texas provide a model for Republicans looking to more successfully navigate multiracial politics in an ever-diversifying nation? Second, does the solidifying of the Latino vote for the Democrats put Texas in play as a swing state in the 2016 or 2020 elections?

Answers to both questions are somewhat mixed. Republicans win Texas not because of their ability to successfully build multiracial coalitions but through their ability to win landslide shares of the white vote. To succeed nationally, Republicans must win significant minorities of the Hispanic and Asian vote, which they do not do in Texas. That landslide share of the white vote—which will remain the majority of the Texas electorate for the next two decades—also explains why Texas will remain a red state in the near future. There are not enough Hispanic votes for Democrats to overcome their massive deficit with white Texans.

With the strong Republican lean of the state, the real focus of Texas political attention in 2012 was on two Republican nomination contests. The first was the disastrous presidential campaign of Rick Perry. Perry's not-ready-for-prime-time performance was due in part to the poor preparation provided by a state dominated by one party. The second contest was in the Republican Senate primary between former state solicitor general Ted Cruz and Lieutenant Governor David Dewhurst, a clash between the Tea Party and the establishment. Cruz's victory not only showed the power of the Tea Party within the state but also marked the first sign of weakness for the Republican political establishment in over a decade.

2012 Elections in Texas

If conservatives want to preserve things and have little change, then the 2012 elections in Texas were certainly conservative. The Texas electorate preserved its tradition of voting Republican for president (every election since 1976) and having an all-Republican delegation to the U.S. Senate (a Democrat last won a Senate election in 1988), a majority-Republican delegation to the U.S. House (every election since 2004), and Republican majorities in the state senate (Republican held since 1998) and in the state house (Republican held since 2002). Republicans also won every statewide election. Indeed, they have not lost a statewide election since 1998.[2]

The gap for Democrats remained very large. Table 12.1 shows that Romney won the state by 16 points, running 10 points above his national vote share. The Senate race in particular showed the impotence of Texas Democrats. The open seat created by the retirement of longtime senator Kay Bailey Hutchison and the nomination of Ted Cruz, who was backed by the most-conservative elements among the state's Republicans, gave Democrats the structural and the ideological opportunity to fight for a statewide seat. The lack of a statewide bench meant that Democrats could only muster a candidate who last won election a decade earlier.[3] Former state representative Paul Sadler brought neither the name recognition, the charisma, nor the fund-raising ability to attract attention from Texas voters. As a result, Sadler limped home 17 points behind Cruz.

There were a handful of victories for Texas Democrats to cheer. State Democratic representative Pete Gallego defeated one-term incumbent Quico Canseco in the state's one swing U.S. House district, and Democrats won two of the state's four new congressional districts. But Republicans drew the new congressional lines in the state and used that advantage to protect Republicans who had taken Democratic districts in 2010 (Bill Flores and Blake Farenthold) and to solidify Republican

Table 12.1. Texas Election Results, 2012

	President	Senate	23rd Congressional District	10th State Senate District
Republican	Mitt Romney 4,569,843 (57.2%)	Ted Cruz 4,440,137 (56.5%)	Quico Canseco* 87,547 (45.6%)	Mark Shelton 140,656 (48.9%)
Democrat	Barack Obama* 3,308,124 (41.4%)	Paul Sadler 3,194,927 (40.6%)	Pete Gallego 96,676 (50.3%)	Wendy Davis* 147,103 (51.1%)

Note: Election results from the Texas Secretary of State.
*incumbent

incumbents in the rest of the state.[4] No Republican won his or her U.S. House seat by less than 12 points in 2012, and no incumbent won by less than 17 points.

Texas Democrats won a handful of victories at the state legislative level, paring down the Republican majority in the state house to ninety-five to fifty-five and holding the one targeted seat in the state senate, Wendy Davis in the Seventeenth District. For the most part, Republicans retained most of their victories in the state house from the 2010 wave, cementing their dominance in that chamber. Democrats have no path to a majority in either house of the legislature in the near future.

Republican Nomination Contests

With a somnambulant general election in the state, the real action in Texas politics in 2012 was earlier in the calendar, during Republican primary contests. Both the fiasco that was the Rick Perry presidential campaign and the upset victory of Ted Cruz over Lieutenant Governor David Dewhurst demonstrated the insular conservatism of the Texas Republican primary electorate, though with different consequences in the two races.

Rick Perry for President

With widespread agreement that the Republican primary field was weak and that conservatives were searching for an alternative to Mitt Romney, momentum built for a Perry campaign through the spring and the summer of 2012.[5] Perry brought substantial advantages to his presidential run. His biography was rooted in rural and traditional values, as the son of farmers from West Texas, an Eagle Scout, and an Air Force pilot,[6] and his record of political success was unmatched—nine victories without a defeat, including six for statewide office.[7] Texas's enviable jobs record—the state "added 1.2 million net jobs since Perry took office as Texas Governor in December 2000, while the U.S. as a whole lost 1.1 million jobs during the same time"—provided Perry with a political asset in a year when the economy was a top issue.[8] Also, Perry had made successful connections with the Tea Party movement in Texas, and his book *Fed Up: Our Fight to Save America from Washington* sounded Tea Party themes by calling for greatly reducing the size and the scope of the federal government.[9]

Put together, Perry held an impressive set of political assets that seemed to make him one of the front-runners for the nomination when he announced his candidacy in August 2011. Despite these assets, however, Perry's campaign flopped from almost his first weekend on the campaign trail. Perry wounded himself with a series of verbal gaffes and weak debate performances.[10] He seemed to lack knowledge of federal government programs, and little evidence existed to show he was learning about these topics as the campaign went along.[11]

Even worse for Perry, he stumbled on two issues where his positions were not fully conservative. Michele Bachmann and Rick Santorum attacked Perry's decision to require thirteen-year-old girls to receive the human papillomavirus (HPV) vaccine.[12] Mitt Romney attacked Perry's signing of a bill offering in-state tuition at Texas colleges and universities to undocumented students as a "magnet that draws people into this country."[13] Perry's ineffectual and tone-deaf responses to both attacks indicated that he failed to understand conservative objections to his policy choices, raising doubts about him in his supposed political base.[14]

Of course, the coup de grâce for his campaign came when in a November debate, he could not remember the name of the third cabinet department he wanted to eliminate. This moment crystallized all doubts about Perry's intellectual capacity to be president. Perry's campaign was a dead man walking after this point—he finished fifth in the Iowa caucuses with 10 percent of the vote. He inexplicably continued his campaign in South Carolina before finally putting it out of its misery a few days before the primary.

The most compelling rationale for the Perry flop was Texas or, really, the nature of Texas politics. The state's key battle is the low-turnout gubernatorial Republican primary, and the state press corps is much less aggressive than the national press corps. Veteran Texas political journalist Paul Burka speculated, "Perry has had it so easy . . . that I wonder if it has dulled his political acumen. . . . He hasn't had any big-league experience, and it shows. Sooner or later, he was bound to pay a price for not engaging in the give and take of a major political campaign."[15] Texas's conservative lean had allowed Perry to avoid tough opponents and tough questions, and thus, he had not learned how to use subtlety and tact in getting his message across to voters.

Cruz versus Dewhurst

That conservative lean of the Texas electorate combined with the populist antiestablishment mood of the Obama era to elevate underdog Ted

Cruz over David Dewhurst in the Republican U.S. Senate primary. To many, the major theme of the Senate runoff was ideological, with Cruz running to Dewhurst's right.[16] The real theme was the clash between the state's Republican establishment, who favored Dewhurst, and its populist Tea Party faction, represented by Cruz.

In many ways, Cruz is an unusual populist figure. While his background is unique (child of a Cuban dissident and an American mother), his résumé is straight establishment—degrees from Princeton and Harvard law and a clerkship for Chief Justice William Rehnquist. His connections in private practice helped him secure a job with the 2000 Bush campaign and positions in the Department of Justice and the Federal Trade Commission in the Bush administration. Governor Perry appointed Cruz the state's solicitor general in 2003.[17] This was not the background of someone who wanted to take down the establishment, yet as someone who had not won elective office and who lacked the support of the state's Republican political establishment, Cruz was the Tea Party's vessel for influencing the Republican Party. Cruz certainly saw the Tea Party as his vehicle for making a case against Dewhurst.

Dewhurst, a member in good standing of Texas's Republican political establishment, won endorsements from the land commissioner, the comptroller, and all eighteen Republicans in the state senate. Dewhurst's biggest supporter was Rick Perry, who appeared in Dewhurst television advertisements and travelled the state backing his lieutenant governor. Cruz's biggest endorsers were out-of-state figures that critiqued the national Republican Party establishment—Sarah Palin and Rick Santorum and senators Mike Lee (Utah), Jim DeMint (South Carolina), and Rand Paul (Kentucky).[18]

The issue differences between the two candidates were few and far between. Instead, the real difference between the two candidates was, according to columnist Ross Ramsay, "one of style and of political culture." He wrote, "Angry and frustrated with politicians and officeholders? Here's the chance to dump one. Send a rebel to Washington instead of someone tainted by 14 years of experience and compromise."[19]

Election and polling results bore out the importance of the Tea Party in Cruz's upset victory. A poll of Republican primary voters released the week before the election showed that while only small splits existed among traditional demographic characteristics (gender, age, race, and evangelical status), the Republican electorate was split with regard to the Tea Party and ideology. Among Republican primary voters who considered themselves a member of the Tea Party, Cruz had a huge 75 to 22 percent lead. Although more Republican primary voters did not consider themselves members of the Tea Party (49 percent were not and 33 percent were), Dewhurst had only a modest 56 to 39 percent lead. Dewhurst led among moderates in the survey (66 to 29 percent) and was tied among those who were "somewhat conservative." Dewhurst trailed significantly, though, among the half of the Republican electorate who were "very conservative" (63 percent for Cruz, 32 percent for Dewhurst).

Geographically, Dewhurst won the vote in Texas's rural counties by 52 to 48 percent, which may have been indicative of his support from traditional parts of Texas.[20] Cruz's margin was provided by voters in suburban counties, which he won 60 to 40 percent, and in urban counties, which he won 58 to 42 percent.[21] The Tea Party movement sprang up primarily in suburban areas impacted by the housing crisis.[22]

The Unique Place of Texas

The 2012 election left Texas in the same place it had been for a while—solidly Republican and conservative. Both Romney and Cruz won the state by 16-point margins. Table 12.2 shows the long-term partisan trend in the state for presidential elections, calculating the difference between the Republican nominee's vote share in Texas and nationally. Like most other southern states, Texas has gone from being a yellow-dog Democratic state to solidly Republican over the past sixty-five years. Most notable in the figures is the maintenance of the Republican lean of the state for the past two elections, neither of which featured a candidate named George Bush on the national Republican ticket.[23] Nevertheless, in the state of Texas, both John McCain and Mitt Romney ran 10 points better than their national numbers.[24]

Texas thus stands at a unique place in American politics. It is not only the largest state to go for Mitt Romney in 2012 but also the only large state to go Republican. Among the seven states with populations over ten million, Obama won six—easily in California, New York, and Illinois and with numbers close to his national percentage in Florida, Pennsylvania, and Ohio. Texas stood out from its fellow megastates, giving the president only 41.4 percent of the vote. If one includes the five other states with double-digit U.S. House delegations, Texas was a bit less alone, since Romney won both Georgia and North Carolina, though

Table 12.2. Texas Republican Vote Trend, 1948–2008

Year	Vote share of Republican presidential nominee		Difference
	Texas	National	
1948	24.3	45.1	-20.8
1952	53.1	55.2	-2.1
1956	55.3	57.4	-2.1
1960	48.5	49.6	-1.0
1964	36.5	38.5	-2.0
1968	39.9	43.4	-3.6
1972	66.2	60.7	+5.5
1976	48.0	48.0	-0.1
1980	55.3	50.8	+4.5
1984	63.6	58.8	+4.8
1988	56.0	53.4	+2.6
1992	40.6	37.5	+3.1
1996	48.8	40.7	+8.0
2000	59.3	47.9	+11.4
2004	61.1	50.7	+10.4
2008	56.3	46.3	+10.0
2012	57.2	47.2	+10.0

Source: Historical data are from *Dave Leip's Atlas of U.S. Presidential Elections*, http://uselectionatlas.org; 2012 data are from Dave Wasserman of *Cook Political Report*, available at https://docs.google.com/spreadsheet/lv?key=0AjYj9mXElO_QdHpla01oWE1jOFZRbnhJZkZpVFNKeVE&toomany=true.

by smaller margins than he won Texas. This set of states also includes the blue states of Michigan and New Jersey and the rapidly trending Democratic Virginia.

Why is Texas different from other large states? The first factor is voting in the state's suburbs. Romney won in the state's suburban counties in a romp—68 to 31 percent. Romney won large margins in the state's largest suburban counties: 65 percent in both Collin and Denton Counties in suburban Dallas, 80 percent in Montgomery County, and 63 percent in Galveston County in suburban Houston. Even in Williamson County in suburban Austin—noted as Texas's one liberal redoubt—Romney won decisively, 59 to 38 percent. Table 12.3 shows Texas suburban counties' sharp contrast with suburban counties such as Westchester (New York), Bergen (New Jersey), Contra Costa (California), and San

Mateo (California), where Obama won comfortably, propelling him to large victories in each of these states. Even in swing states such as Pennsylvania, Colorado, and Virginia, Obama's victories in key suburban counties were essential to winning.[25] Texas's suburban counties stood out by making a significant contribution to Texas's red state status.

Texas also stood out as the nation's only majority-minority state to vote for Obama. The others (Hawaii, New Mexico, and California) were all won quite easily by President Obama. Other states with a large multiracial population—Nevada, New York, Florida, New Jersey, and Illinois—were all won by President Obama, as well, and most, in convincing fashion. Texas, despite having an above-average population of Hispanics, instead voted like southern states such as Louisiana,

Table 12.3. Presidential Votes in Select Large-State Suburban Counties, 2012

County	Metropolitan area	State	Obama %	Romney %
Collin	Dallas–Fort Worth	Texas	33.5	65.0
Denton	Dallas–Fort Worth	Texas	33.4	64.9
Fort Bend	Houston	Texas	46.1	52.9
Montgomery	Houston	Texas	19.0	79.7
Williamson	Austin	Texas	37.9	59.4
Westchester	New York	New York	62.6	36.0
Bergen	New York	New Jersey	55.0	44.1
Montgomery	Philadelphia	Pennsylvania	56.6	42.3
Fairfax	Washington	Virginia	59.3	39.5
Dupage	Chicago	Illinois	49.7	48.7
Oakland	Detroit	Michigan	53.7	45.6
Orange	Los Angeles	California	44.8	53.0
Contra Costa	San Francisco	California	65.7	32.1
San Mateo	San Francisco	California	71.3	26.6
Arapahoe	Denver	Colorado	53.2	44.8
Jefferson	Denver	Colorado	51.0	46.6
Gwinnett	Atlanta	Georgia	44.6	54.0
Cobb	Atlanta	Georgia	42.9	55.3

Source: All county data for Texas elections are from the Secretary of State's website; national data are from "2012 Presidential Election," Politico, last updated November 29, 2012, http://www.politico.com/2012-election/map/#/President/2012.

Mississippi, and Georgia, where the white population had consolidated its vote in support of racial conservatism and against the interests of their large, lower-class African American populations.[26] White Texas voters behaved similarly, voting as a unified block against the votes of the state's minorities.

Texas as a GOP Model

Barack Obama's victory in the 2012 election was notable not only for affirming the political and the policy legacy of his first term but also because of the historically unique political coalition that he built. Obama lost white voters by over 20 points but won the presidency with a comfortable 4-point margin by winning African Americans by monolithic margins (93 to 6 percent) and Hispanic and Asian American voters by landslide margins (71 to 27 percent for Hispanics, 73 to 26 percent for Asian Americans). With minority voters growing to 28 percent of the electorate in 2012 and being projected to increase their voting weight, the ability to appeal to an increasingly diverse and multiracial America is essential to winning future elections.[27]

In light of the Republican Party's struggles with minority voters, some have seen Texas as a model for the Republican Party moving forward. Texas is a majority-minority state, and Hispanics make up 38 percent of all Texans according to the 2010 census. Rather than favoring nationalist anti-immigration policies, the Texas political establishment, led by George W. Bush and Rick Perry, has favored a more lenient and business-friendly approach to immigration (a constant supply of cheap labor helps reduce demands for increased pay and helps to squelch union organizing).[28] As the nation's only large multiracial red state, Texas provides a path that national Republicans can follow.

Texas Republicans have succeeded in dominating the state, however, primarily by dominating the white vote. The 2012 election proves instructive here. Polling results allow us to make an educated guess about the white vote in Texas in 2012. A University of Texas/*Texas Tribune* poll has Romney winning the white vote 67 to 25 percent, and a YouGov poll has Romney up 70 to 25 percent.[29] If one weights the results of these polls to the final results in the state, which eliminates the undecideds, Romney won 72 percent of the white vote in the state. Ted Cruz received similar numbers, winning on average 71 percent of the white vote in the state—again, weighted to the final results for the

Senate race. These results from 2012 were similar to those from 2008, when John McCain won 73 percent of the white vote, and to those from 2010, when Rick Perry won 69 percent of the votes of white Texans.

The Texas model is to win more than two-thirds of the white vote while more or less forfeiting the minority vote. This is a hurdle that seems too high to leap for national Republicans. In order to win the 2012 election, assuming that minority groups turned out at the same rate and voted for Obama at the same rate, Mitt Romney would have needed to defeat Barack Obama by a margin of 61.5 to 36.5 percent among white voters. Considering that Romney's 59 to 39 percent share of the white vote nationally was a record margin, it is hard to see how Romney could have juiced up this number more. More worrisome for Republicans is that as the minority share of the electorate expands in future years, they will need to win even larger shares of white voters.

Can Republicans win two-thirds of all white voters? They do this currently in only two places. One is the rural inner-mountain West. The other is the Deep South, where whites have traditionally voted along racial lines in opposition to civil rights and programs to benefit African Americans. Texas has long followed this political pattern.[30] The original Texas settlers emigrated primarily from the highland areas of the South and followed their southern brothers out of the Union in 1861. Chafing at the occupation of the Union Army and attempts to provide civil rights to freed slaves during Reconstruction, white Texans flocked to a pro-segregation Democratic Party for the next century.[31] In the past two political generations, Texas voters, like those in other southern states, have moved toward the Republican Party, aligning their long-held opposition to the central government and government spending and their traditional views on social issues with the nation's conservative party.

Is this a national model? It is only if Republicans can convince voters across the nation to vote based on racial animus and the results of the Civil War. Since this has not happened in the first 150 years after the Civil War, it will probably not happen in the next 150 years. Thus, Republicans will likely never get two-thirds of the white vote nationwide.

Dreams of a Blue Texas

Texas Republicans like the present, and Texas Democrats dream about the future. No less an election analyst than actress Eva Longoria argued, "Texas is on the verge of a radical shift in our political outcomes."

"This might be the last presidential election during which Texas is not considered a swing state."[32] This theory of a blue Texas holds that the continuing growth of the Hispanic vote in the state combined with the monolithic Democratic African American vote will soon eclipse the white vote, producing a more politically divided state.

This prediction is premature, however. First, note that Mitt Romney won the state comfortably in 2012, defeating Barack Obama by 16 points. It would take a massive shift in the state to change 16 points in four short years. Second, the trend toward Democrats is gradual, so gradual in fact that the Democratic gains between 2008 and 2012 were less than one-tenth of a percent. Certainly, the share of the Hispanic electorate is growing in the state, but Republicans have blunted those gains in recent years by winning increasing shares of the white vote.

Can Democrats overcome the overwhelming Republican advantage among white Texans? It will take time. In 2008, Latinos made up 20 percent of the Texas electorate, while whites made up 63 percent. With the state's white population expected to decrease by about 2 percent each election cycle, it will take some time for the white electoral fortress to erode.[33] If the electorate follows that trend, then the 61 percent of the vote that was white in 2012 will be 59 percent in 2016, 57 percent in 2020, and so on. As long as Democrats are winning 70 percent of the white vote in the state, this will get them 80 percent of their way to a majority in each of these elections. Winning one-third of the votes of Hispanics and Asians will allow Texas Republicans to win the state through 2024. If Republicans can win 73 percent of the white vote and 35 percent of the Hispanic vote, as John McCain did in 2008, then they can maintain their advantage in the state until 2032. Of course, in lower-turnout midterm elections the electorate is even whiter, and Republican will have the advantage there for another decade beyond their advantage in presidential elections.

For Texas to turn blue, one of two things must happen. One would be a massive Democratic landslide victory. In that scenario, nearly every state would turn blue. The second would be for Democrats to reverse their decades-long slide among white voters and convince an appreciable share of white Texans to pull the lever for a Democrat. That Texas Democrats have not been able to do this in any election since 1998 demonstrates the tough task they have and should extinguish Democratic dreams and Republican fears of an impending blue Texas.

The Aftermath of 2012

The 2012 election left Texas as the nation's only large state dominated by Republicans. The results of the 2010 and 2012 elections confirmed that Republicans will remain the dominant, almost monolithic, party in the state. Texas Democrats can put up no more than token opposition at this point.

The biggest political issue in the state moving forward is the fate of the state's top two officeholders in the 2014 elections. Despite their losses at the national level in 2012, Rick Perry and David Dewhurst remain the state's governor and lieutenant governor. These two men have held their jobs for over a decade, and a generation of ambitious Texas politicians has waited to run for higher office. With Rick Perry and David Dewhurst wounded from their 2012 primary defeats, the expectation is that even if Perry and Dewhurst run for reelection, neither will have an uncontested run to the Republican nomination. The political rumor mill suggests that Attorney General Greg Abbott will challenge Perry in the Republican primary and that some combination of Comptroller Susan Combs, Land Commissioner Jerry Patterson, and Agricultural Commissioner Todd Staples will run for Dewhurst's lieutenant governor post.

The success of the unknown Ted Cruz and his Tea Party backers in 2012 makes it possible, if not likely, that someone outside the state's Republican political establishment will go after the governor's and the lieutenant governor's seats in 2014. Both Perry and Dewhurst have expressed interest in running in 2014, though it is possible that the two men are doing so only to maintain political power during the 2013 legislative session.[34] Regardless of who runs, it seems certain that multiple people will run for both of the state's top jobs in 2014 among an unpredictable Republican primary electorate.

From a national standpoint, Ted Cruz has a promising future. As a young Hispanic in a party that seems increasingly old and white, Cruz will be an in-demand speaker among Republican Party groups. As a candidate with an establishment résumé and Tea Party backing, Cruz has much to teach a party that is trying to heal the divisions between these two elements. Cruz may be a potential presidential candidate, but in 2016, he stands behind Marco Rubio of Florida and Bobby Jindal of Louisiana as minority conservatives, and he will likely have to wait to run.

Overall, Texas is and will remain a Republican state. The 2012 election provided no challenge to its deep-red hue and provided no evidence that its Republican lean will change in the immediate future. Yet the 2012 election proved that the state's Republican political establishment was not as dominant as once assumed and that their hold on the state will be up for grabs in future Republican primaries.

13

Virginia

Obama's Unexpected Firewall

John J. McGlennon

Continuing demographic change, a history of Republican success, an expectation of a closer national contest than four years previously, uncertainty about the level of participation among young and minority voters, and anxiety over the impact of federal budget cuts on defense spending all combined to make Virginia a focus for the 2012 presidential campaign. The Commonwealth, which had not voted for a Democratic presidential candidate between 1968 and 2004, was among the top-three states in the nation in terms of campaign resources expended.

Ultimately, President Obama reprised his 2008 victory in Virginia, winning thirteen Electoral College votes. That Virginia proved to be a firewall for the Obama campaign, effectively blocking a number of Mitt Romney's paths to the White House, was a key element of the national election.

Barack Obama's initial election to the presidency in 2008 was accomplished through a number of remarkable results, including his victories in three southern states. Of all those wins his edge in Virginia broke the longest Democratic losing streak in the region.[1] Virginia alone among southern states had resisted the regional appeal of Jimmy Carter in his 1976 election. Not since 1964 had a Democrat won the Old Dominion, and the Johnson landslide of that year marked the only time since 1948 that the state had voted for a Democratic president. Veteran observers were skeptical that Obama would be the candidate to break through that daunting Republican line of success.[2]

In the end, Obama won Virginia by 6.29 percent, within one point of matching his national share of the vote. In 2012, Virginia played an unlikely role again, this time providing a reservoir of support for the president. Republicans were forced to devote time and energy to a state they had taken for granted just eight years earlier and where they now seemed to be at a disadvantage.[3]

Obama's strength in Virginia opened a number of additional options for his path to 270 electoral votes and made the math for any Republican nominee that much more difficult. Democrats became increasingly confident and Republicans more concerned as Obama showed surprising support in approval polls and trial heats throughout 2011 and the first half of 2012.

With multiple polling organizations providing frequent sampling of state-by-state opinions over the year preceding the election, several online publications offered rolling averages of the polls. For a battleground state like Virginia, there were a large number of surveys to consider. Table 13.1 provides a month-by-month snapshot of the average through Election Day, as presented by Pollster.com, one such compendium of polls.[4] Though President Obama's lead dropped somewhat once Romney secured the Republican nomination, it never disappeared, demonstrating remarkable stability among the electorate.

In the end, the election results in the Old Dominion practically matched the national vote and reflected only marginal differences from one contest to the next. Obama drew a 1.4 percent lower share of the total Virginia vote than in 2008, but the outcome reflected some significant changes within the Commonwealth. Patterns that were emerging or first evident in 2004 and 2008 became more pronounced. In other cases, they were confirmed, rearranging the calculations of geography and demography leading to electoral success in Virginia.

The Political Context

The presidential outcome of 2008 upended Virginia politics and reflected more broadly partisan trends. To replace the retiring five-term Republican John Warner, voters elected Democrat Mark Warner (no relation), a

Table 13.1. Virginia Presidential Poll Monthly Averages, January to November 2012

Month	Obama %	Romney %	Margin
January	46.3	42.7	3.6
February	47.4	42.2	5.2
March	48.9	41.1	7.8
April	47.6	42.7	4.9
May	46.8	43.5	3.3
June	46.8	43.4	3.4
July	46.2	44.1	2.1
August	46.7	44.2	2.5
September	46.9	45.1	1.8
October	48.5	46.8	1.7
November	48.7	46.8	1.9

Source: Pollster.com, "2012 Virginia President: Romney vs. Obama Poll," Huffpost Politics Election Dashboard, http://elections.huffingtonpost.com/pollster/2012-virginia-president-romney-vs-obama.

former governor, to the U.S. Senate by a landslide over the former GOP governor and Republican National Committee chair James Gilmore.

Three new Democrats were elected to the U.S. House of Representatives that year. These results continued a string of Democratic accomplishments, including the election of Tim Kaine as governor in 2005, the paper-thin defeat of Republican U.S. senator George Allen by Democrat Jim Webb in one of the biggest upsets of 2006, and the reclaiming of a majority in the Virginia state senate in 2007.

The years following the Obama first-term victory reversed the Democratic surge. Robert McDonnell, the state's attorney general, claimed the governorship in 2009 by a 17 percent margin, as the GOP won all three constitutional offices: governor, lieutenant governor, and attorney general. McDonnell's win came over Sen. Creigh Deeds, the same Democrat he had defeated by 323 votes in 2005 to become the state's chief legal officer. The 2009 GOP victory extended the Virginia Curse, whereby since 1977, the party that had won the presidency the previous year lost the governorship. Given Virginia's unique status in not permitting governors to seek consecutive reelection, these races are always open-seat contests, without the factor of incumbency interfering.

In 2010, the Tea Party dominated midterm elections and restored GOP dominance to the U.S. House delegation with the defeat of three Democratic congressmen, two freshmen and fourteen-term veteran Rick Boucher. Particularly noteworthy was Boucher's defeat, as he had run unopposed in 2008 while Obama lost his southwest Virginia–based Ninth District by 19 percent. Boucher had generally escaped close competition in the past, but the increasingly Republican voting of the district made him a prime target. He was challenged by the majority leader of the Virginia House of Delegates, H. Morgan Griffith, and Boucher fell by 9,000 votes (almost 5 percent). Both Democratic freshmen had finished somewhat ahead of Obama in 2008, but neither Glenn Nye in the Second District nor Tom Perriello in the Fifth could withstand the GOP tide in 2010. Nye lost to first-time candidate and auto dealership owner Scott Rigell, while Perriello lost a closer-than-expected race to state senator Robert Hurt.

Finally, the newly redistricted general assembly in 2011 produced a supermajority for the GOP in the house of delegates and an even split in the forty-member senate, broken by the lieutenant governor's vote, which allowed the GOP the organizing majority. Republican mapmakers in the house of delegates devised a redistricting plan that eliminated or merged districts of Democratic veterans, causing even the house minority leader to move to a new residence in a futile effort to retain a seat. After clawing their way to forty-four seats in the hundred-member house in 2007, following an equally devastating remap in 2001, the Democrats fell to thirty-two seats in the 2012 session. The senate Democrats used their narrow majority to maximize their chances of retaining their only share of state government control. With no room for error, the Democrats lost two seats to the GOP, including one by 226 votes, resulting in the twenty-twenty tie that was broken by Lieutenant Governor William Bolling.

Despite these setbacks, the Democrats made Virginia a top priority in 2012. As a reward for his early support of Obama's presidential candidacy in 2008, the president selected Governor Tim Kaine to chair the Democratic National Committee.[5] Kaine held the post until agreeing to run for the U.S. Senate, despite the poor Democratic performances in 2009 and 2010. Organizing for America (OFA), the interelection incarnation of the Obama campaign, deployed dozens of staffers to maintain a grassroots presence focused on identifying and registering Obama supporters for the next election. The president, Vice President Joe Biden, First Lady Michelle Obama, and other administration officials were frequent visitors to Virginia, with the first lady and Jill Biden focusing particular attention on military families in the Hampton Roads area.[6]

Although the GOP did not have the advantage of an incumbent president, party leaders made clear their intention to fight for the Commonwealth. Governor McDonnell emerged as a frequent national spokesman for Republicans. Both sides saw Virginia's thirteen electoral votes as critical to their 2012 prospects, and each could find evidence to support their optimism about winning the Old Dominion.

Demographic change fueled the hopes of Democrats. The 2010 census showed Virginia's population continuing to grow at a rate somewhat faster than the nation as a whole, and that growth was concentrated in the areas where Democrats had shown the greatest strength in recent years. Suburbs in Northern Virginia, Richmond, and Hampton Roads were all showing movement toward the Democrats. By the end of the decade, central cities and densely populated older suburbs were starting to grow again. New urbanites were often younger people seeking amenity-rich cities and trying to avoid the expensive and time-consuming commutes of their parents.[7]

The increasing diversity of the Virginia electorate was critical to the Obama win in 2008 and continued apace. At the same time, rates of voting had grown considerably over the past several decades, generally to the benefit of the Democrats. Virginia showed significant increases in nonwhite populations and increasing political activism. Hispanic Americans saw the creation of a house of delegates district in Northern Virginia with a Hispanic plurality, and a Hispanic American was elected to the Arlington County Board of Supervisors. Asian American population trends were also sharply upward, again with accompanying political activism and electoral impact. African Americans comprised a stable one-in-five share of the state population, reflecting a continuing growth in total numbers.[8]

The age distribution of the electorate had also moved in a more Democratic direction in recent years. Those between the ages of eighteen and twenty-nine were a growing cohort of the state's electorate, while those over sixty represented a smaller share of the overall voter base. While older voters traditionally cast ballots at much higher rates than did younger voters, the gap had been declining, and the partisan divide showed the young voters to be the most Democratic age group, whereas older voters were most likely to support the GOP. Overall, the state's changing electorate reflected a more Democratic cast.[9]

Republicans pointed to their reclaimed status as the majority party in state government, having taken control of all the institutional centers of power in 2009 and 2011. They had rebounded to take control of the majority of U.S. House races again and cemented those gains in their congressional redistricting plan while increasing the security of the three Democratic congressmen.[10]

Rural white voters moved more strongly toward the Republicans. With a sense of high voter intensity among GOP identifiers, the Republicans felt that Virginia would be among the first states to return to their party after what they saw as the aberration of 2008. Speculation about the Commonwealth possibly providing a vice presidential candidate led to an optimism that seemed well founded. The stage was thus set for the presidential race.

The Nomination Contest

Whereas the Democrats were unified behind Obama's candidacy for reelection, Republicans expected Virginia to play an important role in their nomination contest. Ultimately, however, state ballot requirements created an unexpected impediment to the fluid GOP field. Only two candidates, Mitt Romney and Ron Paul, managed to meet the state requirement of submitting 10,000 signatures (at least 400 from each of the eleven congressional districts). After failing to meet this threshold, Texas governor Rick Perry and former House Speaker Newt Gingrich sued to overturn the requirements but were rebuffed by the courts.[11]

In 2008, the seven main Democrats seeking the nomination recognized the serious effort required to earn a spot on the ballot and agreed to cooperate to get voters to "Sign for Seven," asking voters to sign the petitions for all the candidates. The GOP field in 2012 was too fluid for that, however, with candidates coming in and out of the race. Mitt Romney determined, in particular, to take advantage of the organizational head start provided by his unsuccessful campaign in 2008, to the detriment of his challengers. Only Romney and Paul, another veteran of national campaigns with a dedicated volunteer force, cleared the bar. This gave Romney the opportunity to win a rare majority vote, and it led to the highest vote share for Ron Paul in any state primary.

Had other candidates made it onto the ballot, the results would have been different. In a December 2011 poll, Gingrich posted a large lead over Romney at a time when his stock was generally rising in southern states.[12] Of course, his failure to qualify for the ballot made his performance moot, and in any case, Gingrich suffered a steep decline after losing the Florida primary to Romney. Perry had his moment in the limelight a bit earlier. In an August 2011 survey, he narrowly led Romney in Virginia.[13] Again, Perry's relative strength at this early stage faded, and his failure to qualify for the ballot also made him irrelevant.

Presidential primary turnout was minimal, as the absence of a Democratic contest and the limited GOP menu drew only 265,000 (or less than 6 percent of registered voters) to the polls. In comparison, some 1.47 million Virginians voted in February 2008, with roughly twice as many Democrats as Republicans showing up. GOP participation alone fell by 224,000 votes. Romney won 59.5 percent to Paul's 40.5 percent, with Paul winning only the African American–majority Third Congressional District, which also had the lowest turnout of any congressional district.[14] Unlike the 2008 GOP primary, when John McCain's strength in northern and southeastern Virginia trumped Mike Huckabee's support in the western reaches, the race in 2012 did not follow a clear geographic pattern. Governor McDonnell and Lieutenant Governor Bolling were prominent Romney supporters. Attorney General Ken Cuccinelli, the likely gubernatorial nominee in 2013, declined to make an endorsement.

The General Election

Virginia's central role in the strategies of both campaigns was evident in the days immediately preceding the national conventions. After Governor Romney was acknowledged as the presumptive nominee, speculation about potential running mates prominently featured Virginia's chief executive. Governor McDonnell was tapped as a campaign surrogate, traveling to a number of states in support of Romney, and he was among a handful of prospective vice presidents who traveled with Romney on campaign swings during the summer months. McDonnell was not the ultimate choice, but Romney announced his selection of Rep. Paul Ryan at the site of the mooring of the retired battleship USS *Wisconsin* in the port city of Norfolk, Virginia.[15]

Military- and defense-related issues were a main focus of the GOP campaign in the Commonwealth. Romney sought to take advantage of anxiety over the federal budget relating to the heavy concentration of military bases in Hampton Roads (the Norfolk/Virginia Beach/Newport News area) and of defense contractors there and in Northern Virginia. In resolving a contentious debate over raising the national debt ceiling in the summer of 2011, President Obama signed the Budget Control Act of 2011, which required that Congress agree on a deficit-reducing plan before December 31, 2012, or face automatic tax increases and deep spending cuts equally divided between defense and nondefense programs.[16]

In the final presidential debate, Romney criticized Obama's defense restructuring plan and the coming sequestration, noting that the navy would have fewer ships than it had in World War II. Obama responded with sarcasm, noting that with the advent of aircraft carriers and submarines, we no longer needed to maintain as many small ships nor as many "horses and bayonets." The Romney campaign seized on the comment, running commercials in the state quoting Obama's response and tying it to the loss of defense jobs. Despite the fact that the construction of nuclear submarines and aircraft carriers is a major source of employment in the state, the attacks seemed to gain little traction.[17]

Democrats concentrated on their core constituencies from 2008, including African Americans, Hispanic Americans, Asian Americans, young voters, and women. While Vice President Joe Biden, former president Bill Clinton, and other prominent surrogates campaigned in the western and southwestern parts of the state, President Obama focused his efforts on Northern Virginia, Hampton Roads, Richmond, and Charlottesville, home of the University of Virginia. Obama also chose to prepare for the second debate in Williamsburg, taking a break from preparations to deliver pizzas to campaign volunteers working in the local campaign headquarters.

In total, between June and Election Day, the presidential nominees, their running mates, and their spouses visited Virginia 98 times, which made the state third in visits, behind only Ohio (148) and Florida (118). Romney and his team led the count, with 27 visits from the nominee and a total of 51 for the four GOP campaigners. The Democrats were not far behind, with a total of 47 visits, including 20 by the president.[18]

The allocation of campaign resources also demonstrated the critical role Virginia occupied in both campaigns' strategies. From April to November, the two campaigns and their allies were estimated as spending $151 million in television advertising, second only to the amount spent in the larger (and more expensive) Florida media markets. Democrats spent $68 million compared with $83 million by the GOP, though Democrats were thought to have actually purchased more ads due to their ability to pay for more directly through the campaign and to their earlier and more cost-effective targeting.[19] With ads by the presidential campaigns running at such a high level, along with Senate race advertising and, in several places, heated congressional contests, Virginians were unable to avoid saturation by campaign ads if they viewed commercial television.[20]

Public opinion polling demonstrated the closeness of the contest in Virginia, as Obama began the year with a clear but small lead over candidate Romney. Once the nomination was settled, Obama's advantage narrowed but continued. The average of polls conducted in the state, as measured on the first day of each month, never showed Obama behind, though by Election Day his lead had dwindled to a mere 2 percent (as shown in Table 13.1).

Over the course of the election year, attitudes showed some variance from time to time, as approval or disapproval of Obama's general handling of the presidency closely divided the electorate. Early on, the president's favorability gave him a reservoir of support, while Romney was initially viewed far less positively by the voters in Virginia. Over time, Obama's favorability came into closer alignment with his approval ratings, and Romney closed some of the favorability gap. Obama tended through much of the campaign to be seen more negatively in his handling of the economy, a relative strength for Romney, but public evaluations of the candidates in this area also converged as the election approached on the strength of some positive jobs data and a higher level of confidence in the direction of the economy.

Other Contests

In addition to the presidential race, Virginia featured one of the most competitive Senate contests in the country. With the announcement in the fall of 2011 that U.S. senator Jim Webb would not seek reelection to a second term, two former governors quickly emerged as the favorites to contest for the seat. George Allen, governor from 1994 to 1998, had held the Senate seat from 2001 to 2007. Having ousted two-term senator Charles Robb (himself a former governor) in 2000, Allen had been mentioned as a potential 2008 presidential candidate until he was upset by Democrat Webb, who had served as secretary of the navy in the Reagan administration. Webb's win represented one of the biggest upsets in the nation in 2006 and helped to hand control of the Senate to the Democrats.

Before Allen could attempt to avenge his loss, he had to first win the nomination of his party in a primary election against three candidates.

Ultimately, the better-known Allen prevailed easily. In a June primary where the turnout was about as low as it had been for the February presidential contest, Allen won nearly two-thirds of the vote.[21]

Democrats focused their attention immediately on the Democratic National Committee chair, former governor Tim Kaine. A close confidant of the president, Kaine initially showed little enthusiasm for undertaking the race. Eventually, he yielded to encouragement from state Democrats and the White House and accepted the argument that he would be the strongest candidate and that his efforts would help to deliver Virginia to Obama. Once committed to the race, Kaine demonstrated no lack of effort, even while occasionally deviating from Obama's record and positions.[22]

The U.S. Senate campaign was crucial to GOP hopes of regaining control of the upper chamber, as Democrats held only a three-seat margin and faced retirements and vulnerable incumbents in a number of states. The race in Virginia attracted major expenditures by the national parties, independent expenditure groups, and Super PACs. Kaine raised significantly more campaign money than Allen, but the outside spending more than doubled the overall cost of the race. Outside groups attacking Kaine spent $28 million alone in a race that had hit a record $82 million mark by the beginning of November.[23]

Contests for Virginia's eleven seats in the House of Representatives drew challengers in every case, with all incumbents seeking reelection. The eight Republicans and three Democrats ran under a redistricting plan that was generally expected to preserve the status quo, with the Norfolk/Virginia Beach–based Second District and the Fifth District, spanning an area from the outer reaches of Northern Virginia to the North Carolina border, being on paper the two most competitive races. Both involved freshman Republicans, Scott Rigell and Robert Hurt, who had ousted first-term Democrats in 2010. In both cases, wave elections had produced Democratic wins behind Barack Obama's strong showings. In 2012, however, the new district lines were thought to insulate the Republicans. Both prepared for serious races and faced well-funded opponents.

The Results

Early on Election Night, votes from Virginia's rural western counties showed Mitt Romney and George Allen with substantial leads, but network analysts rated the contests as too close to call. As more precincts reported, it became evident that Kaine would win a close but comfortable victory.

While Obama saw some erosion from his margin of 2008, he was declared the winner well before the national contest was settled. When the last returns came in from Northern Virginia and Norfolk, Obama's margin grew to about 150,000, some 100,000 votes fewer than 2008, although Obama won slightly more votes than he did in his first victory (see Table 13.2). Romney surpassed John McCain's vote, but with overall turnout higher in the state than in 2008, Obama finished 3.87 percent ahead.[24]

Obama's victory confirmed the continuing emergence of the New Dominion, as growing diversity in the rapidly expanding metropolitan

Table 13.2. Virginia Presidential Election Results, 2004–2012

	Vote	%	Margin	Total vote
2004				
George W. Bush (R)	1, 716,959	53.68	262,217	
John F. Kerry (D)	1, 454,742	45.48		
Others	26,666	0.83		
				3,223,156
2008				
Barack Obama (D)	1,959,532	52.62	234,527	
John McCain (R)	1,725,005	46.33		
Others	38,723	0.72		
				3,752,858
2012				
Barack Obama (D)	1,971,820	51.15	149,298	
Mitt Romney (R)	1,822,522	47.28		
Gary Johnson (L)	31,216	0.80		
Virgil Goode (C)	13,058	0.33		
Jill Stein (G)	8,627	0.22		
Write-in	7,246	0.18		
				3,896,846

Source: Constructed from Virginia State Board of Elections, "Election Results," http://www.sbe.virginia.gov/cms/Election_Information/Election_Results/Index.html.
Note: Democratic (D), Republican (R), Libertarian (L), Constitution (C), Green (G).

areas moved the state toward the Democrats (see Table 13.3). The polarization of the parties intensified the support of evangelical Christians for the GOP, and in rural, white areas of the southwest, Obama's vote fell. These regions had been a special problem for Obama, who had performed weakly in this mountainous Appalachian region in both nomination and general election contests. His poor showing against Hillary

Table 13.3. Virginia Presidential Results for Select Localities, 2004–2012

	Party	2004	2004 %	2008	2008 %	2012	2012 %	2004–12 % shift
Southwest								
Tazewell County	D	7,184	41.10	5,596	32.79	3,661	20.64	-20.46
	R	10,039	57.43	11,201	65.65	13,843	78.06	+20.63
	Total	17,480		17,360		18,673		+1,193
Buchanan County	D	5,275	53.67	4,063	46.51	3,094	32.07	-21.60
	R	4,507	45.85	4,541	51.99	6,436	66.72	+20.87
	Total	9,829		8,961		9,830		+1
Dickenson County	D	3,761	50.78	3,278	48.54	2,473	35.81	-14.97
	R	3,591	48.49	3,324	49.22	4,274	61.90	+13.51
	Total	7,406		6,904		7,067		-339
Center Cities								
Richmond	D	52,167	70.19	73,623	79.09	75,921	77.81	+7.62
	R	21,637	29.11	18,649	20.03	20,050	20.54	-8.57
	Total	74,325		94,352		99,379		+25,054
Norfolk	D	43,518	61.67	62,819	71.02	62,687	72.01	+10.44
	R	26,401	37.41	24,814	28.05	23,147	26.59	-10.82
	Total	70,570		88,677		87,652		+17,082
Danville	D	9,436	49.37	12,352	59.12	12,218	60.47	+11.10
	R	9,399	49.18	8,361	40.02	7,763	38.42	-10.76
	Total	19,112		21,136		21,138		+2,026
Alexandria	D	41,116	66.84	50,473	71.73	52,199	71.10	+4.26
	R	19,844	32.26	19,181	27.25	20,249	27.58	-4.68
	Total	61,515		70,923		74,010		+13,495
Older Suburbs								
Virginia Beach	D	70,666	40.22	98,885	49.13	94,299	47.95	+7.73
	R	103,752	59.06	100,319	49.84	99,291	50.49	-8.57
	Total	175,687		202,377		197,961		+22,274

Clinton and John McCain was replicated in sections of West Virginia, Kentucky, Tennessee, and other states, even up to the mountainous sections of Ohio and Pennsylvania. As poor as his performance was in these areas in 2008, Obama

Table 13.3. (continued)

	Party	2004	2004 %	2008	2008 %	2012	2012 %	2004–12 % shift
Henrico County	D	60,864	45.62	86,323	55.70	89,594	55.22	+9.62
	R	71,809	53.82	67,381	43.48	70,449	43.42	-10.40
	Total	133,418		156,527		163,998		+30,580
Fairfax County	D	245,671	53.25	310,359	60.11	315,273	59.56	+6.31
	R	211,980	45.94	200,994	38.93	206,773	39.06	-6.88
	Total	461,379		518,094		532,187		+71,808
New Suburbs								
Loudoun County	D	47,271	43.60	74,845	53.66	82,479	51.53	+7.93
	R	60,382	55.69	63,336	45.41	75,292	47.03	-8.66
	Total	108,430		139,734		160,698		+52,268
Prince William County	D	61,271	46.40	93,435	57.51	103,331	57.34	+10.94
	R	69,776	52.84	67,621	41.62	74,458	41.32	-11.52
	Total	132,063		163,039		181,084		+49,021
Chesapeake City	D	38,744	42.32	53,994	50.21	55,052	49.85	+7.53
	R	52,283	57.11	52,625	48.94	53,900	48.81	-8.30
	Total	91,541		108,139		111,054		+19,513
Chesterfield County	D	49,346	36.88	74,310	45.84	77,694	45.43	+8.55
	R	83,745	62.58	86,413	53.31	90,934	53.18	-9.40
	Total	133,418		162,390		172,227		+29,809
University towns								
Charlottesville	D	11,088	71.77	15,705	78.35	16,510	75.74	+3.93
	R	4,172	27.00	4,078	20.34	4,844	22.22	-4.78
	Total	15,450		20,122		21,902		+6,452
Harrisonburg	D	4,726	42.85	8,444	57.54	8,654	55.49	+14.64
	R	6,165	55.89	6,048	41.21	6,565	42.10	-13.79
	Total	11,030		14,847		15,721		+4,691
Williamsburg	D	2,216	51.30	4,328	63.76	4,903	63.28	+11.98
	R	2,064	47.78	2,353	34.66	2,682	34.61	-13.17
	Total	4,320		6,838		7,770		3,450

Source: Virginia State Board of Elections.

suffered even more erosion of support in 2012. In a string of counties, the Democratic vote dropped 10 to 25 points compared with John Kerry's showing in 2004. Without any particular regional appeal to explain his performance, Kerry's vote appeared to be a good indicator of the base Democratic vote. The drop reflected in Table 13.4 provides strong evidence of wholesale desertion of the Democrats in these areas. The fact that Obama's vote eroded further in these counties raises the question of whether future Democrats can run competitively there.

Ultimately, Democrats do not need to depend on regaining support in these areas if they maintain or increase their performance in the rest of the state. While Obama's support dropped precipitously in the rural, racially homogenous counties, Obama's performance in 2012 far outstripped Kerry's vote in fast-growing exurbs like Loudoun and Prince William Counties, two of the largest jurisdictions in the state. The president's margins in these two counties alone offset the vote loss he experienced in the Ninth Congressional District versus Kerry's vote. Inner suburbs like Fairfax and Henrico Counties and the City of Virginia Beach saw the Democratic to Republican vote shift from a Republican margin of approximately 10,000 votes to a Democratic advantage of around 123,000 votes.

Democratic margins in central cities like Alexandria, Richmond, Portsmouth, and Hampton produced significant increases in turnout and party performance. College towns were mobilized behind Obama in both elections, as cities like Charlottesville, Fredericksburg, Harrisonburg, and Williamsburg all produced massive turnout increases and mostly Democratic landslides. Despite the concern among some Republicans that former Fifth District congressman Virgil Goode might draw votes from the GOP as the Constitution Party candidate, Goode proved to be a nonfactor, drawing only one-third of one percent in his home state.

In the current era of party polarization, the shifting dynamics of partisanship carry beyond the presidential vote. Kaine replicated Obama's pattern of victory, though he was able to improve on Obama's vote in many communities. The congressional races produced a closer reflection of the underlying party dynamics. Few congressional races deviated by more than a few points from the presidential performance within the district. As a result, contests in the First, Second, Fourth, Fifth, Seventh, and Tenth Districts all fell within a 60-to-40-point range. As expected, the Second District was the closest of the eleven races, with Republican Scott Rigell scoring a 5-point win over businessman Paul Hirschbiel. The challenger, who emphasized his close ties to popular U.S. senator Mark

Table 13.4. Virginia Federal Election Results, 2012

	Candidates	Vote	%
President	Barack Obama (D)*	1,971,820	51.15
	Mitt Romney (R)	1,822,522	47.28
U.S. Senate	Tim Kaine (D)	2,010,067	52.86
	George Allen (R)	1,785,542	46.96
U.S. House			
First District	Adam Cook (D)	147,036	41.20
	Robert Wittman (R)*	200,845	56.28
Second District	Paul Hirschbiel (D)	142,548	46.09
	Scott Rigell (R)*	166,231	53.75
Third District	Robert Scott (D)*	259,199	81.26
	Dean Longo (R)	58,931	18.47
Fourth District	Ella Ward (D)	150,190	42.90
	Randy Forbes (R)*	199,292	56.93
Fifth District	John Douglass (D)	149,214	42.86
	Robert Hurt (R)*	193,009	55.44
Sixth District	Andy Schmookler (D)	111,949	34.56
	Robert Goodlatte (R)*	211,278	65.23
Seventh District	Wayne Powell (D)	158,012	41.37
	Eric Cantor (R)*	222,983	58.38
Eighth District	James Moran (D)*	226,847	64.59
	Patrick Murray (R)	107,370	30.57
Ninth District	Anthony Flaccavento (D)	116,400	38.58
	Morgan Griffith (R)*	184,882	61.28
Tenth District	Kristin Cabral (D)	142,024	38.75
	Frank Wolf (R)*	214,038	58.40
Eleventh District	Gerald Connolly (D)*	202,606	60.98
	Chris Perkins (R)	117,902	35.48

Source: Virginia State Board of Elections.
Note: Numbers do not add to 100%, since minor candidates, none of whom received more than 3%, are not listed.
*incumbent

Warner and attacked Rigell's votes for the "Ryan Budget," lagged behind Obama's narrow victory in the district.

Retired general John Douglas did not have the benefit of a Democratic presidential win in the Fifth District and fell to Republican Robert

Hurt. Perhaps the most surprising outcome was a closer-than-expected win for six-term congressman Randy Forbes over former Chesapeake city council member Ella Ward. Forbes had not had a serious challenge in a number of years, but with a surge of African American voters, Obama carried the district narrowly, and Ward, an African American, came within 8 points despite being outspent $1,077,444 to $77,992.[25]

One other race was notable, if not particularly close. In the Seventh District, House Majority Leader Eric Cantor faced an aggressive challenger. Democrat Wayne Powell pursued a highly critical and partisan line of attack on Cantor, forcing the second-ranking House Republican to advertise on television and agree to debate. In the end, Cantor won by more than 16 points, but Powell's challenge required a national leader to focus more attention than usual to his home district.

Exit Poll Results

One of the central questions surrounding the election was the composition of the electorate. Whether Obama would be able to reassemble the coalition of voters he drew to the polls in 2008 and whether these groups would show up in such large numbers were viewed as central to the outcome. Romney's campaign built its projections on the expectation that minorities and young people were less enthused about the realities of the Obama administration than they had been about the promises of hope and change in his first election.

Exit poll data presented in Table 13.5 suggest that Obama met his targets, as whites comprised the same 70 percent of the voters that they had in 2008, though down from 72 percent in 2004. Blacks and Hispanics were 25 percent, while Asian Americans, identified for the first time, were at 3 percent. Though Obama's share of the white vote dropped slightly, his improvements among minority voters remained. Voters under forty-five were slightly less represented in 2012 but more strongly in favor of Obama, whereas those over forty-five backed Romney by a smaller edge.

Women were a substantial 53 percent majority of the electorate, and they favored Obama by 9 points, while the less numerous men backed Romney by a smaller 4 percent margin. While married Virginians constituted more than three out of five voters, their unmarried fellow voters gave the Democrat a 24-point margin, more than double the GOP edge among the married.

Those with postbaccalaureate education preferred the president's reelection. The most highly educated shifted from a 5-point Democratic

Table 13.5. Virginia Presidential Election Exit Poll Results, 2004–2012

	2012 Dem/Rep (% of vote)	2008 Dem/Rep (% of vote)	2004 Dem/Rep (% of vote)
Gender			
Male	47/51 (47)	51/47 (46)	40/59 (46)
Female	54/45 (53)	53/46 (54)	50/50 (54)
Race			
White	37/61 (70)	39/60 (70)	32/68 (72)
Black	93/6 (20)	92/8 (20)	87/12 (21)
Hispanic	64/33 (5)	65/34 (5)	—
Asian American	66/32 (3)	—	—
Age			
18–29	61/36 (19)	60/39 (21)	54/46 (17)
30–44	54/45 (27)	51/47 (30)	40/59 (32)
45–64	46/53 (41)	51/48 (38)	45/55 (32)
65 and over	46/54 (14)	46/54 (11)	51/49 (19)
Education			
No college	49/50 (46)	54/45 (48)	—
Some college	47/51 (25)	53/46 (28)	—
College graduate	48/50 (30)	50/49 (29)	—
Postgraduate	57/42 (24)	52/47 (23)	—
Income			
< $30,000	61/38 (18)	69/30 (—)	58/42 (16)
$30–49,999	60/38 (18)	55/45 (16)	47/52 (21)
$50–100,000	47/52 (65)	49/50 (70)	43/57 (61)
> $100,000	47/51 (34)	—	—
Ideology			
Conservative	11/87 (31)	18/80 (33)	15/85 (38)
Moderate	56/42 (45)	58/41 (46)	57/42 (45)
Liberal	92/7 (24)	90/9 (21)	83/17 (17)
Married			
Yes	44/55 (62)	—	—
No	61/37 (38)	—	—
Party Identification			
Democratic	94/6 (39)	92/8 (39)	92/8 (35)
Republican	5/94 (32)	8/92 (33)	5/95 (39)
Independent	43/54 (29)	49/48 (27)	44/54 (26)

Source: New York Times, "President Exit Polls," http://elections.nytimes.com/2012/results/president/exit-polls.

margin in 2008 to a 15-point margin in 2012. Obama narrowly lost among all other groups classified by level of education, including those with no college education, a group he had carried by 9 points previously. While Romney won those earning more than $50,000, Democrats prevailed much more convincingly among those below $50,000.

Finally, partisanship and ideology had shown some interesting shifts over the past eight years. Both Democrats and Republicans demonstrated consistently high levels of party loyalty, while independents divided more closely. These nonparty voters shifted a bit from Obama in 2012, but the most important change was the growth in Democratic and the decline in Republican identifiers. While the latter comprised 39 percent of the 2004 total, that number had dropped to 32 percent in 2012. Democrats grew, however, from 35 to 39 percent of the electorate.

Similarly, conservatives had held a 21-point advantage over liberals in the 2004 contest but had only a 7-point edge in 2012. Both of these groups intensified the support of their preferred party nominees, and moderates remained the largest segment of voters and gave Democrats a clear edge, as they did throughout the period.

In the end, exit polls demonstrated Obama's ability to reconstruct the basic composition of voters that delivered him success in 2008. Though he suffered some defections among various groups, he made up enough ground among others to attain a reduced but clear margin in his reelection contest.

Virginia's Future in Presidential and Other Elections

The dynamics of the Virginia electorate suggest it is likely that Democrats will be in a competitive position in future races, as the Commonwealth has moved toward greater identification with Democrats. The increasing share of voters who identify as moderates and liberals, their demographic characteristics, and their less-positive view of the Republican Party have caused the Commonwealth to take on a much bluer tinge in presidential election years.

Still to be answered are questions of voter turnout across elections, the impact of Barack Obama's candidacy as a force in motivating supporters and opponents, and the reaction of the Republican Party to consecutive losses in the national contest.

For the moment, Democrats appear to have the edge in being able to identify and mobilize their supporters, and they will undoubtedly try to maintain their advantage. Past experience suggests that the influx of young and minority voters and their overwhelming Democratic affiliation will have an impact for decades. If their levels of participation remain high and the state's demography continues to diversify, Virginia could move more solidly toward the Democrats, in the style of Maryland. The difficulty Democrats had in the years between presidential elections suggests, however, that the higher turnout and Democratic affiliation was driven by President Obama, and thus, the chances of repeat success may be more limited.

The results of the presidential election had barely been certified before Virginia's 2013 gubernatorial election kicked into gear. Democrats and Republicans settled on their nominees before the year came to an end. For the Democrats, after a brief flirtation with a second term in Richmond, U.S. senator Mark Warner opted out of the race, followed by former congressman Tom Perriello, a favorite of activist bloggers. That left former DNC chair Terry McAuliffe, an unsuccessful 2009 candidate, uncontested. McAuliffe signaled that he would run a well-funded, organizationally muscular effort, positioning himself as a businessman–problem solver in the Warner mold. His strategy depended on use of the rich trove of voter information collected by the Obama campaign to generate turnout among young, female, and minority voters, who usually skip the governor's race.

Republicans made clear that they were prepared to make the election an ideological contest with Attorney General Kenneth Cuccinelli as their standard-bearer. Cuccinelli pushed aside the establishment favorite, Lt. Governor William Bolling, by getting the Republican Party of Virginia State Central Committee to adopt a convention nominating process rather than a primary. The convention was sure to be dominated by more ideologically conservative activists, and Bolling withdrew from the nomination contest before the election year began.

On November 5, Virginians narrowly elected McAuliffe and his fellow Democrats to all three statewide offices (though the attorney general's race required a recount). Unlike the previous governor's election, where Democratic turnout was weak, the 2013 electorate nearly matched the 2012 vote in the overall composition of the electorate, though not its total size. African Americans comprised the same 20 percent of voters in both 2012 and 20013, for instance. Both McAuliffe and Cuccinelli performed very well in their bases of support, but McAuliffe had the advantage of a growing portion of the electorate. The outcome offered cheer to Democrats hoping to see their momentum continuing.

Conclusion

Toward Two-Party Competition in the South?

H. Gibbs Knotts

The political realignment of the American South from a solidly Democratic to a reliably Republican region is one of the biggest political transformations in American history. Unlike previous realignments that occurred in a single critical election, this profound change took place over a series of contests, beginning with support for Dwight Eisenhower at the presidential level and then trickling down to federal, state, and local offices in the subsequent decades.[1]

The 2012 elections provide further confirmation of how thoroughly the Republican Party dominates the region's politics. Republican presidential nominee Mitt Romney won nine of the eleven southern states, most by well over 10 percent.[2] Moreover, Republicans hold 99 of 138 U.S. House seats and 18 of 22 U.S. Senate seats. In percentage terms, Republicans make up 72 percent of the region's U.S. House delegation and 82 percent of the U.S. Senate seats.

Republicans also fared well in state-level elections. Following the 2012 contest, the GOP held ten of eleven of the South's governorships. Arkansas governor Mike Beebe is now the lone Democrat leading a southern state. Republicans also control the region's state legislatures, with majorities in ten of eleven southern states.[3] The only reprieve from Republican state legislative dominance is in Virginia. Though Republicans control the Virginia House of Delegates the state's senate is split evenly, with twenty Republicans and twenty Democrats.

While the 2012 results solidified the Republican monopoly in the region, there remain some positive signs for Democrats. Though North Carolina moved back to the Republican column at the presidential level, Democrat Barack Obama once again won closely fought contests in Florida and Virginia.

Of course, Democrats have won in southern states over the past few decades, but the victories in 2008 and 2012 were different. First, Democrats won in the region without having a southerner as the party's nominee. Between 1972 and 2004, the only Democratic wins in the South occurred when a southern governor was atop the ticket. With Georgia governor Jimmy Carter on the ballot in 1976, Democrats won in every state except Virginia. Of course, Democrats had less success in 1980, with Georgia as the sole southern state in the Democratic column. In 1976, Carter benefited from his southern roots and the nation's anti-Republican sentiment following the Watergate scandal. Another southerner, Arkansas governor Bill Clinton, won four states in his successful 1992 campaign—Arkansas, Georgia, Louisiana, and Tennessee. During his reelection bid, he again won in Arkansas, Louisiana, and Tennessee but also added Florida to the Democratic column. Clinton capitalized on his folksy persona, and his victories had a friends-and-neighbors feel, with wins in his home state of Arkansas and the bordering states of Louisiana and Tennessee.[4]

Obama's breakthrough in the South represented the first time since 1972 that a nonsouthern Democrat won in the region. Perhaps most important, the Obama victories occurred in a mix of states with different demographic profiles than the states where Clinton was successful in 1992 and 1996. Though Clinton and Obama both won in Florida, Obama was able to add North Carolina and Virginia to his winning coalition—two of the most prosperous and fastest-growing states in the region.

This concluding chapter takes a broader view of the 2012 contest, with an eye toward the future. Does the competitiveness in Florida, North Carolina, and Virginia represent an emerging trend in southern presidential politics? If so, which southern states hold the best prospects for genuine two-party competition in future presidential elections? The chapter begins with a closer look at the role of race in the 2012 contest before shifting attention to the political consequences of two key demographic trends in the South—increasing urbanization and rapid population growth in several states.

Race and Presidential Politics

The reelection of the nation's first African American president was certainly a historic occurrence, and the fact that he won two states in the American South demonstrates just how much the region has changed since the Jim Crow era. A closer look at the exit polls highlights, however, the level of racially polarized voting in the nation and the region.[5] Nationally, just 39 percent of whites cast ballots for Obama, down from 43 percent in 2008. In the region's three battleground states, there was slightly less support for Obama among the white electorate. In Florida and Virginia, 37 percent of whites supported Obama. These numbers were down from 2008, when 42 percent of whites in Florida and 39 percent of whites in Virginia supported the Democratic nominee. Obama had even less white support in North Carolina, winning just 31 percent, down from 35 percent in 2008. Obama's performance among white voters was even worse in the Deep South. According to exit poll results, Obama won just 15 percent of the white vote in Alabama and a paltry 10 percent of the white vote in neighboring Mississippi.

Among nonwhite voters, Obama once again performed exceptionally well. Nationally, he won 93 percent of blacks, a slight decrease from 2008, and 71 percent of the Hispanic vote, up from 67 percent in 2008. His support among Hispanic voters is particularly important given the projections for a rapid increase in the Hispanic population. According to one study, Hispanics will make up 23 percent of the U.S. population by 2030 and just over 30 percent by 2050.[6]

While race has had a clear effect on individual voting patterns, racial context has also structured southern politics. According to V. O. Key, "The hard core of the political South—and the backbone of southern political unity—is made up of those counties and sections of the southern states in which Negroes constitute a substantial proportion of the population."[7] The 2008 and 2012 contests provided the first occasion to vote for an African American as one of the two major-party presidential nominees and is a good place to explore the role of racial context in electoral outcomes in the southern states.

Figure C.1 plots the state's percent-black population based on figures from the 2010 U.S. Census and the percent of the vote for Obama in 2012. At first glance, the states appear quite scattered, with no discernible pattern. In fact, the incumbent president had some of his lowest support both in states with relatively low black percentages (particularly Arkansas and Tennessee) and among states with the highest black

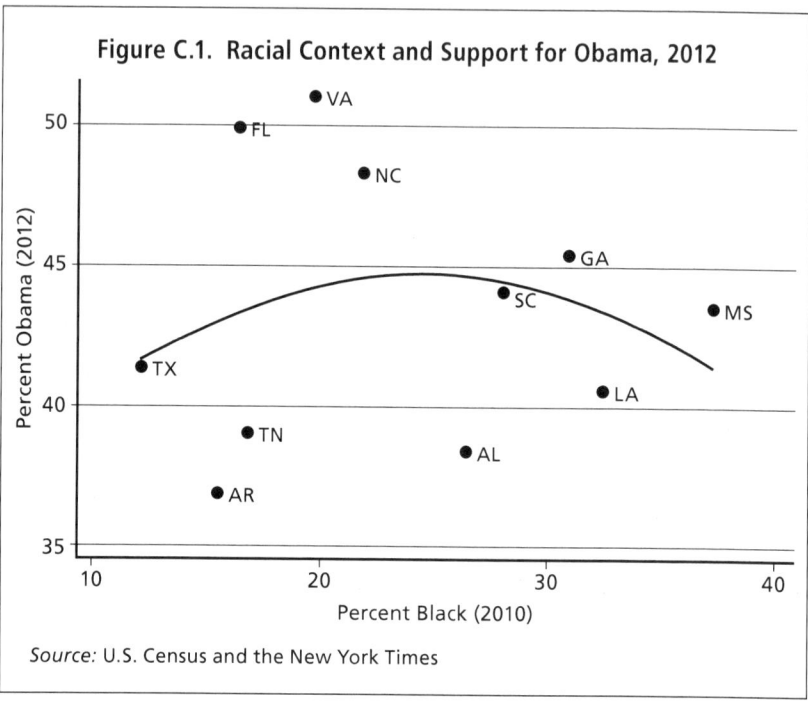

Figure C.1. Racial Context and Support for Obama, 2012

Source: U.S. Census and the New York Times

percentages (such as Alabama and Louisiana). The line of best fit helps uncover a nonlinear pattern, suggesting that there may be an optimal racial context for Democratic presidential prospects. Perhaps, states with too few African Americans in the electorate lack the base of support so important for Democratic success. But it may be the case that in states with the highest percentages of African Americans, Key's notion of racial threat may still play a role in explaining electoral outcomes. Of course, the results in Figure C.1 represent a simple display of what are undoubtedly much more complex dynamics and suggest that more work needs to be done to investigate the effects of racial context on voting behavior in the South.

Urbanization and Presidential Politics

Considerable postelection analyses also focused on the growing urban-rural divide in the American electorate. According to exit polls, 62 percent of voters in cities over 50,000 supported Obama, compared with just 32 percent for Romney. Support was nearly split in the suburbs, with Obama winning 48 percent and Romney garnering 50 percent. Among small-city and rural voters, Romney dominated, winning 59 percent from this group, compared with just 39 percent for Obama. The national voting patterns were similar to voting in the South's three battleground states, though Obama did better among small-city and rural voters in Virginia than he did nationally, winning 45 percent among this group in the Old Dominion.

These results are particularly troubling for Republicans. First, voters in small cities and rural areas, where Romney did the best, make up the smallest proportion of the electorate. According to the exit poll results, 21 percent of the total electorate lived in small cities and rural areas; 47 percent lived in suburbs; and 32 percent lived in cities over 50,000.

Perhaps most important, an increasing number of people live in urban areas. Figure C.2 shows the percent of the population in urban areas over the past sixty years in the South and the non-South. As the figure demonstrates, the South was much less urbanized than the non-South in 1950—less than 50 percent of southerners lived in urban areas compared with nearly 70 percent of people living outside the South. The South experienced rapid urbanization in the 1950s and 1960s and then underwent steady growth in subsequent decades. The rate of urbanization in the non-South also increased, though much less rapidly, with more than 80 percent of the non-South population currently living in urban areas. Figure C.2 also shows the decreasing gap between the level of urbanization in the South and the non-South over the past sixty years. On this important demographic measure, the region is becoming much more like the rest of the United States.

What are the reasons for the urban-rural divide in American politics? A potential explanation is that Republican policies resonate better in rural areas. This is part of the argument made by Thomas Frank in his *New York Times* bestseller *What's the Matter with Kansas: How Conservatives Won the Heart of America*. In this book he argues that the Republicans gained power in rural America by focusing on moral and cultural issues, shifting attention away from economic concerns.[8] Though there is little to dispute the success of Republicans with rural voters, Frank's thesis has been challenged on a number of fronts, including an empirical demonstration of an individualistic ethic in rural America defined by higher levels of self-employment and property ownership.[9]

Another possible explanation for the urban-rural divide is that the

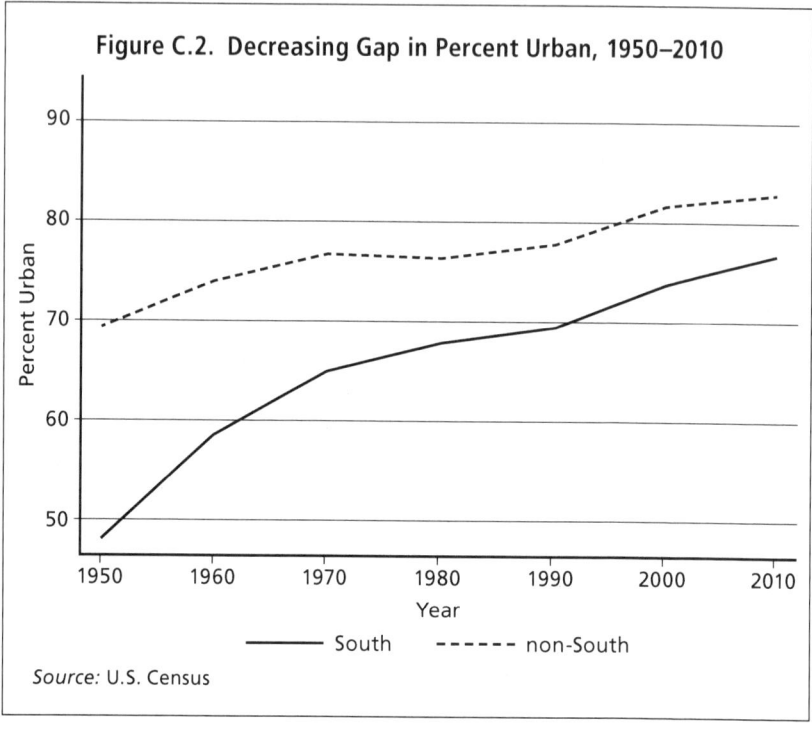

Figure C.2. Decreasing Gap in Percent Urban, 1950–2010
Source: U.S. Census

Democratic Party's message has a greater appeal in urban America. As Princeton University historian Kevin Kruse told the *New Republic*, "There are certain things in which the physical nature of a city, the fact that people are piled on top of each other, requires some notion of the public good."[10] Urban dwellers may be particularly interested in a more active government with support for public transportation, social welfare programs, and recreation facilities.

In the American South there has long been a belief that urbanization would play an important role in the region's political transformation. In his final chapter of *Southern Politics in State and Nation*, Key wrote that "the growth of cities contains the seeds of political change for the South."[11] Likewise, in *Politics and Society in the South*, Earl Black and Merle Black argued that urbanization would dilute but not eliminate traditionalistic political culture, increase state and federal spending to spur growth in cities, increase political choice for gubernatorial and legislative races, and modernize political campaigning.[12]

To explore the relationship between urbanization and electoral outcomes, Figure C.3 plots each state's percent-urban population in 2010 by its vote percentage for Obama in 2012. It is evident that there is considerable variation in the level of urbanization among the eleven states of the Old Confederacy. The South's most urban states are Florida, with 91 percent of the population living in urban areas, and Texas, with 85 percent urban. The least urban states are Alabama, Arkansas, and Mississippi, with 59 percent, 56 percent, and 49 percent, respectively.

As the trend line indicates, Figure C.3 displays a positive correlation between a state's percent urban and support for Obama. In general, states with higher percent-urban populations had higher percentages of voters supporting Obama. Texas is an obvious outlier, with a high urban population and relatively low support for Obama. The state has, however, a particularly unique brand of politics and anti-Washington sentiment, and it is important to remember that "part of the legacy of the Texas frontier ethic has been the state's basic conservatism."[13] Virginia and North Carolina also appear a considerable distance from the fit line.

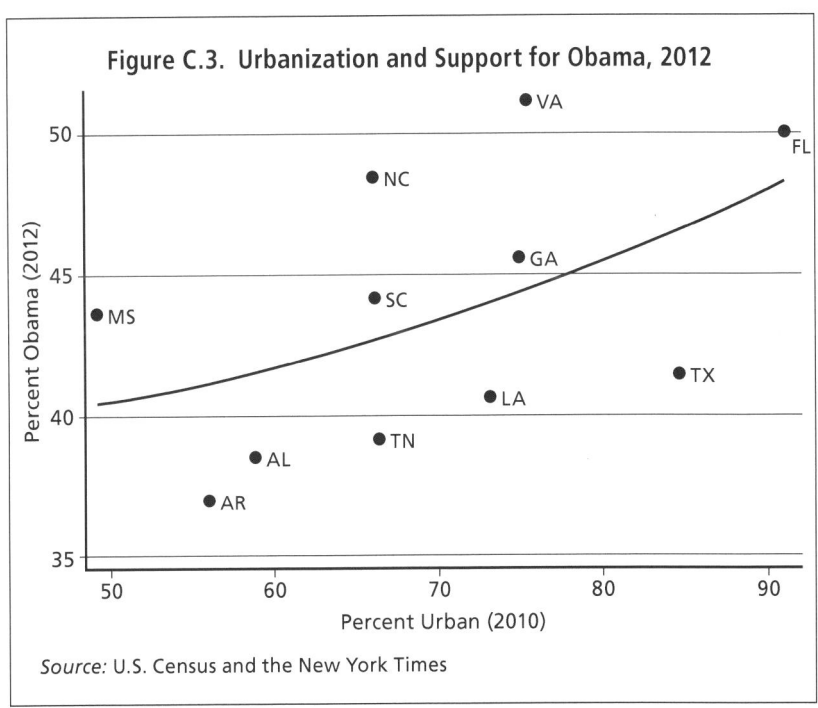

Figure C.3. Urbanization and Support for Obama, 2012

Source: U.S. Census and the New York Times

It is likely that the well-organized voter mobilization efforts in these states, particularly by the Obama campaign, affected the final results. As mentioned earlier, exit polls indicate that Obama also did disproportionately well with rural and small-city voters in Virginia.

Population Growth and Presidential Politics

Population growth is another important demographic change in the American South. Nationally, the population increased by 9.7 percent between 2000 and 2010, down from an increase of 13.2 percent the previous decade.[14] The South, with a 15.5 percent increase between 2000 and 2010, grew, however, at a higher rate than any other region.[15] As a result of the 2010 census and the subsequent reapportionment, four southern states gained additional seats in the U.S. House—South Carolina and Georgia gained one seat; Florida increased by two seats; and the Texas delegation added four seats (the highest increase of any state).[16]

Beyond increased representation in the U.S. Congress, population growth has other critical implications for the region's politics. Writing in the early 1960s, Philip Converse argued for the importance of interregional migration in the transformation of southern politics and wrote, "For the first time the South is not only losing Democrats, but is receiving a significant nonsouthern population more Republican than the native South."[17] Likewise, Black and Black highlighted the continued out-migration of the region's black population and argued that the combination of urbanization and in-migration of northerners was important to the creation of southern Republicanism, particularly in the Peripheral South.[18]

While most scholars have argued that Republicans generally benefit from population changes, some recent evidence may indicate that the current influx of new residents to the South is different. One of the most obvious reasons that the recent in-migration will benefit the Democratic Party is the influx of African Americans moving back to the region. This pattern started in the late 1990s and has been described as the "New Great Migration" by William Frey, the Brookings Institution's chief demographer.[19] Reports also indicate that the new migration consists of "younger and more educated black residents moving out of declining cities in the Northeast and Midwest in search of better opportunities."[20] Fortunately for Democrats, these newcomers are just the types of people likely to vote and participate in the political system.

In addition to the return of African Americans, many new migrants have settled in high-tech corridors like the Research Triangle Park in North Carolina.[21] In fact, one study found that that the in-migration in North Carolina helped Obama win the 2008 election in that state and discovered that the state's newcomers were less ideologically conservative and more likely to register as unaffiliated and to self-identify as independent than were the state's natives.[22]

To take a closer look at these dynamics, Figure C.4 compares the percent population change in southern states, measured by the percent change between 1980 and 2010, to the percent for Obama in 2012. First, it is important to note the substantial differences in population change among the states in the region. Texas, Georgia, and Florida had the greatest population increases, growing at 94.1 percent, 78 percent, and 77.6 percent, respectively. Contrast this breakneck growth with Louisiana (8.4 percent), Mississippi (18.2 percent), and Alabama (23.4 percent), states that grew much less over the same thirty-year period.

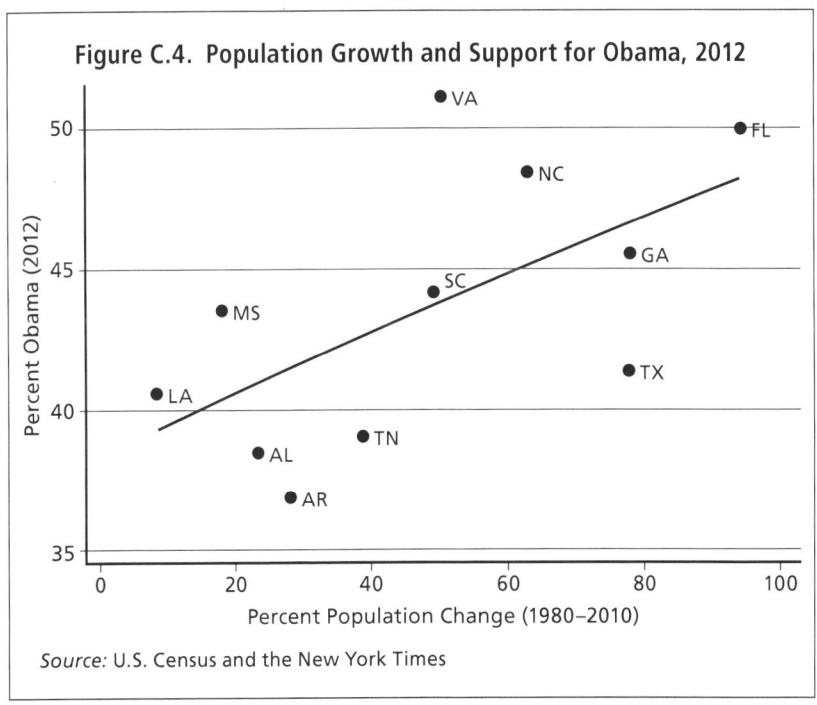

Figure C.4. Population Growth and Support for Obama, 2012

Source: U.S. Census and the New York Times

Figure C.4 demonstrates a positive correlation between percent population change and percent for Obama. States that are growing at higher rates typically had good support for Obama, and states that are growing at lower rates typically had less support for Obama. Again, Texas is an outlier, with much less support for Obama than other high-growth southern states. The state of Virginia is also a good distance from the fit line. While growth during this time period in Virginia was just over 50 percent, the fifth fastest-growing state in the region, support for Obama in this state was the highest in the region.

Looking Forward

Although Republicans dominate modern southern politics, there are signs of hope for Democrats. For the first time since 1968, southern states supported a nonsouthern Democrat for president in both 2008 and again in 2012. Perhaps more important, demographic trends in several states suggest that two-party competition has the potential to accelerate in the region.

To help determine states with increased chances of two-party competition, Figure C.5 plots the percent change in population between 1980 and 2010 by the percent urban in 2010. For presentation purposes, Figure C.5 is subdivided with a vertical line at 50 percent population growth to indicate a high and low category and a horizontal line at 70 percent urban also to show a high and low category.

Not surprisingly, Florida and Virginia appear in the upper-right quadrant, indicating a demographic context favorable for two-party competition. Two states that were less competitive in 2008 and 2012, Texas and Georgia, also appear in the upper-right quadrant. This analysis suggests that future Democratic nominees might consider competing for votes in these states, particularly if the Republican nominee adopts a far-right social platform that would be likely less popular in these urbanized/high-growth states. In addition, the nonwhite population in both Texas and Georgia has grown considerably, making these states possible targets for the Democratic Party.[23] North Carolina will likely remain a battleground state, and it will be interesting to see if Tennessee and perhaps even South Carolina will become more competitive for Democrats in future elections. The prospects for national-level Democrats look much dimmer in Mississippi, Alabama, and Arkansas, states located well within the bottom-left quadrant of Figure C.5.

In *The New Southern Politics*, David Woodard classifies southern

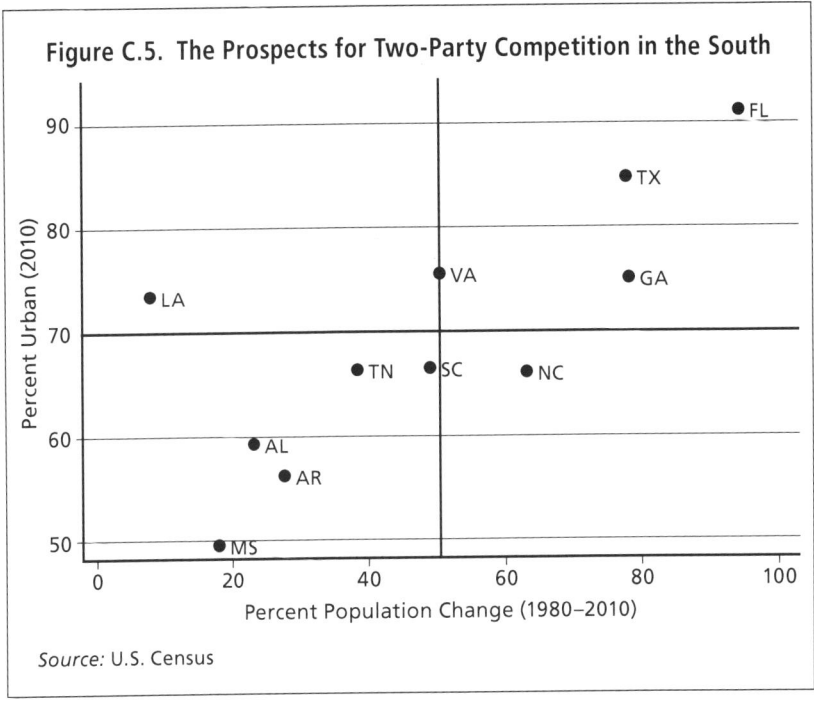

Figure C.5. The Prospects for Two-Party Competition in the South

Source: U.S. Census

states into three broad categories "based on an analysis of their economic and social standing."[24] According to Woodard, Texas, Florida, Georgia, and Virginia are "national states"; North Carolina and Tennessee are "emergent states"; and South Carolina, Alabama, Arkansas, Louisiana, and Mississippi are "traditional states."[25] Later in his book, Woodard compares the overall level of party competition in each of the states and finds that the greatest levels of Republicanism appear in the four national states and in South Carolina.

While these categories and labels may still be useful, a very different political environment has emerged during the past decade. Focusing specifically on the two most recent presidential elections, Woodard's national states hold the greatest hope for genuine two-party competition in presidential contests. Emergent states have some Democratic promise, and it is much less likely that Democratic presidential nominees will be competitive in the most traditional southern states.

As a final indicator of the Democratic Party's potential in the region, it is worthwhile to remember the highly sophisticated, data-driven, and targeted campaign employed by the Obama team. During his successful reelection bid, Obama won in two of the three southern states where he truly competed. He spent very little money outside Florida, North Carolina, and Virginia, and these states were the only southern states with more than ten Obama campaign field offices.[26] If future Democratic nominees build on the Obama team's successes in these states and make targeted efforts in southern states like Georgia, Texas, and perhaps even Tennessee, the prospects for genuine two-party competition will certainly be enhanced.

Notes

Introduction

1. John C. Green, James Guth, and Lyman Kellstedt, "The Soul of the South: Religion and Southern Politics in the New Millennium," in *The New Politics of the Old South*, 3rd ed., ed. Charles Bullock III and Mark Rozell (Lanham, MD: Rowman and Littlefield, 2007), 301–20; Alan I. Abramowitz and H. Gibbs Knotts, "Ideological Realignment in the U.S. Electorate: A Comparison of Northern and Southern White Voters in the Pre-Reagan, Reagan, and Post-Reagan Eras" (paper, Citadel Symposium on Southern Politics, March 2004); Tom W. Rice, William P. McLean, and Amy J. Larsen, "Southern Distinctiveness over Time, 1972–2000," *American Review of Politics* 23 (2002): 193–220.

2. Robert P. Steed and Laurence W. Moreland, "The Importance of the South in Presidential Politics," in *Presidential Elections in the South: Putting 2008 in Political Context*, ed. Branwell DuBose Kapeluck, Robert P. Steed, and Laurence W. Moreland (Boulder, CO: Lynne Rienner Publishers, 2009).

3. Scott E. Buchanan, "The Realignment of 1964?," *Politics and Policy* 30 (2002): 140–58; Scott E. Buchanan, "The Dixiecrat Rebellion: Long-term Partisan Implications in the Deep South," *Politics and Policy* 33 (2005): 754–69.

4. V. O. Key, *Southern Politics in State and Nation* (New York: Alfred A. Knopf, 1949).

5. Robert Field, "Obamacare vs. Romneycare: Is There a Difference?," Philly.com, September 26, 2012, http://www.philly.com/philly/blogs/fieldclinic/Obamacare-vs-Romneycare-Is-there-a-difference.html.

1.

1. All state and county electoral data for all election years referenced were obtained from *Dave Leip's Atlas of U.S. Presidential Elections*, uselectionatlas.org.

2. State-level partisan identification is determined from Gallup Daily tracking polls from January through June 2012. At least one thousand respondents were sampled across the six-month period in most states. Weighting to U.S. Census demographics is used. Data are available at Lydia Saad, "Heavily Democratic States Are Concentrated in the East: Three Western States Are the Most Republican," *Gallup Politics*, August 3, 2012, gallup.com/poll/156437/heavily-democratic-states-concentrated-east.aspx.

3. State-level ideology is based on Gallup Daily tracking polls from January through December of 2012. Methods for calculating point estimates are the same as for party identification in note 2. Data are available at Frank Newport, "Alabama, North Dakota, Wyoming Most Conservative States:

Americans Slightly Less Conservative, Slightly More Liberal," *Gallup Politics,* February 1, 2013, http://www.gallup.com/poll/160196/alabama-north-dakota-wyoming-conservative-states.aspx#1.

4. Christopher Ellis and James A. Stimson, *Ideology in America* (New York: Cambridge University Press, 2012); James A. Stimson, *Tides of Consent: How Public Opinion Shapes American Politics* (New York: Cambridge University Press, 2004).

5. State-level presidential approval is determined from Gallup Daily tracking polls from January through June 2012. Methods for calculating point estimates are the same as for party identification in note 2. Data are available at Jeffrey M. Jones, "Thirteen States and D.C. Give Obama Majority Approval: Highest Ratings in Hawaii, Rhode Island; Lowest n Utah, Wyoming, Alaska," *Gallup Politics,* August 1, 2012, gallup.com/poll/156389/thirteen-states-give-obama-majority-approval.aspx.

6. State-level measures of the uninsured population for 2011 are based on the Gallup-Healthways Well-Being Index, which sampled at least one thousand residents per state. No data on uninsured rates are available from Gallup for 2012. Data are available at Jeffrey M. Jones, "Texas Widens Gap over Other States in Percentage Uninsured: No States Show Consistent Decline in Uninsured since 2008," *Gallup Politics,* March 2, 2012, gallup.com/poll/153053/Texas-Widens-Gap-States-Percentage-Uninsured.aspx.

7. State-level unemployment numbers are from the Bureau of Labor Statistics. Monthly seasonally adjusted data for October 2012 are available at Bureau of Labor Statistics, "Local Area Unemployment Statistics," bls.gov/web/laus/laumstrk.htm.

8. Jon Cohen and Scott Clement, "Networks, AP Cancel Exit Polls in 19 States," *The Fix* blog, *Washington Post,* October 4, 2012, washingtonpost.com/blogs/the-fix/wp/2012/10/04/networks-ap-cancel-exit-polls-in-19-states.

9. For a more thorough discussion of 2008 exit polls in the South, see Scott E. Buchanan, "The Continued Convergence of Demographics and Issues," in *A Paler Shade of Red: The 2008 Presidential Election in the South,* ed. Branwell DuBose Kapeluck, Laurence W. Moreland, and Robert P. Steed (Fayetteville: The University of Arkansas Press), 3–16. Exit poll data are available at "Election 2012: Results," *CNN Politics,* December 10, 2012, cnn.com/election/2012/results/main; "ElectionCenter 2008: Exit Polls," *CNN Politics,* cnn.com/ELECTION/2008/results/polls.main; "America Votes 2004: Election Results," CNN, cnn.com/ELECTION/2004/pages/results.

10. For example, see Earl Black and Merle Black, *Politics and Society in the South* (Cambridge, MA: Harvard University Press, 1987); Earl Black and Merle Black, *The Rise of Southern Republicans* (Cambridge: The Belknap Press of Harvard University Press, 2002); David Lublin, *The Republican South: Democratization and Partisan Change* (Princeton, NJ: Princeton University Press, 2004).

11. Paul R. Abramson, John H. Aldrich, and David W. Rohde, *Change and Continuity in the 2008 Elections* (Washington, DC: CQ Press, 2010).

12. For a discussion of speculation and reality in the youth vote, see Caroline May, "Youth Vote Turned Out in 2012, Despite Enthusiasm Con-

cerns," *Daily Caller,* November 7, 2012, dailycaller.com/2012/11/07/youth-vote-turned-out-in-2012-despite-enthusiasm-concerns.

13. For a discussion of white evangelical support of Romney, with links to Pew Forum data on presidential preferences among this group, see Joanna Brooks, "It's Official: White Evangelical Support for Romney Not Dampened by Mormon Factor," *Religion Dispatches,* December 10, 2012, religiondispatches.org/dispatches/joannabrooks/6678/it_s_official__white_evangelical_support_for_romney_not_dampened_by_mormon_factor.

14. See Black and Black, *The Rise of Southern Republicans.*

15. Jeffrey Passel, Gretchen Livingston, and D'Vera Cohn, "Explaining Why Minority Births Now Outnumber White Births," Pew Research Center, May 17, 2012, pewsocialtrends.org/2012/05/17/explaining-why-minority-births-now-outnumber-white-births.

16. For example, see Larry M. Bartels, "Beyond the Running Tally: Partisan Bias in Political Perceptions," *Political Behavior* 24 (June 2002): 117–50; Geoffrey Evans and Robert Anderson, "The Political Conditioning of Economic Perceptions," *Journal of Politics* 68 (February 2006): 194–207; Alan Gerber and Donald Green, "Misperceptions about Perceptual Bias," *Annual Review of Political Science* 2:189–210.

17. For a discussion of health care opinion with references to survey data, see Jeffrey De Pinto, "Public Opinion of the Health Care Law," CBS News, June 28, 2012, cbsnews.com/8301-250_162-57462689/public-opinion-of-the-health-care-law.

18. Richard Fausset, "Alabama Enacts Anti-Illegal-Immigration Law Described as Nation's Strictest," *Los Angeles Times,* June 10, 2011, articles.latimes.com/2011/jun/10/nation/la-na-alabama-immigration-20110610.

19. John Smith, "President Obama Supports Same Sex Marriage after Amendment 1 Passes in N.C.," Examiner.com, May 9, 2012, www.examiner.com/article/north-carolina-loses-rhythm-as-amendment-1-passes.

20. For example, see José María Mantero, *Latinos and the U.S. South* (Westport, CT: Praeger, 2008); Patrick R. Miller, "Rethinking Racial Threat: A Comparison of Latino Population Change in the North and South," *American Review of Politics* 32 (August 2011): 203–22; Raymond A. Mohl, "Globalization: Latinization, and the Neuvo New South," in *Globalization and the American South,* ed. James C. Cobb and William Stueck (Athens: University of Georgia Press, 2005), 66–99.

21. For a discussion, see Cristina Costantini, "The Problem with Polling Latinos," ABC News/Univision, September 25, 2012, abcnews.go.com/ABC_Univision/Politics/problem-polling-latinos/story?id=17318285#.UMe0-3d5FvI.

22. For a full description of the Latino Decisions methods and their survey data, see *2012 Latino Election Eve Poll,* www.latinovote2012.com/app/#all-national-presidential_vote.

23. For a history of issues surrounding SB 1070, see "A Brief History of SB 1070," *Fronteras,* http://www.fronterasdesk.org/sb1070.

24. For example, see Julia Preston, "Republicans Reconsider Positions on Immigration," *New York Times,* November 9, 2012, nytimes.com/2012/11/10/us/politics/republicans-reconsider-positions-on-immigration.html?_r=0.

25. Mark D. Brewer, *Party Images in the American Electorate* (New York:

Routledge, 2008); Tasha Philpot, *Race, Republicans, and the Return of the Party of Lincoln* (Ann Arbor: University of Michigan Press, 2007).
26. James H. Kuklinski, Michael D. Cobb, and Martin Gilens, "Racial Attitudes and the 'New South.'" *Journal of Politics* 59 (1997): 323–49; Tom W. Rice, William P. McLean, and Amy J. Larsen, "Southern Distinctiveness over Time: 1972–2000," *American Review of Politics* 23 (2002): 190–220; Tom W. Rice and Meredith L. Pepper, "Region, Migration, and Attitudes in the United States," *Social Science Quarterly* 78 (1997): 83–95; Nicholas Valentino and David Sears, "Old Times There Are Not Forgotten: Race and Partisan Realignment in the Contemporary South," *American Journal of Political Science* 49 (2005): 672–88.

2.

1. Clifford W. Brown Jr., Lynda W. Powell, and Clyde Wilcox, *Serious Money: Fundraising and Contributing in Presidential Nomination Campaigns* (New York: Cambridge University Press, 1995), 14–29; Barbara Norrander, *The Imperfect Primary: Oddities Biases and Strengths of U.S. Presidential Nomination Politics* (New York: Routledge, 2011), 36–40.

2. Campaign Finance Institute, "President Obama Is ahead of 2007 Pace, Romney Even: Corporations Supplied a Quarter of the Romney Super PAC Funds," February 2, 2012, http://www.cfinst.org/Press/PReleases/12-02-02/President_Obama_is_Ahead_of_2007_Pace_Romney_Even_Corporations_Supplied_a_Quarter_of_the_Romney_Super_PAC_Funds.aspx.

3. For example, see William G. Mayer and Andrew E. Busch, *The Frontloading Problem in Presidential Nominations* (Washington, DC: Brookings Institution Press, 2004).

4. Not all observers view the disproportionate attention paid to Iowa and New Hampshire to be problematic. See David P. Redlawsk, Caroline J. Tolbert, and Todd Donovan, *Why Iowa? How Caucuses and Sequential Elections Improve the Presidential Nominating Process* (Chicago: University of Chicago Press, 2011).

5. New Hampshire, South Carolina, and Florida lost half of their delegates for holding their primaries in January. Iowa's caucus system does not award delegates, so the rule did not apply. A comprehensive discussion of the 2012 nominating rules and calendar can be found at Josh Putnam's *Frontloading HQ* blog, http://frontloading.blogspot.com.

6. The Democratic Party had long prohibited winner-take-all delegate-allocation systems. Republicans in some states still use them.

7. Perry's "oops" moment took place at a debate on November 10, 2011, with seven other candidates at Oakland University in Michigan. His campaign, already on shaky ground, was never able to recover. He stayed in the race until after New Hampshire before suspending his campaign.

8. The remark was made at a postelection conference hosted by Harvard University's Institute of Politics. See Jonathan Martin, "GOP Scrambles to Fix Its Primary Problem," *Politico*, January 4, 2013, http://www.politico.com/story/2013/01/gop-scrambles-to-fix-its-primary-problem-85726.html.

9. Marty Cohen, David Karol, Hans Noel, and John Zaller, *The Party Decides: Presidential Nominations Before and After Reform* (Chicago: University of Chicago Press, 2008).
10. Redlawsk et al., *Why Iowa?*
11. Robert Behre, "25 GOP Delegates Will Miss the Convention," *Charleston Post and Courier*, August 6, 2012.
12. Felicia Somnez, "Sarah Palin: I'd Vote for Newt Gingrich in South Carolina," *Post Politics* blog, *Washington Post*, January 17, 2012, http://www.washingtonpost.com/blogs/post-politics/post/sarah-palin-id-vote-for-newt-gingrich-in-south-carolina/2012/01/17/gIQA7ZP26P_blog.html.
13. Robert Behre, "GOP Family Feud: Sparks Fly after Moderator's First Question in Rollicking 2-hour N. Charleston Debate," *Charleston Post and Courier*, January 20, 2012.
14. Ben Szobody and Tim Smith, "GOP Voters, in Record Turnout, Give Win to Gingrich," *Greenville News*, January 22, 2012; Schuyler Kropf and Robert Behre, "10 Things Primary Taught Us," *Charleston Post and Courier*, January 23, 2012.
15. Nicholas Confessore, "'Super PAC' for Gingrich to Get $5 Million Infusion," *New York Times*, January 23, 2012.
16. Alex Leary and Patty Ryan, "Mitt Romney Pads Advantage in Florida with Aggressive Early Voting Effort," *Tampa Bay Times*, January 31, 2012.
17. Adam C. Smith, "What We Learned from Fla's GOP Primary," *The Buzz* blog, *Tampa Bay Times*, January 31, 2012, http://www.tampabay.com/blogs/the-buzz-florida-politics/content/what-we-learned-flas-gop-primary-video.
18. For exit poll data, see "2012 Primaries and Caucuses Results," *CNN Politics*, July 26, 2012, http://www.cnn.com/election/2012/primaries.html.
19. Elizabeth Llorente, "Gingrich Campaign Pulls Anti-Romney Ad after Marco Rubio Blasts It," Fox News Latino, January 25, 2012, http://latino.foxnews.com/latino/politics/2012/01/25/gingrich-campaign-pulls-anti-romney-ad-after-marco-rubio-blasts-it.
20. Susan A. McManus with Andrew F. Quecan, David J. Bonanza, Christopher J. Leddy Jr., and Brian D. McPhee, "The Emerging Battleground South: Population Change and Changing Politics," in *Presidential Elections in the South: Putting 2008 in Political Context*, ed. Branwell DuBose Kapeluck, Robert P. Steed, and Laurence W. Moreland (Boulder, CO: Lynne Rienner), 99–136.
21. The question was not asked in the Florida exit poll.
22. Barbara Norrander, *Super Tuesday: Regional Politics and Presidential Primaries* (Lexington: University Press of Kentucky, 1992).
23. Cohen et al., *The Party Decides*.

3.

1. For the most extensive work on the top-down realignment, see Joseph Aistrup, *The Southern Strategy Revisited: Top-Down Republican Party Development in the South* (Lexington: University Press of Kentucky, 1996).
2. Shelly Haskins, "Parker Griffith Wins 5th Congressional District Seat,"

Huntsville Times, November 4, 2008, http://blog.al.com/breaking/2008/11/parker_griffith_wins_5th_congr.html.

3. Stephens, Challen, "Parker Griffith Party Switch Bit Issue in 5th Congressional District GOP Primary," *Huntsville Times,* May 25, 2010, http://blog.al.com/breaking/2010/05/post_309.html.

4. Challen Stephens, "Parker Griffith Concedes, Mo Brooks Is the GOP Nominee for Congress," *Huntsville Times,* June 1, 2010, http://blog.al.com/breaking/2010/06/parker_griffith_concedes_mo_br.html.

5. Challen Stephens and Lee Roop, "Mo Brooks Declares Victory in 5th District Congressional Race," *Huntsville Times,* November 2, 2010, http://blog.al.com/breaking/2010/11/mo_brooks_declares_victory_in.html.

6. For a general discussion of the effects of racial redistricting and partisan change, see John R. Petrocik and Scott Desposato, "The Partisan Consequences of Majority-Minority Redistricting in the South, 1992 and 1994," *Journal of Politics* 6 (August 1998): 613–33; see also Charles Cameron, David Epstein, and Sharyn O'Halloran, "Do Majority-Minority Districts Maximize Substantive Black Representation in Congress?," *American Political Science Review* 90 (December 1996): 794–812

7. Alabama chief justice Sue Bell Cobb retired from office during 2011, citing personal reasons. Public service commission president Lucy Baxley lost her reelection bid in 2012.

8. Aaron Blake, "As Super Tuesday Looms, Republican Primary Heads into Potentially Decisive Phase," *Washington Post,* February 21, 2012, http://www.washingtonpost.com/politics/as-super-tuesday-looms-republican-primary-heads-into-potentially-decisive-phase/2012/02/17/gIQALzmQRR_story.html.

9. Mary Orndorff, "New Alabama Poll Shows Close Three-Way Race for GOP Presidential Primary," *Birmingham News,* February 9, 2012, http://blog.al.com/sweethome/2012/02/new_alabama_poll_shows_close_t.html.

10. Charles J. Dean, "Gingrich, Santorum Work to Sway Voters at GOP Forum at Birmingham's Alabama Theatre," *Birmingham News,* March 12, 2012, http://blog.al.com/spotnews/2012/03/gingrich_santorum_work_to_sway.html.

11. Adam Nagourney, "A Party of Factions Gathers, Seeking Consensus," *New York Times,* August 27, 2012.

12. The Alabama State University Center for Leadership and Public Policy conducted a poll of likely GOP voters between January 23 and February 23, 2012. See *2012 Presidential Primary Survey,* http://www.alasu.edu/academics/research--centers/center-for-leadership-and-public-policy/surveys/index.aspx.

13. Key identified Alabama's regional voting patterns and tied them to a "friends and neighbors" pattern. For more on Alabama voting patterns, see V. O. Key, "Alabama: Populists, Planters, and Big Mules," in *Southern Politics in State and Nation* (New York: Random House, 1949).

14. Thomas Spencer, "Candidate Mitt Romney Blasts Obama, Raises $2 Million at Birmingham Fundraiser," *Birmingham News,* August 15, 2012.

15. Steve Doyle, "Alabama GOP Will Send 200 'Battleground Patriots' to Campaign for Romney in Ohio, Fla., N.C. and Va.," *Huntsville Times,* October 2, 2012.

16. Associated Press, "Artur Davis Finds Opposition Coming from Older Black Leadership," *Mobile Press-Register,* December 29, 2009.
17. George Talbot, "Alabama's Man without a Party," *Mobile Press-Register,* November 2, 2011.
18. Artur Davis, "A Response to Political Rumors," official Artur Davis blog, May 29, 2012, http://www.officialarturdavis.com/2012/05/a-response-to-political-rumors.
19. Mary Orndorff-Troyan, "Artur Davis to GOP: 'America Is a Land of Second Chances,'" *Birmingham News,* August 28, 2012.
20. Mary Orndorff-Troyan, "Artur Davis Named to Mitt Romney's Black Leadership Council," *Birmingham News,* September 5, 2012; George Talbot, "Artur Davis Backs Romney in New Campaign Ad," *Mobile Press-Register,* September 28, 2012.
21. Mary Orndorff-Troyan, "New Alabama Congressional Map Friendly to Incumbents," *Birmingham News,* September 7, 2012.
22. Kim Chandler, "Former Alabama Chief Justice Roy Moore Pulls Off Political Resurrection," *Birmingham News,* March 15, 2012.
23. Roy Moore was removed from office after defying a federal court order to remove a controversial monument of the Ten Commandments he had surreptitiously placed in the lobby of the state judicial building. Moore pledged not to return the monument or pursue the issue further if reelected. On election night at his campaign watch party, supporters placed miniature monuments on the tables. See Kim Chandler, "Roy Moore Wins Chief Justice Race," *Birmingham News,* November 6, 2012.
24. "Alabama Election Chief: No Crowds at Polls Sept. 18," Associated Press, September 7, 2012.
25. George Talbot, "The $437 Million Hustle," *Mobile-Press Register,* September 26, 2012.
26. The controversy over Amendment 111 and its relationship to school funding was salient in the state following a 2008 court case ruling that Alabama's property-tax system denied equal protection to black and low-income students under the Fourteenth Amendment, an example of structural and intentional racism. Judge Lynwood Smith ruled against the challenge, leaving the provisions in place. However, his rebuke of the document and Alabama's continued reluctance to deal with the political, economic, and social legacies were stinging. Among the AEA, the legislature, and other attentive elites, this issue was salient, and political maneuvering began. See Kim Chandler, "Black Lawmakers, AEA Urge Voters to Reject Amendment Taking Jim Crow Language out of Alabama Constitution," *Birmingham News,* October 19, 2012; see also "Alabama Faces Recount over Segregationist Laws," CNN, November 5, 2004, http://www.cnn.com/2004/ALLPOLITICS/11/04/alabama.segregation.
27. President Obama carried Conecuh (50.6 percent) and Bourbon (51.3 percent) Counties by slim margins. In 2008, these counties supported John McCain with 50.1 percent and 53.6 percent of the vote, respectively.
28. Secretary of State Beth Chapman had predicted turnout would be between 72 and 74 percent of registered voters. Turnout rates for 2008

were high at 73 percent. While 2012 levels were not record breaking or on pace with 2008's, they were still robust. See Ryan Vasquez, "Alabama Voting Slightly off 2008 Pace," Alabama Public Radio, http://apr.org/term/alabama-voter-turnout-2012.

29. "Older, Wealthier Alabamians Key to Romney Win, Exit Polls Show," Associated Press, November 6, 2012.

30. Regions of the state are composed of the following counties, as determined by the author: the Tennessee Valley includes the counties of Colbert, Jackson, Lauderdale, Lawrence, Limestone, Marshall, and Morgan; the hill country includes the counties of Autauga, Bibb, Blount, Calhoun, Chambers, Cherokee, Chilton, Clay, Cleburne, Coosa, Cullman, DeKalb, Elmore, Etowah, Fayette, Franklin, Lamar, Lee, Marion, Pickens, Randolph, St. Clair, Shelby, Talladega, Tallapoosa, Walker, and Winston; the Black Belt includes the counties of Barbour, Bullock, Butler, Choctaw, Dallas, Greene, Hale, Lowndes, Macon, Marengo, Perry, Pike, Russell, Sumter, and Wilcox; the Wiregrass includes the counties of Coffee, Conecuh, Covington, Crenshaw, Dale, Escambia, Geneva, Henry, and Houston; the coastal counties include Clarke, Baldwin, Monroe, and Washington; and the metropolitan counties include Jefferson, Madison, Mobile, Montgomery, and Tuscaloosa.

31. Romney support was 77 percent of voters in both Baldwin and Shelby Counties. Baldwin is adjacent to Mobile County, and Shelby County neighbors Birmingham. He surpassed 80 percent support in the north-central area of the state in Blount (87 percent), St. Clair (83 percent), and Cullman (84 percent) Counties.

32. "The Parker Griffith Switch: What Led Him to Join the GOP, and How It Affects District 5," *Huntsville Times,* January 25, 2010.

33. Of course, there were exceptions. Lawrence County, in the Tennessee Valley, went from 63.4 percent Republican to 62.9 percent. While still overwhelmingly supportive of the GOP, it was only slightly less so than in 2008. This was also the case in the northern counties of Lamar and Calhoun. In the southern half of the state, Republican vote share increased in only seven counties, but only two saw increases of more than 1 percent.

34. See Patrick R. Cotter, "Alabama: Electoral Continuity and Racial Voting," in *A Paler Shade of Red: The 2008 Presidential Elections in the South,* ed. Branwell DuBose Kapeluck, Laurence W. Moreland, and Robert P. Steed (Fayetteville: The University of Arkansas Press). Cotter explores these questions and forecasts Artur Davis's gubernatorial run as an expected test case. Although race may have played into Davis's run at the individual voter's level, ultimately his choice not to court leaders of the black establishment led to his early demise in the primary race.

35. Davis had been regarded as a test case to determine if a moderate black candidate could win office outside the Black Belt. Many considered his campaign a gauge for racial politics in the state. For a succinct representation of the combination of forces leading to Davis's downfall, see Elliot Cose, "Fallen Star," *Daily Beast,* June 3. 2010, http://www.thedailybeast.com/newsweek/2010/06/04/fallen-star.html.

36. Population estimates listed in Table 3.3 reflect updated 2010 census data.
37. Charles J. Dean, "After Election Day Beatdown, Are Days Numbered for Alabama Democrats?," *Birmingham News*, November 14, 2010, http://blog.al.com/spotnews/2010/11/days_may_be_numbered_for_alaba.html.
38. Six out of twelve—half—of Alabama's Democratic state senators ran unopposed in the 2010 legislative races. Each unopposed senate district is located in the state's Black Belt region. Of Alabama's Democratic state house representatives, 72 percent ran unopposed. Many of these unopposed house districts were generally split between the Black Belt region and areas of Birmingham and Montgomery with large African American populations.
39. J. D. Crowe, "Redistricting," *Mobile-Press Register,* May 24, 2012; George Altman, "Alabama Legislature Approves Redistricting Plans amid Cries of Racist Maneuvering," *Mobile-Press Register,* May 24, 2012.
40. Doyle, Doyle, "Alabama GOP Will Send 200 'Battleground Patriots.'"

4.

I thank Joel McElhannon for his help and suggestions.
1. Charles S. Bullock III, "Georgia: A Study of Party and Race," in *The New Politics of the Old South: Introduction to Southern Politics,* 4th ed., ed. Charles S. Bullock III and Mark J. Rozell (Lanham, MD: Rowman and Littlefield, 2010), 63.
2. Charles S. Bullock III and Ronald Keith Gaddie, *Georgia Politics in the State of Change,* 2nd ed. (New York: Pearson, 2013), 165.
3. Charles S. Bullock III and Ronald Keith Gaddie, *The Triumph of Voting Rights in the South* (Norman: University of Oklahoma Press, 2009), 103.
4. Because of problems, the exit poll results from 2002 have never been made public.
5. Charles S. Bullock III, "Barack Obama and the South," *American Review of Politics* 31 (Spring and Summer 2010): 13.
6. Charles S. Bullock III and Karen P. Owen, "Marshall vs. Scott in Georgia's Eighth Congressional District: The Power of Incumbency Fails," in *Cases and Congressional Elections: Riding the Wave,* ed. Randall E. Adkins and David A. Dulio (New York: Rutledge, 2012), 181–200.
7. Aaron Gould Sheinin, "Mayor Prods Obama to Fight to Win Georgia," *Atlanta Journal Constitution,* March 16, 2012.
8. For example, see David Wasserman, "Parallel Universes," *National Journal,* December 15, 2012, 16–20.
9. Some observers consider the new Georgia district the most Republican in the nation.
10. The 2012 Republican tsunami proved especially fatal for Blue Dog Democrats. Not all of the Blue Dogs came from the South, but many did. The 2012 election saw the defeat of moderate to conservative white Democrats in Virginia, North Carolina, South Carolina, Alabama, Mississippi, Louisiana, and Texas, as well as Barrow's Georgia colleague Jim Marshall.
11. In 2012, the Democratic primary attracted more than 21,000 votes com-

pared with only 6,500 in the GOP primary. Turnout in the Democratic primary increased by more than 50 percent over the turnout figure for the 2008 primary.

12. Eric Erickson, "Rick Allen for Congress in GA-12," *Red State*, August 13, 2012, http://www.redstate.com/erick/2012/08/13/rick-allen-for-congress-in-ga-12.

13. Sylvia Cooper, "Reserve Judgment of Politicians," *Augusta Chronicle*, January 28, 2012.

14. The 2012 exit poll for the presidential primary showed 94 percent of the ballots coming from whites.

15. Georgia requires that candidates win a majority not just in the primary but also in the general election. In 2008, Chambliss led his Democratic challenger, Jim Martin, but came up short of a majority. In the runoff conservatives returned to the GOP, and Chambliss took 57 percent of the vote. For a fuller discussion of the Chambliss-Martin contest, see Charles S. Bullock III, "One Election Is Not Enough: Chambliss vs. Martin in the Peach State's Senate Race," in *Cases in Congressional Campaigns: Incumbents Playing Defense*, ed. Randall E. Adkins and David A. Dulio (New York: Routledge, 2010), 213–30.

16. If Floridians had not become confused by the butterfly ballot and exercised greater strength in punching out chads, the state might well have voted for Democratic presidential nominees in four of the past five elections.

5.

1. Voting totals are from the Louisiana Secretary of State.

2. Wayne Parent and Huey Perry, "Louisiana: African Americans, Republicans, and Party Competition," in *The New Politics of the Old South: An Introduction to Southern Politics*, 4th ed., ed. Charles S. Bullock III and Mark J. Rozell (Lanham, MD: Rowman and Littlefield, 2010), 116.

3. Parent and Perry, "Louisiana," 113.

4. Nick Corasaniti, "Louisiana: Democrats in Registrants Only," *FiveThirtyEight* blog, *New York Times*, July 30, 2012.

5. Jonathan Tilove, "GOP Presidential Race Twists and Turns through Louisiana Next," *New Orleans Times-Picayune*, March 18, 2012, http://www.nola.com/politics/index.ssf/2012/03/gop_presidential_race_twists_a.html.

6. Trip Gabriel, "Voter Turnout Appears Light in Louisiana Primary," *New York Times*, March 24, 2012.

7. Alana Semuels, "Louisiana Primary: Conservatives Remain Skeptical of Mitt Romney," *Los Angeles Times*, March 24, 2012.

8. Michael O'Brien, "Santorum Wins Louisiana Primary by Significant Margin," *NBC Politics*, March 24, 2012, http://nbcpolitics.nbcnews.com/_news/2012/03/24/10844546-santorum-wins-louisiana-primary-by-significant-margin.

9. Katharine Q. Seelye and Trip Gabriel, "Santorum Gets a Boost in Winning Louisiana," *New York Times*, March 24, 2012.

10. Jonathan Tilove, "LAGOP Agrees to Seating of 17 Ron Paul Delegates to Republican National Convention in Tampa," *New Orleans Times-Picayune*, August 21, 2012.
11. For Republican National Convention final vote counts for Louisiana, see "2012 Presidential Primaries, Caucuses, and Conventions: Louisiana Republican," Green Papers, http://www.thegreenpapers.com/P12/LA-R.
12. "Mitt Romney to Flood Victim: 'Go Home and Call 211,'" *Huffington Post*, September 1, 2012, http://www.huffingtonpost.com/2012/09/01/mitt-romney-211_n_1848432.html.
13. Data obtained from the Federal Election Commission at www.fec.gov.
14. Southern Media and Opinion Research, "Budget Cuts Unpopular in Latest SMOR Survey," October 2, 2012, http://www.laplaintalk.com/news-releases/FALL-2012-LOUISIANA-VOTER-SURVEY-RELEASE-AND-ANALYSIS.pdf.
15. Magellan Strategies BR, "New Poll: Louisiana Presidential, Governor 2015, Landrieu Reelect," October 8, 2012, http://www.realclearpolitics.com/docs/2012/Magellan_LA_1008.pdf.
16. For purposes of this analysis, the sixty-four parishes are divided into the following four regions: (1) Greater New Orleans includes the parishes of Jefferson, Orleans, Plaquemines, St. Bernard, and St. Tammany; (2) the Acadiana region includes the parishes of Acadia, Ascension, Assumption, Avoyelles, Calcasieu, Cameron, Evangeline, Iberia, Iberville, Jefferson Davis, Lafayette, Lafourche, Pointe Coupee, St. Charles, St. James, St. John The Baptist, St. Landry, St. Martin, St. Mary, Terrebonne, Vermilion, and West Baton Rouge; (3) the Florida Parishes include East Baton Rouge, East Feliciana, Livingston, St. Helena, Tangipahoa, Washington, and West Feliciana; and (4) the north-central region includes the remaining thirty parishes.
17. "President: Full Results," *CNN Politics*, December 10, 2012, http://www.cnn.com/election/2012/results/race/president#exit-polls. Note that Louisiana was not included as one of the thirty-one states in the national sample.
18. Robert E. Hogan and Eunice H. McCarney, "Louisiana: From Political Bellwether to Republican Stronghold," in *A Paler Shade of Red: The 2008 Presidential Election in the South*, ed. Branwell DuBose Kapeluck, Laurence W. Moreland, and Robert P. Steed (Fayetteville: The University of Arkansas Press, 2009), 78.
19. Magellan Strategies BR.
20. Hogan and McCarney, "Louisiana," 78.
21. Magellan Strategies BR.
22. CNN 2012 National Exit/Entrance Poll at cnn.com.
23. Hogan and McCarney, "Louisiana," 78.
24. Magellan Strategies BR.
25. CNN 2012 National Exit/Entrance Poll at cnn.com.
26. Magellan Strategies BR.
27. Alex Isenstadt, "Charles Boustany Defeats Jeff Landry in Louisiana House Race," *Politico*, December 8, 2012, http://www.politico.com/story/

2012/12/charles-boustany-defeats-jeff-landry-in-louisiana-house-race-84798.html.

28. Jordan Blum, "District 3 Race 'Charged,'" *Baton Rouge Advocate,* November 2, 2012.

29. Center for Responsive Politics.

30. Lauren McGaughy, "Boustany vs. Landry: Cash, Endorsements Factor in Heated Race in District Three," *New Orleans Times Picayune,* November 1, 2012.

31. Louisiana Secretary of State, Elections Division.

32. Louisiana Secretary of State, Elections Division.

33. Dennis Woltering and Dominic Massa, "Poll: Obama Loses Support in LA: Perry, Romney, Cain Close on GOP Side," WWLTV, October 13, 2011, http://www.wwltv.com/news/politics/Presidential-Poll-131821978.html.

34. Jonathan Martin, "Jindal: End 'Dumbed-Down Conservatism,'" *Politico,* November 13, 2012, http://www.politico.com/news/stories/1112/83743.html.

6.

1. Deborah Barfield Berry, "Congressional Showdown: Childers-Nunnelee Race Gains National Attention," *Jackson Clarion-Ledger,* October 18, 2009.

2. Emily Wagster Pettus, "GOP Targets Mississippi Democrats Childers, Taylor," *Starkville Daily News,* June 8, 2010; Emily Wagster Pettus, "Palazzo Ends Taylor's 21-Year Run in 4th District," *Northeast Mississippi Daily Journal,* November 3, 2010.

3. Bobby Harrison, "Governor's Campaign Race Picks Up," *Northeast Mississippi Daily Journal,* June 5, 2011.

4. Sid Salter, "Forum Good Barometer of Hot 2011 Campaign," *Starkville Daily News,* April 10, 2011.

5. "Editorial: Secretary of State: Hosemann Best," *Jackson Clarion-Ledger,* July 30, 2011.

6. Sid Salter, "Ag Race Could See First Woman Nominated," *Starkville Daily News,* July 10, 2011.

7. Steven Nalley, "Treasurer Candidates Undeterred by Storm," *Starkville Daily News,* April 16, 2011.

8. Emily Wagster Pettus, "Speaker McCoy Not Seeking Re-election to House," *Starkville Daily News,* May 26, 2011.

9. Sid Salter, "Speaker of the House: He's Still the Real McCoy," *Starkville Daily News,* February 25, 2011.

10. "Miss. Tea Party Congratulates Successful Candidates," *Starkville Daily News,* November 11, 2011.

11. "2012 Mississippi Poll On-Line Results," Mississippi State University, http://www2.msstate.edu/~kauai/poll/PollResults12.htm.

12. Emily Wagster Pettus, "Barbour Juggles White House Hopes, State's Past," *Starkville Daily News,* January 30, 2011.

13. Jeff Amy and Laurie Kellman, "Perry Picks Fight with Pelosi," *Starkville Daily News,* November 18, 2011.

14. Jeff Ayres, "Gingrich Hosts His Own Jobs Summit," *Jackson Clarion-Ledger,* December 4, 2009.
15. Jessica Bakeman, "Gingrich Stumps for Votes," *Jackson Clarion-Ledger,* March 9, 2012.
16. Emily Le Coz, "Gingrich in Town: Former Speaker Draws Large Crowd," *Northeast Mississippi Daily Journal,* March 9, 2012.
17. "Romney Announces Support of Lt. Gov. Reeves, Other Leaders," *Starkville Daily News,* January 22, 2012.
18. Jessica Bakeman, "Miss. Officials Make Romney Feel Welcome," *Jackson Clarion-Ledger,* March 10, 2012.
19. Bakeman, "Miss. Officials."
20. Patsy R. Brumfield, "Touring Tupelo: Santorum Hits Miss. ahead of Vote," *Northeast Mississippi Daily Journal,* March 8, 2012.
21. Matt Friedeman, "Santorum Best of the Lot Tuesday," *Jackson Clarion-Ledger,* March 9, 2012.
22. Emily Wagster Pettus, "Conservatives: Who Can Beat Obama?," *Starkville Daily News,* March 12, 2012.
23. Emily Le Coz, "Sunday Joint Appearance May Aid Candidates," *Northeast Mississippi Daily Journal,* March 12, 2012.
24. "Exit Polls: Mississippi," *CNN Politics,* June 26, 2012, http://www.cnn.com/election/2012/primaries/epolls/ms.
25. Dustin Barnes, "Candidate Pulls in More Than $1.7M at Event," *Jackson Clarion-Ledger,* July 17, 2012.
26. Dustin Barnes, "Romney Revs Up Miss. Backers: GOP Hopeful Raises Funds, Hopes of Base," *Jackson Clarion-Ledger,* July 17, 2012.
27. Bobby Harrison, "Hosemann Takes Neshoba National," *Northeast Mississippi Daily Journal,* August 3, 2012.
28. Jeff Amy, "Holder: Civil Rights Still Priority," *Jackson Clarion-Ledger,* September 28, 2012.
29. Dustin Barnes, "Black Caucus Slams Bryant, Hosemann Comments on Voter ID: Governor Stands by Call for Voluntary Display at Polls," *Jackson Clarion-Ledger,* November 5, 2012.
30. "MSGOP Statements on Mitt Romney's Vice Presidential Choice," Mississippi Republican Party, http://www.msgop.org/2012/08/mississippi-republican-party-statements-on-mitt-romneys-vice-presidential-choice.
31. Geoff Pender, "Romney Scores on Key Topics," *Jackson Clarion-Ledger,* October 4, 2012.
32. Carl Smith, "Candidates Discuss Romney's PBS Stance," *Starkville Daily News,* October 14, 2012.
33. Tim Wildmon, "Obama Slides," *Northeast Mississippi Daily Journal,* October 14, 2012.
34. Alan Nunnelee, "Obama's Proposed Tax Hike Would Hurt Mississippians," *Northeast Mississippi Daily Journal,* August 3, 2012.
35. J. B. Clark, "Tea Partiers Gather at Veterans Park," *Northeast Mississippi Daily Journal,* October 28, 2012.
36. Daniel Gardner, "We Need Leader with Real Answers," *Starkville Daily News,* September 20, 2012.

37. Bill Minor, "Life-Saving New Deal at Stake Election Day," *Jackson Clarion-Ledger*, November 5, 2012.
38. Marty Wiseman, "Much at Stake for Mississippi in 2012 Elections," *Columbus, Starkville, and the Golden Triangle Dispatch*, October 16, 2012.
39. Mary Chase Breedlove, "Romney's Comments Reflect the Nation's Deeper Issue," *Mississippi State Reflector*, September 25, 2012.
40. "The Most Important Battle of the Year: Who Will Stand?" *Mississippi State Reflector*, November 6, 2012.
41. "Democrats Energized after Weekend Events," *Starkville Daily News*, June 8, 2012.
42. Steven Nalley, "GOP Candidates Expect Nov. 6 Election Victories," *Starkville Daily News*, October 9, 2012.
43. Ross Adams, "Thompson Defends Record from Opponent," WJTV, March 2, 2012, http://www.wjtv.com/story/21260677/thompson-defends-record-from-opponent.
44. Jeff Amy, "Tea Party Guns for Miss. Incumbents," *Jackson Clarion-Ledger*, March 10, 2012.
45. Emily Le Coz, "Ross Takes Aim at Rep. Nunnelee," *Northeast Mississippi Daily Journal*, February 29, 2012.
46. Paid for by Union County Citizens Against Big Government, "It's Very Simple . . . ," *Northeast Mississippi Daily Journal*, March 12, 2012.
47. "2011 U.S. House Votes," American Conservative Union, http://conservative.org/ratingsarchive/uscongress/2011/house.html. All election returns for primary races are from "Elections: 2012 Election Results," Mississippi Secretary of State, http://www.sos.ms.gov/elections_results_2012.aspx.
48. Emily Wagster Pettus, "2012 Is Not Stressful for Miss. Incumbents," *Starkville Daily News*, October 15, 2012.
49. Bobby Harrison, "Wicker Challenged in Senate Race," *Northeast Mississippi Daily Journal*, October 29, 2012.
50. Cassandra Mickens, "Incumbent Thompson Wins Another Term in Congress," *Jackson Clarion-Ledger*, November 7, 2012. Campaign expenditures are from the Federal Election Commission website, http://www.fec.gov/finance/disclosure/candcmte_info.shtm.
51. Emily Wagster Pettus, "3 Battle Palazzo in 4th District," *Jackson Clarion-Ledger*, October 12, 2012. Campaign expenditures are from the Federal Election Commission website, http://www.fec.gov/finance/disclosure/candcmte_info.shtml.
52. Micah Green, "Harper to Speak at Starkville High's Promote the Vote Event," *Columbus, Starkville, and the Golden Triangle Dispatch*, September 25, 2012.
53. Emily Le Coz, "Morris, Nunnelee Offer Issues Contrast," *Northeast Mississippi Daily Journal*, October 14, 2012. For background on Morris, see Emily Le Coz, "Brad Morris Vows to Protect the Working Family," *Northeast Mississippi Daily Journal*, October 7, 2012.
54. Emily Le Coz, "Alan Nunnelee Offers a Conservative View," *Northeast Mississippi Daily Journal*, October 7, 2012.

55. David A. Breaux and Stephen D. Shaffer, "Mississippi: Democrats Fight for Relevance in an Increasingly Republican State," in *A Paler Shade of Red: The 2008 Presidential Election in the South,* ed. Branwell DuBose Kapeluck, Laurence W. Moreland, and Robert P. Steed (Fayetteville: The University of Arkansas Press), 83–97. These incomplete uncertified election results are from "Election 2012: Results," *CNN Politics,* December 10, 2012, http://www.cnn.com/election/2012/results/main.
56. Breaux and Shaffer, "Mississippi."
57. Breaux and Shaffer, "Mississippi."

7.

1. Scott E. Buchanan, "The Dixiecrat Rebellion: Long-term Partisan Implications in the Deep South," *Politics and Policy* 33 (4): 754–69.
2. Arnold W. Offner, *Another Such Victory: President Truman and the Cold War 1945–1953* (Palo Alto, CA: Stanford University Press, 2002), 14–15.
3. Wayne Washington, "S.C. Has Always Been a Key Political Player," *State,* November 2, 2008.
4. See Tom Benning, "South Carolina Shaping Up as a Focal Point for GOP Race," *Dallas Morning News,* January 5, 2012, http://www.dallasnews.com/news/politics/perry-watch/headlines/20120105-south-carolina-shaping-up-as-focal-point-for-gop-race.ece. Benning identifies two major regions: "Voters in the Upstate area tend to be more conservative and more focused on social issues. Those in the Midlands and Low Country areas, anchored by Columbia and Charleston, are typically more moderate, and the region is home to several military bases." For a discussion of various regions and political culture, see Bob Botsch, "Political Culture and South Carolina," University of South Carolina website, http://www.usca.edu/polisci/apls458/Political%20Culture.htm. Regional analysis has also been conducted by the Winthrop University–South Carolina Educational Television poll, November 2007, conducted October 7–28, 2007. See "The Winthrop Poll," Winthrop University website, http://www.winthrop.edu/winthroppoll/default.aspx?id=9874. *The configuration of counties by region used by the authors in the analysis is devised using a composite of various internal regional configurations.*
5. The South Carolina State Survey included party-identification questions from fall 1989 to fall 2006. It was conducted by the Institute of Public Affairs and Public Policy, University of South Carolina–Columbia.
6. "April 2012 Winthrop Poll," *Fitsnews,* http://www.fitsnews.com/2012/04/24/april-2012-winthrop-poll.
7. "Clemson Palmetto Poll Finds GOP Voters Uncommitted in Presidential Race," Clemson University website, November 9, 2011, http://media-relations.www.clemson.edu/3957/clemson-palmetto-poll-finds-gop-voters-uncommitted-in-presidential-race.
8. "Clemson Palmetto Poll Finds Gingrich Leading, 20% of S.C. Voters Still Uncommitted," Clemson University website, January 20, 2012, www.clemson.edu/media-relations/4047.

9. Adam Beam and Gina Smith, "Haley Endorses Romney," *State*, December 16, 2011. The October 2012 Winthrop University Poll found that Tea Party membership among all registered voters in the sample was only 6.9 percent; 87.9 percent denied membership. There was still a majority approval among identifiers with the Republican Party (62.0 percent) and a 53.7 percent disapproval among registered Democrats. Among all registered voters, the approval/disapproval rate was about the same (33.0 percent approve; 31.1 percent disapprove). See http://www.winthrop.edu/winthroppoll/default.aspx?id=23146.

10. "South Carolina Exit Polls: How Different Groups Voted," *New York Times*, http://elections.nytimes.com/2012/primaries/states/south-carolina/exit-polls.

11. Patrick Ottenhoff, "In South Carolina, the Economy May Favor Romney," *Atlantic*, January 18, 2012, http://www.theatlantic.com/politics/archive/2012/01/in-south-carolina-the-economy-may-favor-romney/251579.

12. U.S. Census Bureau, "State-to-State Migration Flows: 2010," http://www.census.gov/hhes/migration/files/acs/st-to-st/State_to_State_Migrations_Table_2010.xls.

13. Earl Black and Merle Black, *Politics and Society in the South* (Cambridge, MA: Harvard University Press, 1987).

14. Ibid.

15. Adam Beam, "S.C. Democrats Play Key Roles in Obama Campaign," *State*, September 8, 2012. The situation in 2012 was similar to that in 2008, when Obama did not concede South Carolina. His campaign asked his South Carolina volunteers to head to North Carolina, where polls at the time showed him in a dead heat with McCain. Obama eventually lost North Carolina by a narrow margin. See Gina Smith, "Obama's N.C. Staff Looks South," *State*, October 4, 2008.

16. Federal Election Commission, "2012 Coordinated Party Expenditure Limits," http://www.fec.gov/info/charts_441ad_2012.shtml. The number may be adjusted to account for the estimated number of noncitizens included in the 2011 American Community Survey, who are ineligible to vote (3.6 percent, or 129,552). From the 2010 Department of Justice prison report and the year-end 2010 Department of Justice probation and parole report, 23,578 South Carolinians are in prison; 21,144 are on probation; and 6,412 are on parole, a total of 47,298 ineligible felons. The total reduction is 176,850 of the voting-age eligible population. The adjusted VAP is 3,421,825. See "2012 General Election Turnout Rates," United States Elections Project, last updated July 22, 2013, http://elections.gmu.edu/Turnout_2012G.html. The website is maintained by Professor Michael McDonald at George Mason University.

17. The 2012 raw number is actually a record 42,907 more votes than the then record vote for president in the McCain/Obama race in 2008. In the 2004 presidential election, 1,631,148 South Carolinians voted.

18. Jack Bass, "South Carolina: Up for Grabs?," *The Hill*, July 18, 2012, http://thehill.com/blogs/congress-blog/presidential-campaign/238741-south-carolina-up-for-grabs.

19. Among major national polls conducted between October 31 and November 5, three were ties; Romney led in two polls by 1 percent in each, and

Obama led in four polls by an average of 2 percent. The final national poll showed Obama with a 2.8 percent lead. See "General Election: Romney vs. Obama," *Real Clear Politics,* http://www.realclearpolitics.com/epolls/2012/president/us/general_election_romney_vs_obama-1171.html. *Real Clear Politics* reports no polls in South Carolina after the presidential nominating primary in January 2012.

20. A marginal seat requires a smaller change, or swing, in the next election for an opponent to win. Often a marginal seat is targeted by the out party with more campaign resources in an effort to reclaim the seat. The concept may more aptly apply to legislative elections than presidential elections. If states are viewed, however, one at a time with respect to their Electoral College votes and the chances of winning them, then the choice of the states in which to campaign takes on some of the tactics of a legislative election.

8.

1. For an analysis of the dynamics driving the 2008 presidential election in Arkansas, see Jay Barth, Janine Parry, and Todd Shields, "Arkansas: He's Not One of (Most of) Us," in *A Paler Shade of Red: The 2008 Presidential Election in the South,* ed. Branwell DuBose Kapeluck, Laurence W. Moreland, and Robert P. Steed (Fayetteville: The University of Arkansas Press, 2009).

2. "Talk Business Poll: Party ID versus Name ID," *Talk Business,* September 7, 2012, http://talkbusiness.net/2010/09/talk-business-poll-party-id-versus-name-id/851.

3. "Perry Watch: Twenty Arkansas Lawmakers Endorse Perry for President," *Houston Chronicle,* June 14, 2011.

4. "Arkansans Rate Obama Job Performance: 2-to-1 Negative," *Talk Business,* September 18, 2011, http://talkbusiness.net/2011/09/arkansans-rate-obama-job-performance-2-to-1-negative.

5. Jason Tolbert, "Rep. Harris' Unendorsement of Rick Perry," *Talk Business,* November 17, 2011, http://talkbusiness.net/2011/11/rep-harris-unendorsement-of-rick-perry.

6. "Herman Cain Speaks to Sold Out Crowd in Arkansas," *Talk Business,* October 26, 2011, http://talkbusiness.net/2011/10/herman-cain-speaks-to-sold-out-crowd-in-arkansas-update.

7. Frank Lockwood, "Darr, Griffin Endorse Romney," *Arkansas Democrat-Gazette,* October 6, 2011.

8. Peter Urban, "Griffin Convention Speech: 'We Can Do Better,'" *Pine Bluff Commercial,* August 28, 2012, http://pbcommercial.com/sections/news/state/griffin-convention-speech-%E2%80%98we-can-do-better%E2%80%99.html.

9. Chris Cilizza and Aaron Blake, "Barack Obama's Arkansas Primary Problem," *The Fix* blog, *Washington Post,* May 22, 2012, http://www.washingtonpost.com/blogs/the-fix/post/barack-obamas-arkansas-primary-problem/2012/05/22/gIQAV0oihU_blog.html.

10. Associated Press, "Judge Dismisses John Wolfe's Lawsuit against

Arkansas Democrats," *Arkansas Online*, August 30, 2012, http://www.arkansasonline.com/news/2012/aug/30/judge-dismisses-lawsuit-against-arkansas-democrats/?news-arkansas.

11. For a discussion of turnout patterns in Arkansas primary elections, see Diane D. Blair and Jay Barth, *Arkansas Politics and Government: Do the People Rule?* 2nd ed. (Lincoln: University of Nebraska Press, 2005), 104–6.

12. "Arkansas: He's Not One of (Most of) Us," in *A Paler Shade of Red: The 2008 Presidential Election in the South*, ed. Branwell DuBose Kapeluck, Laurence W. Moreland, and Robert P. Steed (Fayetteville: The University of Arkansas Press, 2009).

13. Andrew DeMillo, "Obama Manager on Hand for Ark. HQ Opening," Associated Press, March 27, 2012, http://www.realclearpolitics.com/news/ap/politics/2012/Mar/27/obama_manager_on_hand_for_ark__hq_opening.html.

14. John Lyon, "Romney Raises $2 Million in Little Rock," *Arkansas News*, August 22, 2012, http://arkansasnews.com/sections/news/arkansas/update-romney-raises-2-million-little-rock.html.

15. On this history of pragmatic progressivism, see Jay Barth, *Ripe for Reform: Arkansas as a Model for Social Change* (Little Rock: Arkansas Public Policy Panel, 2012).

16. Report by Democratic Party of Arkansas chair Will Bond at state committee meeting, December 8, 2012.

17. Arkansas Republican House Caucus, "The SIMPLE Plan," April 5, 2012, http://arhouse.org/2012/04/05/the-simple-plan.

18. Jay Barth, "In Arkansas, Dixie's Last Democratic Legislature Faces a Red Tide," *New Republic*, October 29, 2012, http://www.tnr.com/blog/plank/109294/in-arkansas-dixie%E2%80%99s-last-democratic-legislature-faces-red-tide.

19. John Lyon, "Election Results Show Tough Climate for Moderate Republicans," *Southwest Times Record*, May 27, 2012, http://swtimes.com/sections/news/politics/election-results-show-tough-climate-moderate-republicans.html.

20. T. W. Farnam, "Americans for Prosperity Puts Big Money on Legislative Races in Arkansas," *Washington Post*, October 1, 2012, http://articles.washingtonpost.com/2012-10-01/politics/35500590_1_arkansas-afp-presidential-race.

21. Lindsey Millar, "The Obama Effect," *Arkansas Times*, October 21, 2012, 14–19.

22. Andrew DeMillo, "Beebe Focuses on Outside Groups in Election Push," Associated Press, November 3, 2012.

23. Barth, "In Arkansas."

24. See "2012 Presidential Election," *Politico*, last updated November 29, 2012, http://www.politico.com/2012-election/map/#/President/2012.

25. Jon Cohen and Scott Clement, "Networks, AP Cancel Polls in 19 States," *The Fix* blog, *Washington Post*, October 4, 2012, http://www.washingtonpost.com/blogs/the-fix/wp/2012/10/04/networks-ap-cancel-exit-polls-in-19-states.

26. For details, see "2012 Arkansas Poll," http://plsc.uark.edu/7834.php;

for the Hendrix College/*Talk Business* Poll, see "Post-election Poll: What Motivated the Arkansas Voter?," *Talk Business*, November 13, 2012, http://talkbusiness.net/2012/11/post-election-poll-what-motivated-the-arkansas-voter.

27. See Janine A. Parry, *The Arkansas Poll, 2012: Summary Report* (Fayetteville: University of Arkansas, Diane D. Blair Center for Southern Politics and Society, 2012), http://plsc.uark.edu/2012_Arkansas_Poll_Summary_Report.pdf.

28. For national exit poll results, see "President: Full Results," *CNN Politics*, December 10, 2012, http://www.cnn.com/election/2012/results/race/president.

29. Barth, Parry, and Shields, "Arkansas," 136.

9.

1. For a detailed analysis of the emergence of Florida's party development in the past twenty years, see William E. Hulbary, Anne E. Kelley, and Lewis Bowman, "Florida: A Muddled Election," in *The 1992 Presidential Election in the South: Current Patterns of Southern Party and Electoral Politics*, ed. Robert P. Steed, Lawrence W. Moreland, and Tod A. Baker (Westport, CT: Praeger, 1994), 119–37; Kathryn Dunn Tenpas, William E. Hulbary, and Lewis Bowman, "Florida: An Election with Something for Everyone," in *The 1996 Presidential Election in the South: Party Politics in the 1990s*, ed. Laurence W. Moreland and Robert P. Steed (Westport, CT: Praeger, 1997), 147–63; Steven Tauber and William E. Hulbary, "Florida: Too Close to Call," in *The 2000 Presidential Election in the South: Partisanship and Southern Party Systems in the 21st Century*, ed. Robert P. Steed and Laurence W. Moreland (Westport, CT: Praeger, 2002); Susan A. MacManus, "Florida: The South's Premier Battleground State," *American Review of Politics* 26 (Summer 2005): 155–84; Jonathan Knuckey, "Florida: Obama Gives GOP the 'Blues,'" in *A Paler Shade of Red: The 2008 Presidential Election in the South*, ed. Branwell DuBose Kapeluck, Laurence W. Moreland and Robert P. Steed (Westport, CT: Praeger 2009): 137–159.

2. This argument is best expounded upon, for both Florida and the nation, in John B. and Ruy Teixeira, *The Emerging Democratic Majority* (New York: Scribner, 2002).

3. Damien Cave, "Republican Senator Opts against Run for 2nd Term," *New York Times*, December 2, 2008, http://www.nytimes.com/2008/12/03/us/politics/03martinez.html.

4. Crist appointed George LeMieux, his former campaign strategist and chief of staff, to temporarily fill the vacancy.

5. Damien Cave and Gary Fineout, "Restless in Tallahassee, or with Eye on 2012, Governor Rolls Dice," *New York Times*, May 12, 2009, http://www.nytimes.com/2009/05/13/us/13cristq.html.

6. Carol E. Lee, "When a Hug Becomes a Kiss of Death." *Politico*, November 17, 2009, http://www.politico.com/news/stories/1109/29519.html.

7. See "Florida Senate: Rubio vs. Meek vs. Crist," *Real Clear Politics*, September 28, 2010, http://www.realclearpolitics.com/epolls/2010/senate/fl/florida_senate_rubio_vs_meek_vs_crist-1456.html#polls.

8. It was widely reported that to avoid a split in the Democratic vote, Bill Clinton met with Meek in a failed effort to broker a deal in which Meek would withdraw and endorse Crist. See "Clinton asked Meek to drop out," *CNN Politics*, October 28, 2010, http://politicalticker.blogs.cnn.com/2010/10/28/breaking-clinton-asked-meek-to-drop-out.

9. See "Exit Polls: U.S. Senate: Florida," *CNN Politics*, 2010, http://www.cnn.com/ELECTION/2010/results/polls/#FLS01p1.

10. Scott Powers, "It's Official: Rick Scott Is the All-Time Big Spender," *Orlando Sentinel*, February 2, 2011, http://articles.orlandosentinel.com/2011-02-02/news/os-gov-race-finances-20110201_1_rick-scott-big-spender-democrat-alex-sink.

11. Marc Caputo, "Former Office Manager Details Florida GOP's Spending Scandal," *Tampa Bay Times*, July 10, 2010, http://www.tampabay.com/news/politics/stateroundup/article1108238.ece.

12. Jonathan Allen, "Grayson: GOP Wants 'You to Die,'" *Politico*, September 29, 2009, http://www.politico.com/news/stories/0909/27726.html.

13. See "Exit Polls: Governor: Florida," *CNN Politics*, 2010, http://www.cnn.com/ELECTION/2010/results/polls/#FLG00p1.

14. Kathleen Haughney, "Florida Senate to Vote on Elections Law Thursday," *Orlando Sentinel*, May 4, 2011, http://articles.orlandosentinel.com/2011-05-04/news/fl-election-bill-in-senate-20110504_1_early-voting-voter-fraud-election-fraud.

15. Aaron Deslatte and Kathleen Haughney, "Legislature Passes Broad Overhaul of Elections Law," *Orlando Sentinel*, May 5, 2011, http://articles.orlandosentinel.com/2011-05-05/news/os-elections-bill-passes-20110505_1_early-voting-league-of-women-voters-statewide-voter-database.

16. Quoted in Dara Kam and John Lantigua, "Former Florida GOP Leaders Say Voter Suppression Was Reason They Pushed New Election Law," *Palm Beach Post*, November 25, 2012, http://www.palmbeachpost.com/news/news/state-regional-govt-politics/early-voting-curbs-called-power-play/nTFDy.

17. Lizette Alvarez, "Judge to Toss Out Changes in Florida Voter Registration," *New York Times*, August 29, 2012, http://www.nytimes.com/2012/08/30/us/judge-to-block-changes-in-florida-voter-registration.html.

18. Lizette Alvarez, "Florida Steps Up Effort against Illegal Voters," *New York Times*, May 17, 2012, http://www.nytimes.com/2012/05/18/us/florida-attempts-to-scrub-illegal-voters.html.

19. Marc Caputo and Patricia Mazzei, "Hispanics, Democrats Biggest Groups on Florida's List of Potential Noncitizen Voters, Analysis Shows," *Tampa Bay Times*, May 13 2012, http://www.tampabay.com/news/politics/national/hispanics-democrats-biggest-groups-on-floridas-list-of-potential/1229860.

20. Jonathan Martin, "Yes, Florida, You'll Still Get Floor Passes," *Politico*, August 4, 2011, http://www.politico.com/news/stories/0811/60679.html.

21. Alexander Burns, "Priebus: Florida, Other States Will Be Penalized 2012

Calendar Move," *Politico,* October 25, 2011, http://www.politico.com/news/stories/1011/66775.html.

22. Alex Leary, "RNC to Consider Additional Sanctions against Florida Delegation This Week," *Tampa Bay Times,* January 10, 2012, http://www.tampabay.com/news/politics/national/rnc-to-consider-additional-sanctions-against-florida-delegation-this-week/1209834.

23. "2012 Florida Republican Presidential Primary," *Real Clear Politics,* http://www.realclearpolitics.com/epolls/2012/president/fl/florida_republican_presidential_primary-1597.html.

24. Paul Blumenthal, "Mitt Romney Florida Primary Comeback Fueled by Deep Pockets, Big Advertising Spending," *Huffington Post,* January 28, 2012, http://www.huffingtonpost.com/2012/01/28/mitt-romney-florida-primary-newt-gingrich-super-pac_n_1239002.html.

25. "Exit Polls: Florida," *CNN Politics,* June 26, 2012, http://www.cnn.com/election/2012/primaries/epolls/fl (accessed, November 14, 2012).

26. Campaign spending and appearances are taken from the *Washington Post*; see "Presidential Campaign Stops: Who's Going Where," *Washington Post,* last updated November 7, 2012, http://www.washingtonpost.com/wp-srv/special/politics/2012-presidential-campaign-visits; "Mad Money: TV Ads in the 2012 Presidential Campaign," *Washington Post,* last updated November 13, 2012, http://www.washingtonpost.com/wp-srv/special/politics/track-presidential-campaign-ads-2012.

27. Alex Leary and Adam C. Smith, "President Barack Obama Back in Florida This Week for Official Events, But Also Campaigning," *Tampa Bay Times,* February 21, 2012, http://www.tampabay.com/news/politics/national/president-barack-obama-back-in-florida-this-week-for-official-events-but/1216263.

28. Alex Leary and Adam C. Smith, "In Miami, Story of Profits and Layoffs Highlights Debate over Mitt Romney's Tenure at Bain," *Tampa Bay Times,* January 19, 2012, http://www.tampabay.com/news/business/in-miami-story-of-profits-and-layoffs-highlights-debate-over-mitt-romneys/1211253.

29. Catherine E. Shoichet, "Romney Steps Up Effort to Woo Latino Voters in Univision Forum," *CNN Politics,* September 20, 2012, http://www.cnn.com/2012/09/19/politics/romney-univision-forum/index.html.

30. Alexander Burns, "Rick Scott Surfaces at Romney Rally," *Politico,* November 5, 2012, http://www.politico.com//blogs/burns-haberman/2012/11/rick-scott-surfaces-at-romney-rally-148461.html.

31. For polling averages for Florida, see "2012 Florida President: Romney vs. Obama," *Huffington Post,* http://elections.huffingtonpost.com/pollster/2012-florida-president-romney-vs-obama.

32. Scott Powers, "Democrats' Voter-Registration Effort Swamps GOP's," *Orlando Sentinel,* October 2, 2102, http://articles.orlandosentinel.com/2012-10-02/news/os-voter-registration-groups-20121002_1_voter-registration-deadline-registration-efforts-voter-rolls.

33. Michael Van Sickler, "In Voter Registration Fraud Case, It's Not Mickey Mouse You Have to Worry About," *Tampa Bay Times,* October 9, 2012,

http://www.tampabay.com/news/politics/elections/in-voter-registration-fraud-case-its-not-mickey-mouse-you-have-to-worry/1255470.

34. Patricia Mazzei, Kathleen McGrory, and Sergio R. Bustos, "Final Day of Early Voting Goes Late into the Night," *Miami Herald*, November 3, 2012, http://www.miamiherald.com/2012/11/03/3080829/final-day-of-early-voting-mostly.html.

35. Luke Johnson, "Rick Scott on Decision Not to Extend Early Voting: 'The Right Thing Happened,'" *Huffington Post*, November 9, 2012, http://www.huffingtonpost.com/2012/11/09/rick-scott-early-voting_n_2101566.html.

36. Turnout data are from "2012 General Election Turnout Rates," United States Elections Project, last updated July 22, 2013, http://elections.gmu.edu/Turnout_2012G.html.

37. Only one other candidate in Florida's presidential election history received 49 percent of the vote and lost: Samuel Tilden in the "disputed election" of 1876.

38. On the stability in the county-by-county vote in Florida, see Jonathan Knuckey, "The Structure of Party Competition in the South: The Case of Florida," *American Review of Politics* 25 (Spring 2004): 41–65.

39. The model was estimated using weighted least squares (WLS) regression, weighting by a county's population. This method is preferred over ordinary least squares (OLS) regression, as it avoids the problem of heteroskedasticity, which results from using aggregated data with large variation in populations that would give disproportionate weight to the sparsely populated rural counties over the densely populated urban counties and, hence, biased standard errors of the regression coefficients.

40. "President: Florida: Exit Polls," *CNN Politics*, December 10, 2012, http://www.cnn.com/election/2012/results/state/FL/president.

41. A separate exit poll carried out by Bendixen and Amandi International found Romney carrying the Cuban vote 52 to 48 percent. See Juan O. Tamayo, "Did Obama or Romney Win the Cuban-American Vote?," *Miami Herald*, November 12, 2012, http://www.miamiherald.com/2012/11/12/3094299/winner-of-cuban-american-vote.html.

42. Exit poll data for race/age was available in 2008 for Florida, showing Obama winning 76 percent of the Latino vote among those aged eighteen to twenty-nine.

43. Mark Leibovich, "Playing Hardball Runs in the Family," *New York Times*, October 26, 2012, http://www.nytimes.com/2012/10/28/us/politics/connie-mack-iv-takes-his-swings-at-a-senate-seat.html.

44. John Bresnahan, "Top 5 Scandal Races," *Politico*, October 17, 2012, http://www.politico.com/news/stories/1012/82494.html.

45. "Florida Rep Labels Congressional Democrats as Communists," *Political Ticker* blog, *CNN Politics*, April 11, 2012, http://politicalticker.blogs.cnn.com/2012/04/11/florida-rep-labels-congressional-democrats-as-communists.

46. For spending data for congressional candidates, see "Congressional Races," *OpenSecrets.org*, http://www.opensecrets.org/races/index.php.

47. Quoted in Alex Leary, "Obama, Conservatives Woo Hispanic Vote as Deciding Factor in 2012," *Tampa Bay Times*, August 7, 2011, http://www

.tampabay.com/news/politics/national/obama-conservatives-woo-hispanic-vote-as-deciding-factor-in-2012/1184498.

10.

1. Rob Christensen, *The Paradox of Tar Heel Politics* (Chapel Hill: University of North Carolina Press, 2008).
2. The Council of State includes the governor, the lieutenant governor, and eight other executive positions, all elected statewide.
3. For discussions of recent electoral politics in North Carolina, see Charles Prysby, "North Carolina: Continued Two-Party Competition," in *The 2000 Presidential Election in the South: Partisanship and Southern Party Systems in the 21st Century,* ed. Robert P. Steed and Laurence W. Moreland (Westport, CT: Praeger, 2002), 169–80; Charles Prysby, "A Civil Campaign in a Competitive State: The 2002 North Carolina U.S. Senate Election," in *Running on Empty? Campaign Discourse in Congressional Elections,* ed. L. Sandy Maisel and Darrel West (Lanham, MD: Rowman and Littlefield, 2004), 215–28; Charles Prysby, "North Carolina: Color the Tar Heels Federal Red and State Blue," *American Review of Politics* 26 (Spring and Summer 2005): 185–202; Charles Prysby, "The Reshaping of the Political Party System in North Carolina," in *The New Politics of North Carolina,* ed. Christopher A. Cooper and H. Gibbs Knotts (Chapel Hill: University of North Carolina Press, 2008), 61–84; Charles Prysby, "North Carolina: Change and Continuity in 2008," in *A Paler Shade of Red: The 2008 Presidential Election in the South,* ed. Branwell DuBose Kapeluck, Laurence W. Moreland, and Robert P. Steed (Fayetteville: The University of Arkansas Press, 2009), 161–76; Charles Prysby, "North Carolina: Tar Heel Politics in the Twenty-First Century," in *The New Politics of the Old South: An Introduction to Southern Politics,* 4th ed., ed. by Charles S. Bullock III and Mark J. Rozell (Lanham, MD: Rowman and Littlefield, 2010), 155–80.
4. Charles Prysby, "North Carolina: Color the Tar Heels Federal Red and State Blue."
5. Prysby, "North Carolina: Change and Continuity in 2008."
6. John Frank, "Obama Campaign Opens 52nd Local Office," *Raleigh News and Observer,* September 12, 2012.
7. Chelsea Phipps, "N.C. Ranks High in TV Ads," *North Carolina Datanet,* October 2012, http://southnow.org/files/2012/10/ncdn53.pdf.
8. Phipps, "N.C. Ranks High in TV Ads."
9. Rob Christensen, "RNC Political Director: 'We Are Crushing It on the Ground in NC,'" *Raleigh News and Observer,* September 24, 2012.
10. "President North Carolina: Exit Polls," *CNN Politics,* December 10, 2012, www.CNN.com/election/2012/results/state/NC/president.
11. For the results of polls conducted in North Carolina during the campaign, see "2012 North Carolina President: Romney vs. Obama," *Huffington Post,* October 24, 2012, http://elections.huffingtonpost.com/pollster/2012-north-carolina-president-romney-vs-obama.

12. "2012 North Carolina President: Romney vs. Obama."
13. M. V. Hood III and Seth C. McKee, "What Made Carolina Blue? In-migration and the 2008 North Carolina Presidential Vote," *American Politics Research* 38 (March 2010): 266–302.
14. The six largest counties (with the major city in parentheses) are Cumberland (Fayetteville), Durham (Durham), Forsyth (Winston-Salem), Guilford (Greensboro), Mecklenburg (Charlotte), and Wake (Raleigh).
15. For a discussion of the Hispanic vote in the South, see Harold W. Stanley, "The Latino Vote in 2008," in *Presidential Elections in the South: Putting 2008 in Political Context,* ed. Branwell DuBose Kapeluck, Robert P. Steed, and Laurence W. Moreland (Boulder, CO: Lynne Rienner, 2010), 137–52.
16. Alan Abramowitz, *The Disappearing Center* (New Haven, CT: Yale University Press, 2010).
17. John W. Bruce, "The Republican South," in *Presidential Elections in the South: Putting 2008 in Political Context,* ed. Branwell DuBose Kapeluck, Robert P. Steed, and Laurence W. Moreland (Boulder, CO: Lynne Rienner, 2010), 13–38.
18. John C. Green, "The Faith Factor," in *Presidential Elections in the South: Putting 2008 in Political Context,* ed. Branwell DuBose Kapeluck, Robert P. Steed, and Laurence W. Moreland (Boulder, CO: Lynne Rienner, 2010), 215–32.
19. Charles Prysby, "North Carolina: Republican Consolidation or Democratic Resurgence?," in *The 1996 Presidential Election in the South: Party Politics in the 1990s,* ed. Laurence W. Moreland and Robert P. Steed (Westport, CT: Praeger, 1997), 165–82.
20. Jonathan Knuckey, "Generational Changes," in *Presidential Elections in the South: Putting 2008 in Political Context,* ed. Branwell DuBose Kapeluck, Robert P. Steed, and Laurence W. Moreland (Boulder, CO: Lynne Rienner, 2010), 153–74.
21. The Second District was won by a Democrat in 2008, but in 2010 it was the lone district to change party hands. The 2012 district lines were changed to make the district somewhat more Republican, helping the new Republican incumbent, Renee Ellmers, win reelection.
22. The impact of national short-term forces on both federal and state elections in North Carolina in the modern political era is illustrated by the results of elections from 1972 to 2008. For example, in years when the Republican presidential candidate was winning nationally by a comfortable margin (1972, 1980, 1984, and 1988), Republicans did very well in both federal and state elections in North Carolina. The GOP won the gubernatorial elections in 1972, 1984, and 1988, the only three times that the party captured the governorship prior to 2012. Republicans also won every U.S. Senate election held in these years, and they gained several U.S. House seats in 1980 and 1984. In years when the Democratic presidential candidate won a plurality of the national two-party vote (1976, 1992, 1996, 2000, and 2008), the Democratic gubernatorial candidate was victorious, and the Democrats maintained or increased their number of U.S. House seats. The one Democratic victory

in a U.S. Senate race in a presidential election year occurred in 2008, the only time since 1976 that the Democratic presidential candidate carried the state. Midterm elections show similar effects of national forces. In 1994, an extremely good year for the GOP nationally, North Carolina Republicans doubled their number of congressional seats and made substantial gains in the state legislature, going from 34 to 56 percent of the state house and from 22 to 48 percent of the state senate. Conversely, in 2006, a very good year for Democrats nationally, the North Carolina GOP lost a U.S House seat and lost seats in both houses of the state legislature.

11.

1. V. O. Key, *Southern Politics in State and Nation*, 2nd ed. (New York: Alfred A. Knopf, 1984), 75.
2. "Election Polls Eliminated in 19 States," *New York Times*, October 4, 2012.
3. Key, *Southern Politics*, 673.
4. *Memphis: The Biography of a River Town* (Memphis, TN: Gerald Capers Press, 1966).
5. Vanderbilt Poll, January 2011.
6. "Religious Commitment Analysis," Pew Forum on Religion and Public Life, December 21, 2009.
7. John Wolfe Jr. for President, "With Wolfe at the Door, Dems Say Obama Rival Can't Win Delegates in Arkansas," *New Orleans Times-Picayune*, May 18, 2012.
8. "Meet John Wolfe, Candidate Posing a Challenge to Obama in Arkansas," ABC News, May 22, 2012, http://abcnews.go.com/blogs/politics/2012/05/meet-john-wolfe-candidate-posing-a-challenge-to-obama-in-arkansas.
9. "GOP Candidates Ramp up Tennessee Effort as Primary Looms," *Knoxville News Sentinel*, January 24, 2012.
10. "Rick Santorum Brings National Spotlight to Hixon," *Chattanooga Times Free Press*, February 25, 2012.
11. "Exit Polls from the Tennessee Primary," *New York Times*, March 7, 2012.
12. "Dems Nominate Anti-gay Conspiracy Theorist for Senate," *Mother Jones News*, August 3, 2012.
13. "2012's Worst Candidate," *Washington Post*, August 3, 2012.
14. "Fireworks Highlight Election Night as Cohen Retains 9th Congressional Seat," *Memphis Commercial Appeal*, November 6, 2012.
15. OpenSecrets.org.
16. Tennessee Department of State, Division of Elections, Official Results, 2012.
17. Vanderbilt University Poll, December 2012.
18. Tennessee Department of State, Division of Elections, Official Results, 2012.
19. Ibid.

12.

1. Election returns are from the results certified by the Texas Secretary of State; see Office of the Secretary of State, "1992–Current Election History," http://elections.sos.state.tx.us/elchist.exe.
2. This fact is even more remarkable when you realize that between the executive and the judicial branches, Texas has twenty-seven statewide elected offices.
3. Richard Dunham, "Paul Sadler to the Rescue—and the Dems Have a Senate Candidate Again," *Houston Chronicle,* December 19, 2011, http://blog.chron.com/txpotomac/2011/12/paul-sadler-to-the-rescue-and-the-dems-have-a-senate-candidate-again.
4. Jay Root, "Redistricting Map on Its Way to Texas House." *Texas Tribune,* June 9, 2011, http://www.texastribune.org/2011/06/09/redistricting-map-on-way-to-texas-house.
5. Wayne Slater, "Gov. Rick Perry's Consideration of Presidential Run Reflects Weakness of Republican Field," *Dallas Morning News,*. May 27, 2011, http://www.dallasnews.com/news/politics/state-politics/20110527-gov.-rick-perrys-consideration-of-presidential-run-reflects-weakness-of-republican-field.ece.
6. Paul Burka, "Dear Yankee: Eight Things You Ought to Know before You Start Writing Stories about Rick Perry. You're Welcome," *Texas Monthly,* August 2011, 10; Justin Elliot, "What I Learned about Rick Perry from Reading His Bizarre Book about the Boy Scouts," *New Republic,* September 15, 2011, http://www.tnr.com/article/politics/94878/perry-boy-scouts-on-my-honor-aclu; Sheryl Gay Stolberg, "For Perry, Life Was Broadened and Narrowed by the Military," *New York Times,* November 25, 2011.
7. Jake Silverstein, "The Great Campaigner," *Texas Monthly,* September 2011, http://www.texasmonthly.com/story/great-campaigner.
8. Kurt Badenhausen, "Texas Tops the List of the Best States for Jobs," NBC News, December 5, 2011, http://www.nbcnews.com/id/45527495/ns/business-forbes_com/t/texas-tops-list-best-states-jobs/#.UnVJDPmshcZ.
9. Perry, Rick, *Fed Up: Our Fight to Save America from Washington* (New York: Little, Brown, 2010).
10. Paul Burka, "Perry, the EPA, and the Normalcy Compass," *Burkablog* blog, *Texas Monthly,* August 22, 2011, http://www.texasmonthly.com/burka-blog/perry-epa-and-normalcy-compass.
11. William Kristol, "Special Editorial: Yikes," *Weekly Standard,* September 23, 2011, http://www.weeklystandard.com/blogs/special-editorial-yikes_594095.html; Ryan Murphy, "On the Records: Perry Understated Merck Money," *Texas Tribune,* September 13, 2011, http://www.texastribune.org/2011/09/13/records-fact-checking-perrys-merck-contributions.
12. The state legislature, dominated by conservatives, passed a bill to overturn the governor's order. Perry allowed the bill to become law without his signature.
13. Romney's quote is from the September 22, 2011, Fox News/Google debate held in Orlando, FL. See "Transcript: Fox News–Google GOP Debate,"

Fox News, September 22, 2011, http://www.foxnews.com/politics/2011/09/22/fox-news-google-gop-2012-presidential-debate.

14. Paul Burka, "Blood and Irony," *Burkablog* blog, *Texas Monthly*, September 26, 2011, http://www.texasmonthly.com/burka-blog/blood-and-irony.

15. Paul Burka, "The Bush Leagues," *Burkablog* blog, *Texas Monthly*, September 23, 2011, http://www.texasmonthly.com/burka-blog/bush-leagues.

16. It is worth noting that in the first round of voting, Cruz consolidated support among voters skeptical of Dewhurst, holding Dewhurst below 50 percent and forcing the runoff. Former Dallas mayor Tom Leppert provided little contrast to Dewhurst, and football player Craig James's campaign was cheered only by college football bloggers and fans desperate to see the end of his ESPN broadcasting career.

17. Rachel Weiner, "Who Is Ted Cruz?," *The Fix* blog, *Washington Post*, August 1, 2012, http://www.washingtonpost.com/blogs/the-fix/post/who-is-ted-cruz/2012/08/01/gJQAqql8OX_blog.html.

18. Aman Batheja, "In Senate Race, Out-of-State Stars Outshined Texans," *Texas Tribune*, August 3, 2012, http://www.texastribune.org/2012/08/03/senate-race-out-state-stars-outshined-texans.

19. Ross Ramsey, "Runoff's Storyline Doesn't Begin and End with Ideology," *Texas Tribune*, July 31, 2012, http://www.texastribune.org/2012/07/31/no-tea-party-cruz-and-dewhurst.

20. I define rural as counties that are not part of a metropolitan area as defined by the U.S. Census Bureau. The urban counties are those at the center of a metropolitan area. So Bexar (the home of San Antonio) is the urban county in the San Antonio metropolitan area. I include both Dallas and Tarrant (Fort Worth) Counties as urban. Counties that are part of a metropolitan area but are not the center of the urban area are coded as suburban.

21. It is worth noting that Texas's urban counties—especially Harris and Bexar—contain huge amounts of suburban sprawl, and in a party that has little support among inner-city voters, suburban voters make up the majority of Republican primary voters in these areas.

22. Wendy K. Tam Cho, James G. Gimpel, and Daron R. Shaw, "The Tea Party and the Geography of Collective Action," *Quarterly Journal of Political Science* 7, no. 2 (2012): 105–33.

23. Between George H. W. Bush's runs for president and vice president and his son's two presidential campaigns, only once between 1980 and 2008 did a Republican ticket not feature a Texan named George Bush.

24. All historical election data come from *Dave Leip's Atlas of U.S. Presidential Elections*, http://uselectionatlas.org. National data and results from other states are from Dave Wasserman of *Cook Political Report*, available at https://docs.google.com/spreadsheet/lv?key=0AjYj9mXElO_QdHpla01oWE1jOFZRbnhJZkZpVFNKeVE&toomany=true.

25. All county data for Texas elections are from the Secretary of State's website; national data are from "2012 Presidential Election," *Politico*, last updated November 29, 2012, http://www.politico.com/2012-election/map/#/President/2012.

26. Nicholas A. Valentino and David O. Sears, "Old Times There Are Not

Forgotten: Race and Partisan Realignment in the Contemporary South," *American Journal of Political Science* 49, no. 3 (2005): 672–88; Merle Black and Earl Black, *The Rise of Southern Republicans* (Cambridge, MA: Harvard University Press, 2002).

27. See "Election 2012: President Exit Polls," *New York Times*, http://elections.nytimes.com/2012/results/president/exit-polls.

28. Jim Henson, "Immigration, Perry, and a Divided GOP," *Texas Tribune*, July 27, 2011, http://www.texastribune.org/2011/07/27/immigration-gop-vs-gop-and-perry.

29. For crosstabs on race and presidential vote choice, see University of Texas/Texas Tribune, *Texas Statewide Survey: Crosstabs*, http://www.laits.utexas.edu/txp_media/html/poll/files/201210-crosstabs.pdf, 112–13. For the YouGov crosstabs, see YouGov, *November Wave: TX*, http://cdn.yougov.com/cumulus_uploads/document/uj7wo27oq7/ygTabs_november_likelyvoters_TX.pdf.

30. V. O. Key, *Southern Politics in State and Nation*, rev ed. (Knoxville: University of Tennessee Press, 1949).

31. Randolph B. Campbell, *Gone to Texas: A History of the Lone Star State*, 2nd ed. (New York: Oxford University Press, 2012).

32. Gilberto Hinojosa and Eva Longoria, "The Sleeping Giant of Texas's Latino Vote," *Politico*, October 31, 2012, http://www.politico.com/news/stories/1012/83081.html.

33. For projections of future Texas populations, see the Texas Population Projections Program website at http://txsdc.utsa.edu/data/TPEPP/Projections/Index.aspx.

34. On Perry, see Emily Ramshaw, "Perry Adviser Says Governor Will Run for Re-election," *Texas Tribune*, October 16, 2012, http://www.texastribune.org/2012/10/16/perry-adviser-says-governor-will-run-re-election. On Dewhurst, see Mike Ward, "Dewhurst: Running for Re-election '101 percent,'" *Austin Statesman*, January 4, 2013, http://www.statesman.com/news/news/breaking-news/dewhurst-running-for-re-election-101-percent/nTnJr.

13.

1. John McGlennon, "Virginia: The New Math of Blue Virginia," in *A Paler Shade of Red: The 2008 Presidential Election in the South*, ed. Branwell DuBose Kapeluck, Laurence W. Moreland, and Robert P. Steed (Fayetteville: The University of Arkansas Press, 2009), 215–34.

2. For instance, see "2008 Presidential Race: Virginia," *New York Times*, November 4, 2008, elections.nytimes.com/2008/president/states/Virginia.

3. Micah Cohan, "In Virginia, It's Tradition versus Change," *FiveThirtyEight* blog, *New York Times*, November 4, 2012, http://fivethirtyeight.blogs.nytimes.com/2012/11/04/in-virginia-its-tradition-versus-change.

4. "2012 Virginia President: Romney vs. Obama," *Huffington Post*, http://elections.huffingtonpost.com/pollster/2012-virginia-president-romney-vs-obama last.

5. Adam Nagourney, "Virginia Governor Is Named D.N.C. Chief," *New York Times,* January 4, 2009, http://www.nytimes.com/2009/01/05/us/politics/05dnc.html?_r=0.

6. Julian Walker, "Michelle Obama to Welcome Sailors in Norfolk Today," *Virginian-Pilot,* July 30, 2009, http://hamptonroads.com/2009/07/michelle-obama-welcome-sailors-norfolk-today.

7. Dustin A. Cable and Michele P. Claibourn, "Red State, Blue State: Demographic Change and Presidential Politics in Virginia" (paper, Demographics and Workforce Group, Weldon Cooper Center for Public Service, University of Virginia, July 2012).

8. Cable and Claibourn, "Red State, Blue State," 4–6.

9. Cable and Claibourn, "Red State, Blue State," 8–10.

10. Anita Kumar, "Bob McDonnell Signs Va. Congressional Redistricting Bill into Law," *Washington Post,* January 25, 2012, http://www.washingtonpost.com/blogs/virginia-politics/post/bob-mcdonnell-signs-va-congressional-redistricting-bill-into-law/2012/01/25/gIQADxR0QQ_blog.html.

11. "Virginia's Primary Failure," *Washington Post,* January 2, 2012, http://www.washingtonpost.com/opinions/virginias-primary-failure/2011/12/30/gIQApws3WP_story.html.

12. Tom Jensen, "Gingrich, Allen, Cuccinelli lead GOP primaries," Public Policy Polling, December 13, 2011, http://www.publicpolicypolling.com/main/2011/12/gingrich-allen-cuccinelli-lead-gop-primaries.html.

13. Tom Jensen, "Virginia Republican Numbers," Public Policy Polling, August 2, 2011, http://publicpolicypolling.blogspot.com/2011/08/virginia-republican-numbers.html.

14. "March 2012 Republican Presidential Primary Official Results," Virginia State Board of Elections, https://www.voterinfo.sbe.virginia.gov/election/DATA/2012/A64F1220-CC02-4DED-AB71-09E34ED36339/Official/1_s.shtml.

15. Jonathan Karl, "Mitt Romney Picks Paul Ryan for VP," ABC News, August 11, 2012, http://abcnews.go.com/Politics/OTUS/mitt-romney-selects-paul-ryan-running-mate/story?id=16983499#.UNfBx6yKV8E.

16. Cameron Joseph, "Romney's Strategy of Winning Va.: Ripping Obama on Defense Cuts," *The Hill,* October 19, 2012, http://thehill.com/blogs/ballot-box/presidential-races/262937-romneys-strategy-of-winning-va-ripping-obama-on-defense-cuts.

17. Laura Vozzella, "Obama's 'Horses and Bayonets' Debate Jab Makes Few Ripples in Va.'s Navy Country," *Washington Post,* October 23, 2012, http://articles.washingtonpost.com/2012-10-23/local/35499637_1_horses-and-bayonets-navy-base-navy-families.

18. See "Presidential Campaign Stops: Who's Going Where?," *Washington Post,* http://www.washingtonpost.com/wp-srv/special/politics/2012-presidential-campaign-visits.

19. Peter Bell and Reid Wilson, "Ad Spending in Presidential Battleground States," *National Journal,* June 20, 2012, http://www.nationaljournal.com/hotline/ad-spending-in-presidential-battleground-states-20120620.

20. Tom Hamburger, "Romney Spent More on TV Ads But Got Much Less,"

Washington Post, December 11, 2012, http://articles.washingtonpost.com/ 2012-12-11/politics/35767760_1_romney-campaign-officials-obama-campaign-ad-strategy.

21. "June 2012 Republican Primary Official Results," Virginia State Board of Elections, https://www.voterinfo.sbe.virginia.gov/election/DATA/2012/ A2E23EAB-7EA6-40E2-AF41-3CE22C787EA4/Official/5_s.shtml.

22. Ben Pershing, "Tim Kaine Splits with Obama on Birth Control Rule for Religious Groups," *Washington Post,* January 8, 2012, http://www.washingtonpost.com/blogs/virginia-politics/post/kaine-splits-with-obama-on-birth-control-rule/2012/02/08/gIQAVGrWzQ_blog.html.

23. David Grant, "Virginia Senate: How Tim Kaine Survived a Record Barrage of Attack Ads," *Christian Science Monitor,* November 7, 2012, http://www.csmonitor.com/USA/Elections/Senate/2012/1107/ Virginia-Senate-how-Tim-Kaine-survived-a-record-barrage-of-attack-ads.

24. "November 6, 2012 General Election Official Results," Virginia State Board of Elections, https://www.voterinfo.sbe.virginia.gov/election/DATA/ 2012/68C30477-AAF2-46DD-994E-5D3BE8A89C9B/Official/1_s.shtml.

25. "Virginia Congressional Races in 2012," OpenSecrets.Org, http://www.opensecrets.org/races/election.php?state=VA&cycle=2012.

Conclusion

1. For a nice overview of the top-down realignment, see Joseph A. Aistrup, *Southern Strategy Revisited: Republican Top-Down Advancement in the South* (Lexington: University Press of Kentucky, 1996), and for an excellent account of the transformation in the U.S. Congress, see Earl Black and Merle Black, *The Rise of Southern Republicans* (Cambridge, MA: Harvard University Press, 2001).

2. "Election 2012: President Map," *New York Times,* http://elections.nytimes.com/2012/results/president.

3. Information about the partisan makeup of state legislatures was found at the National Conference of State Legislatures website at http://www.ncsl.org/ legislatures-elections/elections/statevote.aspx.

4. For more on localism in southern politics, see V. O. Key, *Southern Politics in State and Nation* (New York: Alfred A. Knopf, 1949).

5. See "2012 Fox News Exit Polls," Fox News, http://www.foxnews.com/ politics/elections/2012-exit-poll.

6. David G. Waddington and Victoria A. Velkoff, "Projecting Race and Hispanic Origin for the U.S. Population and an Examination of the Impact of Net International Migration" (paper, Joint Eurostat/UNECE Work Session on Demographic Projects, April 28–30, 2010, Lisbon, Portugal), http://www.unece.org/fileadmin/DAM/stats/documents/ece/ces/ge.11/2010/wp.34.e.pdf.

7. Key, *Southern Politics in State and Nation,* 4.

8. Thomas Frank, *What's the Matter with Kansas? How Conservatives Won the Heart of America* (New York: Metropolitan Books, 2004).

9. See Larry Bartels, "What's the Matter with *What's the Matter with*

Kansas?," *Quarterly Journal of Political Science* 1 (2006): 201–26; James G. Gimpel and Kimberly A. Karnes, "The Rural Side of the Urban-Rural Gap," *PS: Political Science & Politics,* July 2006, 467–72.

10. Lydia DePillis, "The GOP Can't Afford to Ignore Cities Anymore," *New Republic,* November 12, 2012, http://www.newrepublic.com/article/110074/republicans-cant-afford-ignore-cities-anymore.

11. Key, *Southern Politics in State and Nation,* 673.

12. Earl Black and Merle Black, *Politics and Society in the South* (Cambridge, MA: Harvard University Press, 1987), 45.

13. James W. Lamare, J. L. Polinard, and Robert D. Winkle, "Texas: The Lone Star (Wars) State," in *The New Politics of the Old South,* 4th ed., ed. Charles S. Bullock III and Mark J. Rozell (Boulder, CO: Rowman and Littlefield, 2010), 269.

14. Paul Mackun and Steven Wilson, *Population Distribution and Change: 2000 to 2010,* U.S. Census Bureau, March 2011, http://www.census.gov/prod/cen2010/briefs/c2010br-01.pdf, 1.

15. See Mackun and Wilson, *Population Distribution and Change: 2000 to 2010,* 2. Population change in the South was 14.3 percent between 2000 and 2010 and 15.5 percent among the eleven states of the Old Confederacy. The U.S. Census uses a broad definition of the South with three divisions. The South Atlantic includes Delaware, the District of Columbia, Florida, Georgia, Maryland, North Carolina, South Carolina, Virginia, and West Virginia. The East South Central consists of Alabama, Kentucky, Mississippi, and Tennessee. The West South Central includes Arkansas, Louisiana, Oklahoma, and Texas.

16. For a nice reapportionment map, see "Apportionment of the U.S. House of Representatives Based on the 2010 Census," U.S. Census Bureau, http://www.census.gov/population/apportionment/files/2010map.pdf.

17. Phillip E. Converse, "A Major Political Realignment in the South?," in *Change in the Contemporary South,* ed. Allan P. Sindler (Durham, NC: Duke University Press, 1963), 206–10.

18. Black and Black, *Politics and Society in the South,* 19.

19. William H. Frey, *The New Great Migration: Black Americans' Return to the South, 1965–2000* (Washington, DC: Brookings Institution, 2004), http://www.frey-demographer.org/reports/R-2004-3_NewGreatMigration.pdf.

20. Sabrina Tavernise and Robert Gebeloff, "Many U.S. Blacks Moving South, Reversing Trend," *New York Times,* March 24, 2011, http://www.nytimes.com/2011/03/25/us/25south.html?pagewanted=all&_r=0.

21. William M. Rohe, *The Research Triangle: From Tobacco Road to Global Prominence* (Philadelphia: University of Pennsylvania Press, 2011).

22. M. V. Hood and Seth C. McKee, "What Made North Carolina Blue? In-migration and the 2008 North Carolina Presidential Vote," *American Politics Research* 38 (2010): 266–302.

23. See Becca Aaronson, "On the Records: Texas 1 of 5 'Minority-Majority' States," *Texas Tribune,* May 17, 2012, http://www.texastribune.org/texas-counties-and-demographics/census/on-the-records-majority-texas-minority-races; Aaron Gould Sheinin, "Shifting Population Could Help Democrats in

Georgia," *Atlanta Journal-Constitution,* September 2, 2012, http://www.ajc
.com/news/news/shifting-population-could-help-democrats-in-georgi/nR2JH.
   24. J. David Woodard, *The New Southern Politics* (Boulder, CO: Lynne
Rienner, 2006), 15.
   25. Woodard, *The New Southern Politics,* 16.
   26. John Sides, "Mapping Romney and Obama Field Offices," *Monkey
Cage,* November 6, 2012, http://themonkeycage.org/blog/2012/11/06/
mapping-romney-and-obama-field-offices.

Contributors

Scott E. Buchanan is associate professor of political science at The Citadel. Professor Buchanan has been the executive director of The Citadel Symposium on Southern Politics since 2009. His research focuses on southern politics and elections, and he is the author of the only published biography of former Georgia governor Marvin Griffin.

Branwell DuBose Kapeluck is associate professor of political science at The Citadel. Since 2004, Professor Kapeluck has been codirector of the Citadel Symposium on Southern Politics. He is the author and editor of a number of publications, including *A Paler Shade of Red: The 2008 Presidential Election in the South*.

Patrick Miller is assistant professor of political science at the University of Kansas. His primary research areas include public opinion, political psychology, elections, and survey and experimental methods. He has recently published research in *Political Psychology, American Review of Politics*, and *IRB: Ethics & Human Research*. His professional background includes a year as a postdoctoral associate at the Duke Initiative on Survey Methodology at Duke University and two years teaching fifth grade in Atlanta public schools through Teach for America.

John A. Clark is professor of political science at Western Michigan University. His research focusing on political parties, elections, and legislative politics has appeared in a variety of academic journals and edited volumes. He is coeditor of *Party Organization and Activism in the American South* and *Southern Political Party Activists: Patterns of Conflict and Change, 1991–2001*.

Shannon L. Bridgmon is assistant professor of political science at Northeastern State University. Her primary research areas are southern politics and state political party issues. She has published in the *American Review of Politics* and the *Criminal Justice Policy Review*. Other research projects have examined party responsibility in various policy areas, state party legislative performance, and the Alabama Constitution of 1901. She earned her PhD in 2009 from the University of Alabama. Since 2003, she has taught at James Madison University, the University of Alabama–Tuscaloosa, the University of Alabama–Huntsville, and Northeastern State University.

Charles S. Bullock III is the Richard B. Russell Professor of Political Science and Josiah Meigs Distinguished Teaching Professor at the University of Georgia. He has authored, coauthored, edited, or coedited 28 books and more than 150 articles. His most recent books are the fifth edition of *The New Politics of the Old South* and *The Oxford Handbook of Southern Politics*, both coedited with Mark Rozell; the second edition of *Georgia Politics in a State of Change*, coauthored with Keith Gaddie; *Redistricting: The Most Political Activity in*

America; and *The Triumph of Voting Rights in the South,* coauthored with Keith Gaddie and winner of the V. O. Key Award as the best book published on southern politics in 2009. In 2011 and 2012, *Georgia Trend Magazine* named Bullock one of the 100 Most Influential Georgians.

Robert E. Hogan is associate professor of political science at Louisiana State University. He conducts research on various aspects of American electoral politics in the states. His most recent projects focus on the role of candidate decision making and its effects on the representation process. His work has appeared in journals such as *Social Science Quarterly, Legislative Studies Quarterly,* and the *Journal of Politics.*

Joshua D. Hostetter is a PhD candidate at Louisiana State University in the Political Science Department. His research focuses on the effects of institutional differences in state elections and voting behavior.

David A. Breaux is dean of the graduate school and professor of political science at the University of Louisiana–Lafayette. He has published articles in various journals, including *Legislative Studies Quarterly, American Review of Politics, American Politics Quarterly,* and *Public Administration Review.* Dr. Breaux has also published numerous book chapters on state political party activists, state electoral politics, state policy making, and southern politics. In addition, he has been the recipient of various research grants, including three from the National Science Foundation.

Stephen D. Shaffer is professor of political science at Mississippi State University. He has published extensively on Mississippi party organizations and political campaigns, as well as on national public opinion and federal elections. Professor Shaffer directs the Mississippi Poll. He coauthored *Mississippi Government and Politics* and the 2006 V. O. Key award–winning *Politics in the New South: Representation of African Americans in Southern State Legislatures* and has published in the *American Journal of Political Science, Western Political Quarterly,* and *Social Science Quarterly.*

Cole Blease Graham Jr. is visiting professor at the George H. W. Bush School of Government and Public Service at Texas A&M University–College Station. His specialty is American state and local government politics and administration.

Janine A. Parry is professor of political science at the University of Arkansas and has directed the Diane D. Blair Center's Arkansas Poll since its inception in 1999. Her major fields of teaching and research include state politics and policy, public opinion and voter mobilization, and gender, politics, and policy. Her work has appeared in *Political Behavior, State Politics and Policy Quarterly, Social Science Quarterly,* the Presidential Elections in the South series, and other outlets.

Jay Barth is M. E. and Ima Graves Peace Professor of Politics and the chair of the Department of Politics and International Relations at Hendrix College in Conway, Arkansas. Barth's academic work includes research on the politics of the South, state government and politics, LGBT politics, political communication (particularly, radio advertising), and the achievement gap in Arkansas. He is the coauthor, with the late Diane D. Blair, of the second edition of *Arkansas Politics and Government: Do the People Rule?* Barth has authored or coauthored chapters on Arkansas in four previous books in the Presidential Elections in the South series.

Jonathan Knuckey is associate professor of political science at the University of Central Florida and the director of research at the Lou Frey Institute for Politics and Government. His research interests include voting behavior and political parties and elections, with particular emphasis on the American South.

Tyler Branz is a lecturer in the Department of Political Science at Valencia College. His research interests focus on political parties, elections, and Florida politics.

Charles Prysby is professor of political science at the University of North Carolina–Greensboro. His principle research interests include southern politics, political parties, campaigns and elections, and religion and politics. His work has appeared in journals such as *Political Research Quarterly*, *Social Science Quarterly*, and the *American Review of Politics*.

J. David Woodard has taught at Clemson University since 1983 and at Vanderbilt University and Southern Methodist University as a visiting professor. He is the author or coauthor of books on political conservatism and the presidency of Ronald Reagan and of a book with former U.S. senator and now–Heritage Foundation president Jim DeMint. The second edition of his book *The New Southern Politics* was published in 2013. He is a political consultant, campaign manager, and pollster for Republican candidates. Dr. Woodard teaches courses in political theory, political parties, politics and film, and American government, as well as southern politics.

Brian Arbour is assistant professor of political science at John Jay College, City University of New York. His research focuses on campaign message strategy and ethnic voting in American elections. Professor Arbour also works on the Decision Desk at Fox News Channel, the Election Night group that analyzes exit poll results and calls races for the network.

John J. McGlennon is professor and chairman of the Government Department at the College of William & Mary in Virginia. He specializes in state and local government and southern politics. His research has appeared in the *Journal of Politics*, *International Political Science Review*, *American Review of Politics*, and the *Australian Political Science Review*. He has contributed to a number of books and is the coeditor of *The Life of the Parties: A Study of Presidential Activists* and a coauthor of *Party Activists in Virginia*, both with Alan Abramowitz and Ronald Rapoport.

H. Gibbs Knotts is professor and chair of political science at the College of Charleston. His work on southern politics, public administration, and public policy appears in a range of journals, including the *Journal of Politics*, *Social Forces*, *Southern Cultures*, *Social Science Quarterly*, the *American Review of Public Administration*, and *Public Administration Review*. He is also coeditor of *The New Politics of North Carolina*.

Index

Abbott, Greg, 211
abortion and the 2012 presidential election, 16
Adams, Sandy, 146, 166
age and the 2012 presidential election, 9
Alabama: comparison with national voting, 37, 45; down-ticket voting in, 42–45; income voting patterns in 45–46, 48; nomination process, 32; previous elections, 38–39, 47; realignment, 38–39, 48–49; race and voting in, 45, 46–49; regional voting in 40–41, 46–48; religion and voting, 40, 45–46; 2012 general election in, 41–42, 45; 2012 Republican primary, 39–41; Tea Party in, 38, 40, 42
Alexander, Lamar, 196, 197
Allen, George, 215, 221, 222
Americans for Prosperity, 128
Anderson, Lee, 62
Arkansas: age and voting in, 135; campaign in, 126–129; comparison with national voting, 129; down-ticket elections in, 127–128, 139–140; education and voting in, 137; gender and voting in, 134, 137; general election in, 126–139; income and voting in, 136, 139; issues and voting in, 138; nomination process in, 124–126; party identification patterns in, 138; party identification and voting in, 135, 138; race and voting in, 126–127, 128, 129–130, 134–137; regional voting in, 129–134; residential voting patterns in, 127, 136, 138; 2008 results in, 126, 138; turnout in, 125–126, 139; urban voting in, 136; voting patterns in, 125, 134–137

Bachmann, Michelle, 26, 27, 105, 203
Bachus, Spencer, 42
Bain Capital, 151
Baker, Howard, 197
Barbour, Haley, 83, 84, 86
Barnes, Roy, 52
Barr, Bob, 52
Barrow, John, 61, 62–63
Baxley, Lucy 44
Beasley, David, 118
Beason, Scott, 42
Beaven, Heather, 166

Beebe, Mike, 127
Bennett, Mike, 148
Berra, Yogi, 101
Biden, Jill, 217
Biden, Joe, 153, 216, 220
biracial coalition, 19
Black, Earl, 238
Black, Jim, 182
Black, Merle, 238
Blanco, Kathleen, 70
Blair, Diane, xi
Bolling, William, 216, 219, 231
Bonner, Jo, 42
Boucher, Rick, 216
Boustany, Charles 80–81
Boyd, Allen, 147
Breaux, John, 70
Brooks, Mo, 38, 41, 42, 47
Brookings Institution, 240
Bryant, Phil, 83, 84, 89, 90, 93
Burka, Paul, 203
Bush, George W., xvi, 22, 113, 145, 160, 190, 193, 194, 205, 208
Bush, Jeb, 145, 153, 168, 169
Byrnes, James F., 102–103

Cain, Herman, 26, 27, 28, 53, 54, 105, 124
Campbell, Carroll, 103
Campfield, Stacey, 192
Canseco, Quico, 201
Cantor, Eric, 228
Carter, Jimmy, 38, 103, 189, 213, 234
Cavanaugh, Andress, 44
Chambliss, Saxby, 67
Chaney, Mike, 85
Childers, Travis, 84, 92
Christensen, Rob, 171
Christie, Chris, 26
Citizens United v. Federal Election Commission, 23
civil rights movement, ix
Clayton, Mark, 193–194
Clinton, Hillary, 224–225
Clinton, William Jefferson (Bill), xi, xvi, 53, 153, 169, 179, 183, 220, 234
Clyburn, Jim, 117
Cole, Rickey, 87, 88, 89
Collins, Mac, 54
Combs, Susan, 211
Connally, John, 22, 103
Cohen, Steve, 194

281

comparison with national voting and South, 235
Constitution Party, 226
Converse, Philip, 240
Corker, Bob, 193, 196
Cornyn, John, 145
Cotton, Tom, 139
Crawford, Rick, 139
Crist, Charlie, 145, 153, 167
Cruz, Ted, 199, 200, 201, 203–205, 208, 211
Cuccinnelli, Ken, 219, 231

Daniels, Mitch, 26
Dalton, Walter, 181
Darr, Mark, 125
Davis, Artur, 41–42, 47
Davis, Wendy, 201, 202
Deal, Nathan, 54, 60, 67
Deeds, Creigh, 215
Demings, Val, 167
DeMint, Jim, 106, 116, 204
demographic change in the South, x, 3, 6–12
DeSantis, Rob, 166
Dewhurst, David, 200, 202, 203, 211
Diane D. Blair Center of Southern Politics and Society, x
Dixiecrats, xv, 102
Dole, Elizabeth, 179
Douglas, John 227
down-ticket elections in the South, 233
Dukakis, Michael, 93
Dunn, Winfield, 186, 187
DuPree, Johnny, 84

Easley, Mike, 181
economy and the 2012 presidential election, 13–14
Edwards, James, 103
Eisenhower, Dwight D., 70, 103, 189, 193, 233
Electoral College, ix, xv
Ellington, Scott, 139
evangelical whites and the 2012 presidential election, 9–10, 31

Farenthold, Blake, 201
Federal Election Campaign Act, 22
Feeney, Tom, 146
Fitch, Lynn, 85
Flores, Bill, 201
Florida: age and voting in, 147, 163; comparison with national voting, 155; down-ticket elections in, 165–167; geographical regions in, 157–158; general election in, 151–156; gender and voting in, 163; ideology and voting in, 150, 164; income and voting in, 163–164; issues and voting in, 151, 164–165; Latino vote, 144, 147, 152, 160, 169–170; nomination process in, 27, 30–32, 149–150; party identification patterns in, 168–170; party identification and voting in, 164; race and voting in, 145, 147, 160,163; race relations in, 144; recent political history in, 144–147; religion and voting in, 150; registration drives in, 153–154; residential voting patterns in, 156–157,167–170; 2010 midterm elections in, 144–147; Tea Party in, 145, 147, 150; turnout in, 154–156; voting patterns in, 144, 147, voting rights in, 147–149
Forbes, Randy, 228
Frank, Thomas, 237
Frankel, Lois, 167
Frey, William, 240
Frist, Bill, 190
frontloading, 23–24

Gallego, Pete, 201
Garcia, Joe, 166
gay marriage and the 2012 presidential election, 16, 86
gender and the 2012 presidential election, 9
Georgia: age and voting in, 55, 57, 66; down-ticket voting in, 51–53, 60–64; gender and voting in, 54, 57; income voting patterns in 55; nomination process, 32; previous elections, 54; realignment, 51–53; race and voting in, 52, 55, 57, 64–66; regional voting in 55, 58–60; religion and voting, 55, 58, 66; 2012 general election in, 57–60; 2012 Republican primary, 53–56; Tea Party in, 55
geographic size and the 2012 presidential election, 10–12
Gilmore, James, 215
Gingrich, Newt: and Alabama, 39–41; and Florida, 150; and Georgia, 53–55; and Louisiana, 71, 72; and Mississippi, 86–87, 88; and South Carolina 103, 105–106, 108, 111, 117; and Tennessee, 192; and Texas, 218–219; and the 2012 nomination, 26, 27, 28, 29, 30, 31, 32, 33
Goldwater, Barry, 51, 70, 103
Goode, Virgil, 226
Gore, Albert N., Jr., 89, 91, 189, 190, 193, 194

Graham, Lindsey, 116
Grayson, Alan, 146–147, 167
Greer, Jim, 146, 148
Griffin, Tom, 125
Griffith, H. Morgan, 216
Griffith, Parker, 38, 42, 47

Haley, Nikki, 19, 29, 106, 111, 116, 117, 118
Harper, Gregg, 92
Harrell, Bobby, 29
Harwell, Beth, 196
Haslam, Bill, 191, 196
Hasner, Adam, 167
health care reform and the 2012 presidential election, 3, 5–6, 14
Hirschbiel, Paul, 226
Hispanics and the 2012 presidential election, 16–18
Hodges, Jim, 118
Holder, Eric, 88–89
Hood, Jim, 85, 89, 93, 98
Hosemann, Delbert, 84, 88
Hubbard, Jon, 128
Huckabee, Mike, 41, 55, 72
Huntsman, Jon, 26, 27, 105
Hurricane Sandy, 153
Hurt, Robert, 216, 222, 227–228
Hutchison, Kay Bailey, 201
Hyde-Smith, Cindy, 85

invisible primary, 26–27
Isakson, Johnny, 54
issues and the 2012 presidential election, 12–16

Jeffress, Gene, 139
Johnson, Gary, 105
Johnson, Lyndon B., 214
Jindall, Bobby, 19, 70, 71, 75–76, 82, 211

Kaine, Tim, 215, 216, 222, 226
Kefauver, 193
Kennedy, John F., 103, 186
Kerry, John, 9, 45, 47, 49, 57, 93, 157, 226
Key, V.O., xvii, 40, 185, 186, 235–236, 238
King, John, 106
Kissel, Larry, 180
Klein, Rob, 147
Koch brothers, 128
Kosmas, Suzanne, 146
Kruse, Kevin, 238

Landrieu Mary, 71
Landry, Jeff, 80–81

Lee, Mike, 204
LeMieux, George, 165
Lewis, John, 90
Long, Todd, 167
Longoria, Eva, 209–210
Lott, Trent, 83
Louisiana: comparison with national voting, 69, 81; down-ticket voting in, 80–81; gender voting patterns in 79–80, 81; nomination process, 32; previous elections, 69–71; realignment, 81–82; race and voting in, 77–78, 79; regional voting in 77–78; religion and voting, 69, 71, 73–74; 2012 general election in, 75–78; 2012 Republican primary, 71–75
Lourie, Joel, 118

Mack, IV, Connie, 165
Marcy, Bill, 92
Marshall, Jim, 53
Martin, Jim, 52
Martinez, Mel, 144
McAullife, Terry, 231
McCain, John, 26, 28, 45, 55, 58, 60, 69, 71, 78, 91, 96, 114, 154, 157, 205, 209, 210, 219, 223, 225
McCollum, Bill, 146
McCoy, Billy, 85
McCrory, Pat, 181
McDonnell, Robert, 215, 217, 219
McIntyre, Mike, 180
McTeer, Heather, 91
McWhorter, Mike, 196
Meek, Kendrick, 145
Mencken, H.L., 187
Messina, Jim, 127
Mica, John, 166
Miller, Brad, 180
Miller, Zell, 54
Mississippi: age and voting patterns in, 96–98; comparison with national voting, 98–99; congressional voting in, 91–92; ideology and issues in, 85–86, 90, 93–96; income voting patterns in 96; nomination process, 32; previous elections, 83–86; realignment, 83–84, 98–99; race and voting in, 86, 96, 98–99, 114; regional voting in 88; religion and voting, 87–88, 96; 2012 general election in, 92–98; 2012 Republican primary, 86–90; and Tea Party in, 85, 90, 91, 92
Moore, Matthew, 92
Moore, Roy, 42
Morris, Brad, 92
Mulvaney, Mick, 117

Murphy, Patrick, 166
Musgrove, Ronnie, 83

Naifeh, Jimmy, 196
Nelson, Bill, 165
New Great Migration, 240
New Republic, 238
Nixon, Richard, xvi, 70, 103, 186, 187
North Carolina: age and voting in, 175–176, 178, 179, 182; campaign in, 173; comparison with national voting, 174, 175, 182, 183; down-ticket elections in, 171–172, 179–182, 184; geographical regions in, 174–175; gender and voting in, 178; general election in, 173–179; ideology and voting in, 175–177; income and voting in, 178; issues and voting in, 177; Hispanic vote in, 175–176, 178, 182; party identification and voting in, 175, 177; political history of, 171; race and voting in, 175–176, 178; recent political history in, 171–172, 175; redistricting and congressional elections, 179–181; religion and voting in, 176, 178, 182; 2008 results in, 172; turnout in, 173; voting patterns in, 181, 183
Nosef, Joe, 89, 90
Nunnelee, Alan, 84, 87, 89, 91, 92
Nye, Glenn, 216

Obama, Barack: and Alabama, 39, 41, 45, 46–48, 49; and Arkansas, 123–125, 127–130, 134, 137–138, 141; and Florida, 144, 145, 147, 151–160, 163–169; and Georgia, 52, 58, 60; and Louisiana, 69, 76, 78–80, 81; and Mississippi, 84, 86–87, 88, 90, 92, 93, 96, 98; and North Carolina, 173–179; and South Carolina, 111, 114; and Tennessee, 189, 190, 191, 194; and Texas, 200, 201, 203, 205, 207, 208, 209, 210; and Virginia, 213–214, 215, 216–218, 220–221, 222, 223–231; and the South, 233, 234–236, 237, 239–240, 241–242, 244; and the 2012 election, xvi, xvii, 3; and the 2012 nomination, 21, 26
Obama, Michelle, 41, 42, 216
Organizing for America, 216

Palazzo, Steven, 84, 91, 92
Palin, Sarah, 26, 114, 204
Patterson, Jerry, 211
Paul, Rand, 204
Paul, Ron: and Georgia, 55; and Louisiana, 72, 75, 86; and South Carolina, 105, 106, 108; and Tennessee, 192; and Texas, 218, 219; and the 2012 election, xvi; and the 2012 nomination, 26, 27, 29, 30, 32
Pawlenty, Tim, 26, 27, 105
Pelosi, Nancy, 62, 84, 85, 86
Perdue, Bev, 181
Perdue, Sonny, 52
Perriello, Tom, 216, 231
Perry, Rick, 24, 26, 27, 28, 71, 86, 152, 200, 202–203, 204, 208, 209, 211, 218, 219
Pickering, Stacey, 85, 87
political history in South: recent, 234
population change in South, 3, 234, 237, 240–242
Powell, Wayne, 228
presidential debates and the 2012 election, 24–25, 29–30

Raby, Steve, 38
race and voting in South, 235–236; and the 2012 presidential election in the South, 6–8, 31
racially polarized voting, 20
Ramsay, Ross, 204
Ramsey, Ron, 196
Reagan, Ronald, 19, 70, 83, 103, 189
realignment, xvii, 4–6, 233–234
redistricting, 49, 61
Reeves, Tate, 84
Rehnquist, William, 204
Republican nomination process, 21–22
Research Triangle Park, 241
residential voting patterns in the South, 236–240
Richmond, Cedric, 71
Rigell, Scott, 216, 222, 226, 227
Rivera, David, 166
Robb, Charles, 221
Romney, Mitt: and Alabama, 39–41, 42, 45, 46–48, 49; and Arkansas, 124–125, 127, 129, 130, 134, 137–139; and Florida, 144, 149–155, 155, 157, 160, 163–165, 167–169; and Georgia, 54, 55, 57, 58, 67; and Louisiana, 69, 71, 72, 73, 75, 76, 79–80; and Mississippi, 87, 88, 92–93, 96, 98; and North Carolina, 171, 173–179, 182; and South Carolina, 105, 106, 108, 111, 112, 113, 114; and Tennessee, 192; and Texas, 199, 201, 202, 203, 205–206, 208, 209, 210; and Virginia, 213, 214, 218–221, 222–223, 227–230; and the 2012 election, ix, 3; and the 2012

nomination, 21, 26, 27, 29, 30, 31, 32, 33; and the South, 233, 237
Roosevelt, Franklin D., 102–103
Ross, Henry, 91
Ross, Mike, 139
Rove, Karl, 111
Rubio, Marco, 31, 144, 145, 151–152, 168, 169, 211
Ryan, Paul, 75, 89, 152, 219

Sadler, Paul, 201
Sanford, Mark, 118
Santorum, Rick: and Alabama, 39–41; and Arkansas, 125; and Florida, 150; and Georgia, 54; and Louisiana 72, 73, 75, 82; and Mississippi, 87, 88; and South Carolina, 105, 106, 108; and Tennessee, 192–193; and Texas, 203, 204; and the 2012 nomination, 26, 27, 29, 30, 32
Sewell, Terri, 38
Scott, Rick, 144, 146, 148, 152, 154, 167
Scott, Tim, 116
Sheheen, Vincent, 118
Shelton, Mark, 201
Shipley, Tony, 192
Shuler, Heath, 180
Sink, Alex, 146
Smith, James 118
Solid South, ix
South Carolina: comparison with national voting, 111, 117; down-ticket voting in, 116–117; income voting patterns in; nomination process, 27–30, 31–32; party identification in, 104–105; previous elections, 101–103; realignment, 101–103, 118–119; race and voting in, 101–102, 111; regional voting in 103–104, 108–111, 112–114; religion and voting, 106; 2012 general election in, 111–117; 2012 Republican primary, 105–111; Tea Party in, 102, 106
Southerland, Steve, 147
Southern Manifesto, 185
Staples, Todd, 211
Stearns, Clifford, 166
Stevenson, Adlai, 103
Super PACs, 23, 29, 63
Super Tuesday, 32, 33, 150, 191–192

Taylor, Gene, 84
Tennessee: down-ticket elections in, 196–197; geographical regions in, 185–189, 193, 194–195; Nomination process in, 32, 191, 196; political culture in, 185–186; public opinion in, 189–191; race relations in, 185; recent political history in, 186, 189–190, 191, 197; residential voting patterns in, 186–188, 194
Texas: age and voting in, 204; comparison with national voting, 199, 207, 205–208; down-ticket elections in, 201–202, 211; gender and voting in, 204; Hispanic vote in, 199–200, 207–208, 210; ideology and voting in, 203, 204–205; nomination process in, 202–205; party identification patterns in, 205–206; political history of, 209; race and voting in, 200, 207–210; recent political history in, 200–201; religion and voting in, 204; residential voting patterns in, 205, 206–207; Tea Party in, 200, 202, 204–205, 211
The Citadel, x
The Citadel Symposium on Southern Politics, xvi
Thompson, Bennie, 91, 92, 93
Thurmond, Strom J., 102, 103
Treen, David, 70
Truman, Harry S, 103
Trump, Donald, 26
two party competition in the South, 234, 235, 238, 242, 243–244

urban voting in South: 234, 236–240

Vance, Robert, Jr., 44
Virginia: age and voting in, 217, 228–229; campaign in, 219–221; down-ticket elections in, 221–222, 226–228, 231; education and voting in, 228–230; gender and voting in, 228–229; general election in, 219–221; Hispanic vote in, 217; ideology and voting in, 32, 229–230; issues and voting in, 219–220; nomination process in, 218–219; party identification patterns in, 230; party identification and voting in, 228, 229–230; race and voting in, 217, 228, 228–229, 231; recent political history in, 213–219; redistricting in, 216, 222; regional voting in, 220, 222–223, 226; religion and voting in, 224; residential voting patterns in, 217–218, 223–224, 226; 2008 results in, 214, 223, 225–226; Tea Party in, 216; turnout in, 217, 219, 222, 230–231
Virginia Curse, 215
voter ID, 88, 89
Voting Rights Act of 1965, 61

Wallace, George, xvi
Wamp, Zach, 196
Ward, Ella, 228
Warner, John, 214
Warner, Mark, 214–215, 226, 231
Watergate, 234
Webb, Jim, 215, 221
Webster, Daniel, 146, 167
West, Allen, 147, 166
White, Brad, 84

Wicker, Roger, 83, 91, 93
Wilder, John, 196
Wildmon, Don, 87, 89
Williams, Darrin, 128
Williams, Juan, 106
Wolfe, Jr., John, 125, 191
Woodard, David, 242–243

Yoho, Ted, 166